Monstrous Progeny

==================================

Monstrous Progeny

A History of the Frankenstein Narratives

LESTER D. FRIEDMAN
AND ALLISON B. KAVEY

==================================

RUTGERS UNIVERSITY PRESS
NEW BRUNSWICK, NEW JERSEY, AND LONDON

823.7
FRI

a.xx-16 ac

Library of Congress Cataloging-in-Publication Data

Names: Friedman, Lester D., author. | Kavey, Allison, 1977–author.
Title: Monstrous progeny: a history of the Frankenstein narratives /
Lester D. Friedman, Allison B. Kavey.
Description: New Brusnwick, New Jersey: Rutgers University Press, 2016. |
Includes bibliographical references and index.
Identifiers: LCCN 2015047575| ISBN 9780813564241 (hardback) |
ISBN 9780813564234 (pbk.) | ISBN 9780813564258 (e-book (web pdf))
Subjects: LCSH: Shelley, Mary Wollstonecraft, 1797–1851. Frankenstein. | Shelley,
Mary Wollstonecraft, 1797–1851–Adapatations. | Frankenstein, Victor (Fictitious
character)—Miscellanea. | Frankenstein's monster (Fictitious character)—
Miscellanea. | Monsters in mass media. | BISAC: PERFORMING ARTS / Film & Video /
History & Criticism. | LITERARY CRITICISM / Gothic & Romance. | SOCIAL SCIENCE /
Popular Culture. | LITERARY CRITICISM / European / English, Irish, Scottish, Welsh.
| LITERARY CRITICISM / Semiotics & Theory. | SOCIAL SCIENCE / Media Studies. |
LITERARY CRITICISM / Science Fiction & Fantasy.
Classification: LCC PR5397.F73 F785 2016 | DDC 823/.7—dc23
LC record available at http://lccn.loc.gov/2015047575

A British Cataloging-in-Publication record for this book is available
from the British Library.

Visit our website: http://rutgerspress.rutgers.edu

Manufactured in the United States of America

For Bob Congemi, who inspired me to become a teacher

–LDF

For Kraken, my own monster though never my creation

–ABK

Something was waiting for him in the darkness, a part of himself he couldn't deny.

—Alice Hoffman, *The Museum of Extraordinary Things*

The world will teach them about monsters soon enough. Let them remember there's always the poker.

—Terry Pratchett, *Hogfather*

CONTENTS

ACKNOWLEDGMENTS

The common ground between an early modern intellectual historian and a film scholar of post–World War II American cinema might seem to be very small indeed. Oddly enough, however, our feet have trod the same path twice: first with J. M. Barrie's *Peter Pan*, which was Allison's fascination, and now with Mary Shelley's *Frankenstein*, a text that has captivated Les for decades. That said, however, this book took an inordinately long time to come together, and our first thanks must be to each other. Our second collaboration demanded a great deal of patience, tact, and hard work from each of us, and we hope you will find it as worthwhile and engaging as we did. We will certainly never hear "50 Ways to Leave Your Lover" quite the same way ever again. We also need to thank our many students, both undergraduate and graduate, who have enriched our thinking about *Frankenstein* and challenged our understandings of this text and the films. For those legions of students at Syracuse, Northwestern, Hobart and William Smith, Johns Hopkins, Drexel, and CUNY John Jay College and the Graduate Center—thank you. Allison in particular would like to thank Luke Reynolds, whose research help on the Royal Navy's attempts to explore the Arctic was exceptionally helpful.

We also want to extend some personal appreciation. We owe our spouses, Rae-Ellen and Andrea, at least a year before we begin the next project and a million thanks for their patience (saintly) and support. We promise: no more Frankencalls! We are also grateful for the supportive and stern guidance of Leslie Mitchner at Rutgers University Press. Without her help, this book would have been dead on the slab. The staff at Rutgers—especially Carrie Hudak, India Cooper, Anne Hegeman, Jeremy Grainger, and Lisa Boyajian—were also immensely helpful during this process. Les would like to thank Randall Brune, Jillian Collins, Wheeler Winston Dixon, Delia Temes, Murray Pomerance, and Fred Wiebel Jr. for their contributions and feedback on his work, and Jerry Ohlinger's Movie Material Store for the movie stills. Allison would like to thank Ben Kerschberg, Andrea Woodner, and Bettina Drummond for their contributions and feedback on her work. She would also like to thank Larry Principe, whose unerring guidance on Renaissance magic and alchemy, as always, tempered her flights of fancy.

Monstrous Progeny

Introduction

Singing the Body Electric

I think your mother was right. *Frankenstein* should be required reading for all scientists.

–Dr. Forbin, *The Forbin Project*

The "incessant rain" that soaked the Swiss countryside during the summer of 1816 confined nineteen-year-old Mary Shelley inside Lord Byron's Villa Diodati for days on end, placing her into almost constant contact with one uncommon and two extraordinary men. However wretched the weather that unseasonably cold and stormy "Year without a Summer," it nonetheless generated a period of extraordinary creative productivity for these four people fate hooked together near the shores of Lake Geneva. During their days in Switzerland, the world-famous poet Byron (1788–1824) worked on Canto III of *Childe Harold's Pilgrimage* (1816), wrote "Prometheus" (1816), and began *Manfred* (1817). His friend and Mary's young husband, Percy Shelley (1792–1822), completed "Hymn to Intellectual Beauty"(1817) and "Mont Blanc" (1817) and undoubtedly began thinking about what would eventually become his masterful epic poem *Prometheus Unbound* (1820). Even the least accomplished of the quartet, the young physician John Polidori (1795–1821), wrote a very popular novella, *The Vampyre* (1819), that envisioned a romantic and aristocratic vampire, Lord Ruthven, a tale that exerted considerable influence on future stories of the undead, including Bram Stoker's (1847–1912) renowned *Dracula* (1897).

Yet harrowing personal tragedies enveloped the Shelleys during this extended period of confinement and fertile inspiration. Mary still lamented the death of her premature, two-week-old daughter on March 5, 1815; the suicide of her half sister, Fanny Imlay, by an overdose of laudanum at the age of twenty-two (October 9, 1816) was closely followed by the suicide/drowning of twenty-one-year-old Harriet Westbrook (December 10, 1816), Percy Shelley's first wife. Although he deserted her while she was pregnant to run away with seventeen-year old Mary Godwin, Harriet still wore his wedding ring when her body was

The Villa Diodati and its inhabitants during the summer of 1816: Lord Byron, John Polidori, Mary Shelley, and Percy Shelley.

recovered from the Serpentine River in Hyde Park. Death would continue to haunt the Shelleys after that summer. Their daughter Clara would die of heat exhaustion in Venice on September 24, 1818, nine months after the first publication of *Frankenstein*, and malaria took their son William in Rome on June 7, 1819. Several years later, in 1822, the author herself would barely survive a miscarriage. Mary also suffered from ongoing guilt over the death of her mother, the eminent feminist Mary Wollstonecraft (1759–1797), due to septicemia eleven days after giving birth to her. Strikingly similar, within Mary's novel, Elizabeth causes the death of Victor's mother by infecting her with scarlet fever [1.2, 99–100].)[1] Within this churning cauldron of prolific creativity and personal grief from June of 1816 to July of 1817, both in Switzerland and in England, Mary Shelley wrote her famous tale of Victor Frankenstein and his immortal Creature.

Frankenstein remains as popular today as it was during Shelley's era—and perhaps it has become even more so. It is the fountainhead for seemingly endless rivers of remakes, sequels, and various other types of productions that continue to flood our TV, Internet, and movie screens. The philosopher Stephen T. Asma, for example, contends that Mary Shelley's creature "may be the most famous monster of the past two centuries."[2] Susan J. Wolfson and Ronald L. Levao, editors of the lavishly annotated *Frankenstein*, proclaim that the novel "may be the most famous, most enduring imaginative work of the Romantic era, even of the last two hundred years."[3] Elaine L. Graham, in *Representations of the Post/Human*, claims that the novel's "ability to shape the Western cultural imagination has been immeasurable . . . (and) *Frankenstein* stands as one of the quintessential representations of the fears and hopes engendered by new technologies."[4] Praising *Frankenstein* as "a remarkable work," the novelist Joyce Carol Oates notes its "double significance as a work of prose fiction and cultural myth."[5] The office of the horror film director Guillermo del Toro overflows with his expansive collection of Frankenstein memorabilia, and he characterizes the novel as "a beautiful book" suffused with "teenage angst."[6]

But what combination of conjoined elements makes this narrative relevant and popular across decades? Oates provides one answer: Victor Frankenstein become the prime example of the scientist whose ingenuity creates his own nightmare, what she calls a "manufactured nemesis." Recognizing how very few fictional characters "have made the great leap from literature to mythology," Oates asserts that the novel's figures remain compelling to modern readers because none of Shelley's characters are truly evil: their "universe is emptied of . . . theistic assumptions of "good" and evil"; instead, the novel depicts a "flawed god . . . eventually overcome by his creation." She further contends that *Frankenstein* becomes "a parable for our time and enduring prophecy, a remarkably acute diagnosis of the lethal nature of denial: of denial for one's actions, denial of the shadow-self locked within consciousness."[7] Unlike Marlowe's (1604) and Goethe's (1808) Faust or Rabbi Loew's Golem (1920), all of whom invoke supernatural presences and magical incantations to achieve their goals, the swarm of Frankensteins that spring from the novel clearly signify their protagonists as "men of science," and as a result their mechanical (re)invention of life automatically intersects with the defining moral quandaries that characterize modernity.

Fair enough, but what makes a monster monstrous? The "monster" is the category we use to frame those things that violate or transgress upon our conventional ideas of what is natural. It calls into question the assumptions inherent to our definitions of natural law and progression, as well as our relationship to life's creations and endings. Yet the monster does not necessarily do bad things; in fact, most literary monsters are surprisingly good, save for the twisted acts commit in reaction to their hysterical, often violent, receptions by human beings. The monster enters the scene as the hapless, misbegotten accident of a warped genesis; his very being is so problematic that it outweighs his actions.

Frankenstein's monster neatly corresponds with the most significant late eighteenth- and early nineteenth-century questions about life, death, and human attempts to control nature. Composed of dead flesh reanimated by a man wielding electricity rather than, as would have been the case a century earlier, a magician commanding demons or manipulating occult forces, he embodies the central question of how far humans should seek to mimic the powers of God or nature in the name of scientific investigation. Put within a context of moral reflection, Shelley asks: What *ought* a research scientist do, regardless of what he/she is able to do? The Monster, through its precise performance of humanity, demonstrates the pathetic hubris—and the innate limitations—of its inherently human creator. The tragedy of Frankenstein's monster is that he desires acceptance by a group frightened by his very existence, horrified at his physical appearance, and bent on his destruction. Such vicious rejections result in the Monster exacting a terrible revenge, thus validating the aggressively hostile vision that initially inspired his exclusion. Such an unending cycle of desire, rejection, violent action, and death forms the basic narrative arc of Shelley's *Frankenstein* and the vast majority of its offspring.

Four Critical Approaches to Reading *Frankenstein*

Because of *Frankenstein*'s longevity and popularity, scholars from diverse critical camps read the novel from a variety of perspectives. Below are very brief sketches of four popular interpretative approaches that attest to Shelley's fluid imagination and the continuing relevance of her work.

Psychological Readings of *Frankenstein*

The conception of monsters as embodied projections escaping from deep caverns within our individual and collective unconscious forms the basis of all psychological analysis of the horror/monster tale, including *Frankenstein*. Over the decades, therefore, critics have relentlessly plowed into both Mary Shelley's biography, analyzing her life as if she were a patient on a couch, and her text, as if her fictional characters were flesh-and-blood human beings, using insights drawn from a variety of psychoanalytic sources but most often Freud, Jung, and Lacan. The common Freudian approaches expose Victor's hidden sexual desires (including homosexuality, incest, oedipalism, and narcissism) and reveal how the creature functions as his lethal doppelganger. Victor's horrific dream, in which he kisses a healthy Elizabeth for the first time, only to dissolve into horror as her lips become livid with death and she morphs into the corpse of his dead mother, has drawn reams of attention from these critics. These commentators also stress how *Frankenstein* juxtaposes Victor's creation of the Creature and his marriage to Elizabeth as irreconcilable events, the former dangerously illicit and the latter socially acceptable. Victor's secret life of nocturnal experiments hidden from his friends, his family, and certainly his fiancée, who represents the domestic pleasures of hearth and home, results in Elizabeth's murder on her wedding night before their marriage is consummated, foregrounding the sexuality-perversity perspective rendered by scholars employing Freudian concepts.

Initially a pupil of Freud, Jung later rejected some of his mentor's theories. Although he also believed that the unconscious was a deep reservoir of repressions, he held that it consisted not only of sexual drives, as Freud alleged, but also of universal archetypes that he labeled the "collective unconscious"—a shared cultural legacy of recurring themes and symbols that we respond to emotionally, that influence both individual and societal actions, and that function as a stage between the unconscious and conscious mind to reveal what was buried. For Jungians, therefore, creative works are not solely the manifestation of an individual psyche's submerged desires but rather a symbolic embodiment of the repressed wishes of the entire human race. Those using Jungian insights to read *Frankenstein*, therefore, would seek a collective symbolic framework, one that often focuses on how the novel incorporates archetypal situations, themes, and characters, such as the hero's quest and the travails of the outcast. In particular, they would explore Shelley's masculine (animus) and feminine (anima) representations for their communal symbology. Taking into account Jung's concepts about the darker part of our unconscious, what he labels "the shadow," they would explore how the novel expresses those threatening and concealed urges.

Like Freud, Lacan explores childhood development, but with a more comprehensive emphasis on the acquisition of language and how this affects an individual's progression into a broader social context. Thus, Lacanian critics emphasize Shelley's language, particularly how she describes the manner in which the Creature learns to read and to speak and, consequentially, how language shapes his conception of the world and interaction with others throughout the course of the novel. David Collings's sophisticated Lacanian approach, for example, interprets the novel as primarily contrasting a realm of law and language against one of secrecy and solitude to "expose the way ideology operates in modern societies." Collings conceives of society as "the product of a collective fantasy, as a psychoanalytic construct in its own right," and then proceeds to "decipher the significance of the uncanny and clarify the relation between the construction of desire and of modern society."[8] All these psychological readings approach the surface elements of plot and character as pathways to explore deeper issues of both the individual and the communal psyche, teasing out buried meanings that reveal broader truths about the human condition that Mary Shelley herself was not aware that she was transmitting to her readers.

Feminist Readings of *Frankenstein*

In her article exploring Mary Shelley's novel within the context of feminist and literary theory, Diane Long Hoeveler claims that with the possible exception of Jane Eyre, "*Frankenstein* has figured more importantly in the development of feminist literary theory than perhaps any other novel."[9] At least initially, Hoeveler's sweeping assertion seems incongruous given that the book she elevates to such exalted heights contains conventional female characters without any agency, kills off the major female figures in the narrative (Elizabeth, Justine, and Caroline), and eradicates women from the procreative process. Throughout the novel, women, Elizabeth and Mrs. Saville in particular, epitomize a conventional domesticity juxtaposed to lives lived outside the home by men like Victor and Walton, whose imaginations and bravery compete for center stage with their hubris and failures. Anne K. Mellor concludes that "one of the deepest

horrors of this novel is Frankenstein's implicit goal of creating a society for men
only. . . . There is no reason that the race of immortal beings he hoped to propa-
gate should not be exclusively male."[10]

So why has Shelley's novel been celebrated as a landmark in feminist writing? One answer is that *Frankenstein*'s emphasis on pathogenesis, a process that
erases the need for woman to procreate, remains one of the most significant
aspects of the novel and, along with the stratums of parental/familial relations layered throughout the novel, offers abundant soil for feminist writers
to till. In her groundbreaking book *Literary Women: The Great Writers*, Ellen
Moers describes how the devastating deaths of children and mothers in Mary
Shelley's life were instrumental in making her novel into a "birth myth . . . not
as realism but gothic fantasy." Moers cites the maternal biography set forth
in Shelley's journals as the catalyst for her fictional depictions, viewing the
novel as mythmaking from the perspective of a teenage mother who has, in the
author's own words, had cause to "think of, and to dilate upon, so very hideous
an idea"; such wording, for Moers, turns Mary Shelley into a female mythmaker
and *Frankenstein* into a "trauma of afterbirth" that "transforms the standard
Romantic matters of incest, infanticide, and patricide into a phantasmagoria
of the nursery."[11]

In similar biographical approaches, U. K. Knoepflmacher considers that
the novel "resurrects and rearranges an adolescent's [Mary's] conflicting emotions about her relation both to the dead mother she idolized and . . . the . . .
father-philosopher she admired and deeply resented," while Peter Dale Scott
sifts through the connections between Victor and Percy Shelley, concluding that
the novel "depicts the tragic consequences of sexual isolation through artificial
roles of 'masculinity' and 'femininity,' and . . . focuses on one-sided parenting
. . . as the ultimate source of these roles . . . whereby psychic and social depriva-
tions reinforce one another in history."[12] Rebecca Solnit notes that Mary Shelley
grew up in a household of two adults and five children, none of whom had the
same pair of parents, and that upon her elopement with Percy, her father cut
her off, thereby providing her with a personal example of a "parent who dis-
owns a child as one version of the irresponsible distancing inventor that is her
Victor Frankenstein."[13]

A short time after Moers, Sandra M. Gilbert and Susan Gubar published
their influential feminist volume *The Madwoman in the Attic: The Woman Writer
and the Nineteenth-Century Literary Imagination*, with a significant section devoted to interpreting *Frankenstein* as a rewriting of one of the key literary works
of the Romantic era, a "fictionalized rendition of the meaning of *Paradise Lost* to
women." Gilbert and Gubar, like Moers, seek to understand and analyze *Frankenstein* by delving into the biography of its creator, a motherless child (who
created a motherless creature) who read extensively and, from the ages of sev-

enteen to twenty-one, was "almost continuously pregnant, 'confined,' or nursing." Despite its lack of a leading female character, Gilbert and Gubar consider *Frankenstein* as a "woman's book" and a "female fantasy of sex and reading." For them, Shelley was so "caught up in such a maelstrom of sexuality at the time she wrote the novel" that the combined confluence of "her family studies, her initiation into adult sexuality, and her literary self-education" resulted in a "gothic psychodrama" displaying a "keen sense of the agony of female sexuality, and specifically of the perils of motherhood."[14]

Much additional feminist writing about *Frankenstein* has appeared since the books by Moers and by Gilbert and Gubar, not all of it as heavily influenced by the biographical or psychoanalytic approaches to the fictional work. Here is a small sample of varying approaches. Mary Poovey (*The Proper Lady and the Woman Writer*, 1984) contextualizes Shelley within the English society of her time. Returning to the novel, Mary Jacobus ("Is There a Woman in This Text?," 1982) concentrates on how the women in the novel fall prey to the struggle between paternity and scientific endeavors. Anne Mellor focuses in a 1988 essay ("Possessing Nature: The Female in *Frankenstein*") and later in a book (*Mary Shelley: Her Life, Her Fiction, Her Monsters*, 1989) on Victor's "womb envy" and "heroic self-aggrandizement," which motivates him to violate nature and reap his punishment. Writing as a postcolonialist feminist, Gayatri Spivak ("Three Women's Texts and a Critique of Imperialism," 1985) explores the novel in terms of English cultural identity. Kate Ellis ("Monsters in the Garden: Mary Shelley and the Bourgeois Family," 1974) scrutinizes the examples of domestic affection and its limitations in *Frankenstein*, while Peter Brooks ("What Is a Monster? [According to *Frankenstein*]," 1993) argues that Mary Shelley attempted to escape the generic cultural codes that constrained fictional heroines during the nineteenth century. Female poets such as Liz Lochhead (*Dreaming Frankenstein*, 1984) and Margaret Atwood ("Speeches for Doctor Frankenstein," 1996) have been sufficiently intrigued by Shelley's creation to use it as a springboard for their own writings.

Queer Readings of *Frankenstein*

Rereading Mary Shelley with a contemporary eye, one can see the foundations for a queer reading of the novel. In the second letter to his sister, Walton speaks of a never-satisfied want that he now feels "as a most severe evil": "I desire the company of a man who could sympathize with me; whose eyes would reply to mine. . . . I greatly need a friend who would have sense enough not to despise me as romantic, and affection enough for me to endeavour to regulate my mind" (L2, 70–71). Almost immediately after meeting Victor, Walton begins to love him as "the brother of my heart" and considers him "like a celestial spirit" and a "divine wanderer" (L2, 82, 84). For him, Victor is a "noble . . . creature destroyed by misery," a man "gentle, yet so wise; his mind is so cultivated," and his words "are culled with the choicest art and flow with rapidity and unparalleled eloquence (L4, 82). In essence, Walton becomes a nurse tending to Victor's physical and psychological wounds while being captivated by how, when he is treated well, "his whole countenance is lighted up, as it were, with a beam of benevolence and sweetness that I never saw equalled" (L4, 80). Walton's feelings about Victor are equally matched by Victor's admiration of his dearest childhood friend, Henry Clerval (who nurses Victor earlier), "the most noble of human creatures" whose form was "so divinely formed, and beaming with beauty," and whose "soul overflowed with ardent affections, and [whose] friendship was of that devoted and wondrous nature that the worldly-minded teach us to look for only in the imagination" (L4, 84; 3.1, 241–42). This authorial focus on powerful male connections, particularly as seen in Henry's and Walton's preference for spending time with other men, does lend support to seeing *Frankenstein* as having a homoerotic subtext that, if not consciously reflecting Shelley's intention, still provides sufficient material for intelligent speculation when viewed through a modern perspective.

Drawing on the writings of Harold Bloom, Eve Kosofsky Sedgwick (who made *Frankenstein* a synecdoche for an entire age of extreme homophobia), and Jonathan Dollimore, James Holt McGavran's analysis bridges the gap between feminist criticism and queer theory, noting Mary Shelley's repeated use of "the language of passionate attachment" throughout the novel and arguing that Victor's creation is "a self at least partially liberated from heterosexual stereotypes of desire." McGavran cites the virulent antigay persecution that characterized early nineteenth-century Europe, acknowledges that Mary Shelley did not consciously pen a novel with an overt homoerotic current, and recognizes that no overt homosexual activity occurs in the novel. Yet by juxtaposing Victor's safe homosocial relationships with Clerval and Walton with the lethal homoerotic desire (and ensuing homosexual panic) between the creator and his creation, combined with how frequently heterosexual relations are delayed and interrupted, McGavran concludes that Victor's "pursuit of his creature reads like a secret yet scarcely disguised gay adventure." He contends the novel warns that "the intimate relations between (and within) men, if not acknowledged and understood, can lead to the destruction not just of heterosexual relationships but of both men's and women's lives."[15] Mitch Walker analyzes double archetypes and homosexuality in the novel in "The Problem of *Frankenstein*," a six-part gay Jungian reading on YouTube inspired by the Christopher Isherwood TV series that aired in late 1974 and focusing on homosexual love, vicious cultural bigotry, and the importance of self-acceptance.[16] Perhaps the most radical queer reading may be found in John Lauritser's *The Man Who Wrote Frankenstein* (2007), in which he posits that the novel's author is not Mary but rather her husband,

Percy. He claims the novel represents Percy Shelley's coming-out narrative—an assertion that infuriates feminist scholars who claim Mary Shelley as one of their own. Two plays have also incorporated this homosexual context, the Living Theatre's adaptation of the novel (1966) and the modern off-Broadway musical *The Gay Bride of Frankenstein* (2008).

Social Metaphor Readings of *Frankenstein*

Over the decades, Shelley's monster has frequently been adopted as a metaphor for a wide variety of social issues. In recent years, for example, Frankenstein's Creature has come to embody people with disabilities fighting for their civil rights. Unlike commentators whose psychoanalytic slant envisions the Creature and his creator as reflecting some repressed part of Mary Shelley's life, social metaphor critics bind *Frankenstein* to events of a particular era, starting with those that occurred during the author's lifetime. They note that Mary Shelley, the daughter of two of the most radical thinkers in the nineteenth century, was quite aware of the most controversial social and political issues of her day. As a result of being raised in a household filled with famous literary and political figures, and then joining the company of acutely political artists like Shelley, his friend T. J. Hogg, and Lord Byron, Mary could not help but pack *Frankenstein* with her thinking about current social and political situations, including her castigation of primogeniture (1.1), capital punishment (1.7; 2.1), and the corrosive effects of poverty (2.4; 3.2), among others.

With this biographical background in mind, many commentators, typified by Chris Baldick's *In Frankenstein's Shadow: Myth, Monstrosity, and Nineteenth-Century Writing*, mine the novel for its connections to its author's era. They cast the Creature into various roles, including as an embodiment for the French and American revolutions that traumatized England. Lee Sterrenburg's Creature, for example, emerges as a hybrid between "the Burkean tradition of horrific, evil, and revolutionary monsters" and "the republican tradition of social monsters. . . oppressed and misused by the social orders above them."[17] David Hirsch contends that the novel criticizes the French Revolution's failure to achieve its utopian promise, but his Creature becomes "the figural embodiment of the republican Revolution's aspiration toward a new form of social federation."[18] Judith Weissman also construes *Frankenstein* as a disguised political warning; her Creature enters the world as "Rousseau's natural man," but vicious deeds transform him into the embodiment of English fears that "they would be overwhelmed by a violent revolution like the one in France."[19] Noting that the figure of the Monster "takes on a multitude of different forms and functions in British political life immediately after the French Revolution," Fred Botting sees *Frankenstein* "as a novel that provides reflections on, as much as reflections of, revolutionary and counter-revolutionary texts."[20]

Believing that Shelley drew upon contemporary attitudes toward non-whites, H. L. Malchow sees a Creature who personifies "the fears and hopes of the abolition of slavery in the West Indies."[21] Such a reading takes into account George Canning's direct reference to "the splendid fiction of a recent romance" in 1824 when confronting this controversial issue, and later Prime Minister William Gladstone's description of hybrid mules as "Frankensteins of the animal creation" in 1838—both within Mary Shelley's lifetime.[22] In a similar racial reading, Anne K. Mellor notes that Frankenstein's Creature has "yellow skin" (1.4, 114) and concludes that "most of Shelley's nineteenth-century readers would have immediately recognized the Creature as a member of the 'Mongolian' race"; the novel thus "initiates a new version of this Yellow Man, the image of the Mongol as a giant . . . who finally becomes a murdering monster, destroying all those dear to his maker."[23] Edith Gardner connects the novel to the highly publicized Luddite uprisings (1811–1817) that epitomize the volatility of the working class during the time of the novel's gestation, and Paul O'Flinn suggests that *Frankenstein* imaginatively confronts the possibility of working-class insurrections manifest in both the Luddite violence and the Pentridge uprising of 1817 (a revolt of three hundred unemployed textile workers). In this light, Victor corresponds to "the upper classes and the British government," while Gardner's Creature "represents the lower, or working-class: the Luddites."[24]

Other associations during Shelley's lifetime abound. Because the Shelleys lived in Geneva during a time that historians label "the Poverty Year," when extremely cold weather caused crop failures that resulted in widespread famine, food riots in France and Switzerland, and deaths from hunger and a typhus epidemic, some commentators relate the coldness evident throughout the novel (it begins and ends in the Arctic) to these aberrant environmental conditions. Tim Marshall cites the connections between the 1832 Anatomy Act and *Frankenstein*, which he characterizes as a classic story of the bodysnatching era, and his Creature literally embodies the stigma that the law of that time imposed. Fuson Wang believes that "the patchwork body of the creature . . . rehearses early nineteenth-century vaccination anxieties" associated with Edward Jenner and smallpox.[25] Steven Forry points out that, whatever Mary Shelley's overt intention, *Frankenstein* became a staple in political cartoons (he includes several of these in his book) of the day—appearing in publications such as *McLean's Monthly Sheet of Characters*, *Figaro in London*, *Punch*, and the *Tomahawk*—most importantly attacking the 1832 Reform Act that altered the electoral system of England and Wales, general labor unrest, and the continuing Irish Question.[26]

Other commentators employ the social metaphor approach more generally rather than limiting it to Shelley's era. Almost all these readings adopt the premise that the Creature is born benevolent and good and that social circumstances turn him evil: "I am malicious because I am miserable; am I not shunned and hated by all mankind?" (2.9, 227). For them, a callous and selfish capitalistic society has turned a naturally good being into a monster. Franco Moretti, for example, characterizes the novel from a Marxist perspective; his Creature represents the proletariat: "Reunited and brought back to life in the monster are the limbs of those—the poor—whom the breakdown of feudal relations has forced into brigandage, poverty, and death.[27] Using a similar Marxist methodology, Elsie B. Michie interprets the descriptions of what Victor does while making her Creature as a way "to deal with the issues of material production and the problems that arise from it . . . a reflection of the relation between workers and those who control the forces of production."[28]

Paul O'Flinn concurs that *Frankenstein* incorporates the "central tensions and contradictions of the industrial society," specifically distinguishing his Creature as a "contradictory figure, still ugly, vengeful and terrifying but now also human and intelligent and abused."[29] Pointing out that the novel was "written at a time when the oppressive and dehumanizing effects of capitalism were all too obvious," Warren Montag links "the image of the monster to the industrial proletariat: an unnatural being, singular even in its collective identity, without a genealogy and belonging to no species."[30] Anca Vlasopolos focuses on the class selection and inbreeding that, for her, makes the novel subversive and a threat even in modern times: her Creature "embodies the punishment of taboo breaking"—the incest between Victor and Elizabeth—and "reveals the crack at the center of English society."[31]

Modern commentators adopt this notion of a political idea disguised as Shelley's Creature as well, making similar social metaphor analogies. On his blog, the filmmaker Michael Moore equates Saddam Hussein to his version of the Frankenstein monster: "We like playing Dr. Frankenstein. We created a lot of monsters. . . . And, just like the mythical Frankenstein, Saddam eventually spun out of control."[32] Michael C. Dorf claims, "Large-scale catastrophes such as the 2010 Deepwater Horizon Gulf oil spill and the 2011 tsunami-induced radiation leakage at the Fukushima nuclear power facilities are only the latest reminders of the limits of human ingenuity and the continuing relevance of the *Frankenstein* story."[33] Examples like this can be seen at least weekly in various media outlets across the United States.

One of the most extended examples of the monster-as-social-metaphor approach is Elizabeth Young's book *Black Frankenstein: The Making of an American Metaphor*: "The Frankenstein story of monstrous sons and haunted fathers throws U.S. racial formations into high relief and, in so doing, illuminates how these formations have been shaped, reinforced, and opposed in American culture." Young's goal is threefold: 1) to show how the black Frankenstein metaphor affirms, and at the same time challenges, structures of race and masculinity in US culture; 2) to offer a study in form about the making of the

Frankenstein metaphor in aesthetic terms; and 3) to explore the metaphor's politics. Although she notes that Shelley describes Victor's creation as "yellow," Young asserts that her "monster's color nonetheless signifies symbolically, on the domestic American scene, as black . . . [and] intertwined with fantasies and anxieties about masculinity." Like others mentioned above, Young understands that Mary Shelley's contemporaries saw Frankenstein's Creature as a revolutionary threat to English society, but she contends that her monster also serves as "the embodiment of racial uprisings," particularly in an America whose independence was "founded on the imagery of filial revolt."[34]

To some degree, any new scientific theory, technological invention, or medical breakthrough inevitably changes the ways people think, behave, and interact with others, causing alterations in our daily lives and belief systems that engender doubts and anxieties. Whatever its flaws, ongoing iterations, and unanticipated mutations in popular culture, Shelley's narrative has become a primary text for a host of these issues in the contemporary world and an indispensable part of serious (and some not so serious) discussions about the role of science, medicine, and technology in our culture. As such, *Frankenstein* has arguably become more relevant to apprehensive concerns omnipresent in the twenty-first century than it was in the nineteenth. As Paul Wolpe observes, the fundamental issues raised in *Frankenstein* "have become, if anything, more immediate and trenchant as the power to alter our nature has actually emerged . . . the power and longevity of the novel is due to the primordial nature of its social and ethical insights about science."[35] At its core, then, the novel explores the increasingly blurry boundaries and distinctions between what we label human and nonhuman/the natural and the unnatural, and the interconnected relationships between social responsibility and scientific or medical research.

As is the case with every great work of literary art, generations of readers have discovered not only a home amid the luxuriant materials embedded within *Frankenstein* but one that is comfortable and well furnished. To twist a phrase: every academic gets the *Frankenstein* he/she wants to see. As Joyce Carol Oates asserts, "It is a measure of the subtlety of this moral parable" that it "strikes so many archetypal cords and suggests so many variant readings."[36] Such extensive, and at times quite dissimilar, interpretations of Mary Shelley's work might upon first glance seem far-fetched examples of academic overreaching, but they ultimately provide a deeper appreciation of the flexibility and power of her fertile narrative, particularly the allure of her Creature. Indeed, the summation of approaches above barely scratches the surface of the diverse ways critics have conceptualized the novel over the decades—not to mention the creative artists inspired by Mary Shelley's portrayal of her characters and their stories in a wide assortment of interpretations and a growing mixture of digital formats. We owe a debt to the multitude of authors who have preceded us in this Frankensteinian venture. But we have also tried to do something new, combining historical contextualization and cultural readings into a single volume that reads the novel and the films as intellectual and cultural products of their time and then as cultural producer.

By considering the story as a historical product that reflects the ideas that came before and surrounded it, we strongly embed it in the intellectual and cultural milieu of the early nineteenth century. And by reading the Frankenstein legacy as the product of an extraordinarily prolific cultural producer, we take seriously the idea of changing intellectual contexts making use of a single source in fluid, multiple ways. To demonstrate the longevity and flexibility of the Frankenstein narratives, we have focused on what we believe to be the significant themes that have made it an enduring text for two centuries, particularly those of natural versus artificial life, the limits of experimentation, scientists' ethical obligations, the relationship between the creator and the created, and the bond between science and nature. The ideas that animate the novel did not spring full-blown from Mary Shelley's head. They were an intrinsic part of the intellectual zeitgeist that characterized her age and can be traced back to philosophical arguments that dominated earlier centuries as well. Such a strategy does not denigrate the uniqueness of Shelley's intellect; whatever inspired her that famous dark and stormy night resulted in a classic work of fiction that continues to resonate far beyond her time and has engaged millions of readers—and will likely continue to do so. Instead, we seek to contextualize the novel's thematic strands by exploring the intellectual trends that animate it and then progress to the subsequent works—primarily the films—that drew their inspiration from it.

In the first chapter, an analysis of the intellectual roots of the Frankenstein story provide the context for understanding the scientific questions to which it responds, particularly the importance of pursuing new knowledge within a community, the differentiation between investigation for its own sake and for personal aggrandizement, and the rising role of institutions, such as universities and the Royal Society, in defining good and useful scientific work. This chapter also tackles the theology resonating through *Frankenstein*, contending that the debt to the Bible extends beyond the story of the fallen angel to the lesser-known story of the half-angel, half-human Nephilim, the giants who nearly destroyed the earth and were, in turn, destroyed by God-sent natural disasters. The second chapter provides insight into the medical culture from which *Frankenstein* emerged and discusses its manifold debts to ongoing debates about the nature of life and death, the increasing importance of anatomy in medical education and scientific work, current ideas of madness and the nascent field of psychiatry, and the relationship between the body and the soul. Shelley weaves such issues into overlapping patterns throughout the novel, and they function as a thematic foundation for the ongoing narrative variations well into modern times. The third chapter provides a bridge, much as the latter half of the nineteenth century did, bringing *Frankenstein* from the page to the stage and then onto celluloid, thereby generating a mass audience that exists to this day and signaling the first variations to the original narrative. In the final three chapters, we trace the ongoing cinematic power of the Frankenstein narrative, identifying key aspects of the original tale that surface and resurface in films, and addressing biological modifications such as artificially created bodies, cyborgs, and robots. In short, we try to capture the continuing evolution of the Frankenstein narrative, beginning with the ideas that engaged Mary Shelley and spawned the creation of the world's most famous mad scientist and his Creature, read the novel in light of these questions, and investigate the various iterations of the fundamental moral questions posed in the novel that continue to agitate contemporary readers and audiences. And, so, we begin.

1

=================================

In a Country of Eternal Light
Frankenstein's Intellectual History

> Everywhere science is enriched by unscientific methods and unscientific
> results, . . . the separation of science and non-science is not only artifi-
> cial but also detrimental to the advancement of knowledge. If we want
> to understand nature, if we want to master our physical surroundings,
> then we must use all ideas, all methods, and not just a small selection
> of them.
>
> —Paul K. Feyerabend, *Against Method*

Commentators traditionally regard Mary Shelley's *Frankenstein; or, The Modern Prometheus* as the most influential cautionary tale ever written. To this day, it remains a compelling illustration of how the seductive temptations offered by scientific research can drive researchers both to reckless excesses and a blatant disregard for ethical limitations. Such a black-and-white reading, however, fails to account for the spectrum of scientific investigation embraced and condemned by the novel. A more nuanced and historically contextual view articulates the ways in which *Frankenstein* walks the line trodden by many earlier scientists who struggled to defend and more clearly define their profession, thereby providing the foundation for contemporary research practices. Reviewing the variety of natural philosophies forwarded by the Renaissance authors at whose feet Shelley lays Victor's corruption provides insight into how the rich entanglements of magic, theology, and natural philosophy function in the novel, establishes the ethical boundaries that shape the scientific revolution and its later adherents, and forms the framework for our modern conceptions of legitimate research aspirations and experimental protocols.

Frankenstein aggressively attacks the path advocated by many Renaissance magi who believed that the study of the natural world necessarily led to an understanding of the divine plan within nature and, consequently, to their control over it. While rejecting Renaissance natural philosophy, Shelley simultaneously embraces a very different kind of scientific investigation, one that places her work squarely in the middle of the ongoing struggles to define "science" in the late eighteenth and early nineteenth centuries. Her approach to knowledge production, especially chemistry and polar exploration, ultimately develops a definition of the kind of science championed by many at the dawn of the nineteenth century. Controlled, occurring within institutions and the confines of peer review, and deliberately within the realm of the visible and the natural, this kind of science provided a greater understanding of the world people inhabited and illustrates how they believed science could help them to better control that world. The new approach to scientific information depended on codes of gentlemanly conduct and the ties binding scientific men to produce a culture of peer review and an emphasis on method, replicability, and witnessing that made honor among men an integral part of scientific culture and that features prominently in the binding relationship between Robert Walton and Victor Frankenstein in the novel.

Juxtaposed to the tenets of Renaissance natural philosophy, Shelley provides readers with three crucial litmus tests for separating "good" from "dangerous" science that reflect the scientific culture that spawned *Frankenstein*. Several windows provide readers access to the types of science and sources the novel deems legitimate and helpful versus those categorized as dangerous and potentially harmful. For example, science within the context of the university or, in the case of Arctic exploration, with governmental and institutional support emerges as beneficial, especially when it occurs in a peer-governed environment that maintains boundaries that distinguish acceptable and desirable endeavors from dangerous and harmful projects. Isolated investigations, on the other hand, veer into dangerous territory and can encourage scientists to indulge their egos and desires for personal power rather than to gain knowledge for the greater good. Motive is another defining factor for damning or lauding specific scientific endeavors. Tightly articulated efforts to better understand a specific aspect of the natural world or, in the case of exploration, to locate new sources of desirable materials or potential trade routes are suitable intellectual work. Conversely, grandiose projects that aim to eliminate all disease or solve the mystery of life remain inherently problematic and demonstrate the practitioner's hubris, as well as a risky failure to grasp the collaborative nature of scientific work. Finally, the novel approves of work that seeks to better understand the way objects function within the natural world, but it rejects elaborate projects that endeavor to attain power over other objects or systems within nature as overreaching and potentially destructive.

As a result, *Frankenstein* calls into question the scientific context its period inherited, juxtaposing the opposing ideas and concerns that shaped the world of late eighteenth-century and early nineteenth-century scientific investigation.

The science it champions is closely tied to the formal rules for experimentation established and enforced during the seventeenth and eighteenth centuries by institutions such as the Royal Society in England, the Académie Royale in France, and major European universities. Such approaches to scientific explorations were also embraced by the men who embarked upon expeditions to better understand the biology and anthropology of exotic locations, such as the Arctic, the Antarctic, and the tropics. Because their governments often subsidized these voyages, the knowledge gained—and any new property discovered—belonged to the states that sponsored them. This arrangement meant that the process of gaining knowledge was subject to the ethical standards adopted—or at least publicly held—by their governments, and the explorers necessarily represented those regimes during their travels.

Offshoots of the Royal Society developed to provide peer review for this kind of natural science as well, including the Royal Geographical Society. Efforts to publicize the findings of natural scientists, often packaged for public consumption to stress the moral compass of the lead investigator and his selfless devotion to knowledge production, provided significant public access to—and widespread support for—natural science and scientific expeditions. Shelley's novel falls into an interesting place within this arena because it provides two examples of scientists whose labors flirt with disaster. It damns Victor for his grandiose ambitions and refusal to join the scientific enterprise of his era and saves Walton from his personal quest for glory with a stern reminder about his social status and responsibilities to the men who serve him. Shelley also delivers a severe reminder to Walton about his socioeconomic place in society and his responsibility to the English nation.

But the actual emergence of this scientific culture is far less clear-cut than the gentlemen of the Royal Society would have wished—or publicly admitted. A review of their transcripts reveals a shared space between what we would recognize as science and early modern pursuits of natural knowledge that reflect the sixteenth century better than the nineteenth. For example, the expeditions undertaken by early nineteenth-century explorers and natural scientists in search of the open polar sea, especially in the face of extensive evidence supporting its nonexistence, are as steeped in the English imagination as any alchemical quest. The difference lies in the framing integral to understanding both the science of this period and the scientific vision in *Frankenstein*. Embraced by members of the Royal Society and the Royal Navy as a means of extending the power of the English nation—through both the gathering of new natural knowledge and the potential discovery of a highly lucrative and useful trade route—the investigation of the Arctic was separated from the myths still permeating the English vision of the region and embedded in the realm of useful and meaningful scientific investigation.

Part of the transition from imagined geography to formal scientific exploration involved making exploration a governmental project and, as a subsidiary goal, a viable means of employing the Royal Navy in the military vacuum following the Napoleonic wars. Such a shift separated gentlemen scientists devoted to the discovery of natural knowledge for the sake of the nation from benighted dreamers, like Shelley's Robert Walton, bent on pursuing personal greatness through the realization of their Arctic-twilight fantasies of Hyperboreans and earthly paradise. This project was not unique to the nineteenth century. Steven Shapin writes at length about the importance of gentlemanly status in determining the worth of scientific observation in seventeenth-century England; various scholars clearly demonstrate how the shared roles of personal observation—with the value of that observation depending to some extent on the social role occupied by the observer—and historical authority merge in sixteenth-century European natural philosophy.[1] But an urgency characterizes these late eighteenth- and early nineteenth-century iterations, emerging at least in part because of the increasing institutionalization of science and its practitioners' need to legitimize the discipline by differentiating between worthy and unworthy practice.

In *Frankenstein*, both Victor and Robert Walton derive their scientific imaginations from historical sources, and many literary critics characterize their failed quests as an overt rejection of the Romantic imagination, particularly its hyperbolic language and grandiose gestures. Shelley does, indeed, chastise both men for their actions in the novel; she places the malformed Creature squarely at the feet of the ambitious Victor, who inherits his ideas from natural philosophers such as Heinrich Cornelius Agrippa and his peers, and reproves Walton for his near-fatal search for unknown places and undiscovered people inspired by his childhood reading of exploration tales. But Shelley's attitudes—given the sources she credits for seducing Victor away from the legitimate pursuit of knowledge—are also a rejection of the Renaissance magi who hoped to gain knowledge of the natural world. Such a goal was inspired by a desire to better understand, and even mimic, God, a narcissistic quest doomed to failure and set against natural and religious prohibitions.

Walton, Natural Science, and the Contest over Authority

Victor Frankenstein's scientific enterprise has attracted meaningful scholarly attention during the last thirty years, much of which contributes to our understanding of how this novel reflects research currents within late eighteenth- and early nineteenth-century English science. Samuel Vasbinder, for example, states, "All of Victor's scientific studies can be traced in eighteenth-century science. There is not a statement made by [Shelley] that does not have at least one, sometimes dozens, of echoes in the scientific literature of her age."[2] That literature included a slew of theories attempting to explain how energy moved in the body—and how this activity related to sickness and health and to life itself. Mesmerism and galvanism attacked the first two of these, while the ongoing debates at the Royal College of Surgeons between 1814 and 1816 about how life begins and the interest in what constituted the "spark of life" concentrated on the third. The proliferation of these themes in *Frankenstein* demonstrates that Shelley was very familiar with the principal scientific questions of her day. Her careful delincation of scientific education under the watchful eyes of professors within the university community establishes that she also understood the ways in which scientific knowledge was produced, both legitimately and illegitimately, according to the conventions of her age.

The novel favors a particular approach to scientific work and explicitly supports certain kinds of investigations, most notably those grounded specifically in the natural world and not delving too deeply into loftier questions about how life begins, the unifying power behind all living things, and whether that power could be replicated. As such, *Frankenstein* can easily be read as a warning to scientific experimenters inclined to seek the glory promised by solving the great mystery of life. That said, however, a more subtle reading that champions a stricter version of science is also plausible. In addition to warning readers to avoid the problems of what constitutes life and how it begins, Shelley also condemns the misguided, solipsistic approach Victor adopts. The novel presents the treacherous pitfalls of working in isolation, thereby detached from communal advice and, if necessary, collegial intervention. Instead, Shelley suggests that researchers function most productively when operating under the watchful eyes of their peers, rather than removed from society in a laboratory with only their egos to judge their progress and guide their decisions. In this sense, then, *Frankenstein* reflects the emergence of a clearly defined scientific community that maintained its own rules for producing and assessing natural knowledge.

The perspective regarding scientific research that Shelley presents in the novel was not unique to the early nineteenth century. The Royal Society, for example, was awarded its first charter in 1662, in which King Charles II granted its members access to unclaimed bodies to pursue anatomical investigations, among other natural philosophical queries, along with the land and buildings necessary to house a great institution. This charter also recognized the importance of an international scientific community when he granted its members the right to "enjoy mutual intelligence and knowledge with all and all manner of strangers and foreigners . . . in matters of things philosophical, mathematical, or mechanical."[3] Similar institutions formed across Europe during the seventeenth century, including the Accademia dei Lincei in Rome in 1603 and the Académie Royale in Paris in 1666 (formally incorporated and chartered by the king in

1699).[4] The rise of these institutions, which provided a place to discuss and pass judgment on scientific questions and approaches, increasingly brought natural philosophy into the purview of a knowledge community. The participation of the government in these institutions was matched by various European monarchs' interest in what their kingdoms could gain from science. By investing in exploration, for example, all of the major European governments pinned their hopes for gold, new transport routes, and other treasures on the coats of scientists whose goals were often very different. When the Royal Navy and the Royal Society undertook quests for the open polar sea, for example, they had different goals for the missions they funded, but they shared the commitment to exploration as an integral part of nation- and knowledge-building.

Take, as an example of Shelley's viewpoint, Walton's naval quest for an open polar sea as a manifestation of the intersections between widely known scientific events and *Frankenstein*. England approved the renewed quest for that polar chimera in 1818, the year Shelley's novel was first published. Yet the importance of the social communities governing and contributing to scientific knowledge production and the relationships and their helpers remained a vexed question, especially in the ice-choked waters of the polar seas, where experienced seamen were frequently endangered by library-trained experts with minimal (or no) practical knowledge. In retrospect, the learned scientific men who refused to accept the expertise of sailors, whalers, and even less formally educated but more practically experienced men defined nineteenth-century English Arctic exploration. In choosing people to embark upon major, crown-funded expeditions, for instance, the Royal Navy regularly granted expert status to educated men of higher social class over those with practical experience, even if they came with an acknowledged reputation for expertise in natural science. This preferential treatment favored men whose theories about the Arctic ran parallel to the Admiralty's own, rather than those with prior experience in the region.

The contest over the relative authority of eyewitness testimony and classical texts, such as Pliny, has its roots in the Renaissance, and thus its appearance in a novel whose scientific framework owes a great debt to that period is not coincidental. Walton, Frankenstein's final friend, is exactly the kind of man whose social class and lack of formal experience should have attracted Royal Navy funding, but he fails to gain a place on a national expedition because he lacks a formal education. Even so, his social class still guarantees him some consideration, while whalers and other uneducated but highly experienced men were rejected outright. William Scoresby, for example, was a veteran whaler and acknowledged expert in natural science who achieved international scientific recognition for his seventeen years of observations and drawings of polar ice. Yet he was refused a place on the government-sponsored and Royal Society–backed Arctic expedition in 1818 for two reasons: first, he lacked an Oxbridge

This image of the icy waters of the summer Arctic as observed during one of the expeditions to find the Northwest Passage was published in a very popular book about the expedition.

education, and second, he took the opposite view of Sir John Barrow, the second secretary of the Admiralty and the director of polar expeditions, about whether an open polar sea was likely, contending that its absence from the reports of whalers, fishermen, and expert sea captains proved that it did not exist.[5]

Presented as a real thing in ancient books once accepted without question as authoritative, the existence of an open polar sea was increasingly being questioned because no individual had witnessed it. Its foothold in the English imagination of the Arctic notwithstanding, the open polar sea was under attack in Shelley's time, and the fact that Walton saw a frozen wasteland, not a tropical paradise and open water, and a gigantic creature whose existence had only been verified by its creator puts his testimony on shaky ground.. The reiteration of scientific procedure as central to confirming old tales and making new knowledge underscores the importance of the emerging scientific method in Shelley's model for research investigations. The struggle to determine whether the experience of many individuals was more relevant than the theories contained in aged tomes went on for centuries, ultimately becoming foundational to the creation of the modern scientific approach accepted as legitimate today.

The transition from accepting single authoritative ancient reports to trusting only multiple testimonies by different witnesses to determine an experiment's or object's legitimacy took a long time. Its ascendency owes much to the oversight of institutions such as the universities and the Royal Society, both of which stressed the value of peer-reviewed knowledge production and experimentation over text-driven theorizing. The kind of witnessing that Victor Frankenstein does when he brings the Creature to life and later views its destruction would be considered as inherently untrustworthy because he is almost always the lone witness. Victor's social class and education notwithstanding, his testimony remains unreliable according to the standards of scientific evidence emerging during this period. Robert Walton and his crew also witness the Creature, and their testimony lends credence to its existence. But their lack of formal education and their unfamiliarity with scientific work also make their testimony untrustworthy.

For Shelley, Walton illustrates the temptation faced by so many gentlemen who strayed into natural science without formal training, weighted down by the myths of previous generations and their own misconceptions about the social relationships required to generate beneficial scientific knowledge. Walton, in Victor's thrall, initially disregards his crew's threats to mutiny when his quest to follow the Creature endangers the ship and its inhabitants. His willingness to pursue an obsessively personal goal reflects the original misapprehension behind his expedition; he seeks the Arctic for personal gain and to rescue his reputation from previous errors, rather than for the greater good of society and England's glory. By finally accepting his crew's demands to return home should the ice break up, rather than overwintering in the Arctic with a strong chance of losing their lives and any scientific evidence they had gained, he reinstates the social order of the ship. Although Walton's socioeconomic status endows him with the right to command, it also obliges him to be governed by those whose practical knowledge outweighs his own. The crew, despite Victor's urging to pursue the original goal for glory even in the face of certain death, reminds Walton about the source of a gentleman's and a captain's honor: knowledge produced at the expense of those subject to the whims of the expedition's leader is morally suspect because the man who generates it has abdicated his social responsibilities in a quest for personal aggrandizement and thus sacrificed his status as a gentleman. While Walton will get the credit for the knowledge gleaned from the expedition, the shipboard community is responsible for keeping him obedient to the principles governing legitimate knowledge production and upholding the rules of social obligation.

The possibility of an open polar sea tantalized many early modern and nineteenth-century navigators. Conceived partially from the Renaissance maps that showed the four main rivers of the world meeting in the Arctic and from the vivid imaginations of those obsessed by the Arctic as the final frontier possible to house an Edenic paradise, the tempting prospect of finding an open polar sea lured the suddenly underemployed Royal Navy into Arctic exploration.[6] The navy was not the first to attempt to find the sea. In 1773, Daines Barrington led the Royal Society Council into a discussion of the scientific merits to be gained from an Arctic expedition that would search for a passage through the North Pole to the East Indies. This passage necessarily depended on the existence of an open polar sea, and at the behest of the Royal Society, the Earl of Sandwich backed the search for the sea. He billed the voyage as a specifically scientific one, which differentiated it from earlier attempts to combine natural history and science with whaling and other commercial pursuits. The letter from the Royal Society to the Earl of Sandwich asking his support for the mission reminds its recipient: "And as a voyage made towards the north-pole might be of service to the promotion of natural knowledge, the proper objective of their institution, they cannot but be much interested in the prosecution of the same. They therefore beg leave to recommend it to your Lordship who have always shewn such readiness in promoting science and geographical knowledge, whether it might not be proper to take some steps towards the making such a discovery."[7]

Barrington, an enthusiastic member of the Royal Society who wrote on natural history topics ranging from birdsong to the Arctic, was elected its vice president in 1772. His standing in the Royal Society and his personal relationship with the Earl of Sandwich helped to launch the 1773 expedition led by John Phipps, captain of the *Racehorse*, and Skeffington Lutwidge, who captained the *Carcass*. The Admiralty reiterated the scientific goals of the expedition and the hope that it would bring back legitimate reports of an open polar sea. The directions proceeded to provide guidance for what Phipps should do once he found the open polar sea, something that seems—from the letter at least—to be the possible result of following the Admiralty's cautions. "If you arrive at the Pole and should even find the sea so open as to admit of a free navigation on the opposite meridian, you are not to proceed any further, but having made such observations there of every kind as may be useful to navigation or tend to the promotion of natural knowledge (which you are also to do during the whole course of your voyage) you are to return to the Nore exploring on your way back."[8] The command to bring back as much natural knowledge as possible from all points of the journey reflects the Royal Society's conviction that those embarked on Arctic expeditions should remain committed, perhaps in the face of common sense and the greater wisdom of those piloting the ships, to their natural philosophical goals. The learned men who were theoretically in charge of these expeditions knew almost nothing about the challenges of navigating the ice through which they had to travel, and their ambition to collect as many samples as possible often ran counter to the experienced sea captains' plans for bringing their ships home intact with their crew alive.

Walton's experiences in the Arctic, both before the journey featured in the novel and on that doomed sailing, reflect this dispute over expertise, a contest over whose knowledge and expedition goals were more valuable and reliable, that played a significant role in the Royal Society debates over the open polar sea. Walton describes his efforts "inuring my body to hardship" by signing on to whaling ships, and his pride when a whaling captain "entreated me to remain with the greatest earnestness" (L2, 68, 69). The crew he hires, from his captain through his sailors, is also comprised of whaling men. He entrusts these men, whose knowledge of the Arctic comes from the hard necessity of catching enough whales before the end of the season to cover their expenses and make a profit, with the logistics of navigation and the timing of their trip (L2, 71). His scientific quest for the open polar sea will be conducted, then, according to the limits defined by men whose knowledge of the Arctic far exceeds his own, and for whom the dream of a paradise locked in the ice must run in the face of their extensive accumulated experience. Their experience, however, does not dissuade Walton from his conviction that an Eden lies in the Arctic, and he weights the theories of a few scientific men over the accumulated evidence of many whaling expeditions: "I try in vain to be persuaded that the pole is the seat of frost and desolation; it ever presents itself to my imagination as the region of beauty and delight. Here, Margaret, the sun is for ever visible; its broad disk just skirting the horizon, and diffusing a perpetual splendor. There—for with your leave, my sister, I will put some trust in preceding navigation—there snow and frost are banished; and, sailing over a calm sea, we may be wafted to a land surpassing in wonders and in beauty every region hitherto discovered on the habitable globe (L1, 65). Despite all the theorizing by Royal Society experts, such a thing had never been observed by any of the whalers who regularly sailed the Arctic. They came home with reports of ships trapped in ice and then crushed when the floes moved, and detailed descriptions of the seasonal variations in the ice pack that could allow open water to remain in some areas when others were iced in, but they never reported a consistently open body of water in the Arctic winter or an Edenic paradise of light and warmth in the midst of the ice.

The friction over what kind of expertise was more valuable, especially in the context of Arctic explorations, sheds light on the tension surrounding science becoming more accessible to a broader population and thus losing value as a hallmark of gentlemanly virtue. Even fifty years later, the debate over what kind of knowledge should prevail in determining Arctic expeditions was still taking place on the floor of the Royal Society. In 1868, Captain Sherard Osborn presented his arguments to the Royal Society for why an approach through Baffin's Bay produced the best possible chance for success in discovering an open polar sea. He testified that practical experience with the Gulf Stream and the reports of sailors and whaling captains should be given greater credence than the theories of academic experts, at least until a route was established. Ironically, of course, his steadfast belief in the open polar sea flew in the face of all the experience these men had gained, but nonetheless he prized it as a critical part of knowledge production. He begged his audience, "Let us explore first; then let knowledge be perfected by men of perhaps greater scientific acquisition than the sailor-officer."[9] Here, he creates a divide between exploration and scientific knowledge production that would remain an important part of nineteenth-century expeditions, with the routes and approaches increasingly determined by previous experience by traders and sailors.

Walton, to an even greater extent than Victor Frankenstein, lacks the educational and social grounding that would protect his efforts from his tremendous ambition and thus ensure their scientific value. His interest in the Arctic is fostered not by a strong background in the sciences but instead by his childhood reading about voyages of discovery.[10] He tries and fails to become a poet and averts ignominy only by inheriting a cousin's fortune. This same fortune funds his efforts to become an experienced Arctic sailor and the expedition to find the open polar sea. He never has a formal scientific education but is instead entirely self-taught in "the study of mathematics, the theory of medicine, and those branches of physical science from which a naval adventurer might derive the greatest possible practical advantage" (L1, 69). This lack of an institutionally defined curriculum, along with his poetic imagination, is reflected in Walton's conviction that his earlier failures and redoubled efforts should result in his achieving "some great purpose" (L1, 69). While self-made men are the fodder of great stories, they did not correspond well with the emerging expectations for peer-governed and -reviewed knowledge production.

Walton's community is limited to his sister, who has no scientific training and whose sex disqualifies her anyway, and the men he hires to sail the ship for him. He laments the lack of a like-minded man on board, but even his ardent desire for a friend to share his ambitions reflects his isolation from the emerging standards of the scientific community. In describing his own strengths and weaknesses to his sister, he cites the need for a friend: "It is true that I have thought more, and that my day dreams are more extended and magnificent; but they want (as the painters call it) *keeping*; and I greatly need a friend who would have sense enough not to despise me as romantic, and affection enough for me to endeavour to regulate my mind" (L2, 71). In pointing to his need for an external agent to help "regulate" his mind, Walton emphasizes not his lack of education, which originally prompted this part of the narrative, but the greater lack perpetuated by that—discipline. Having floated from an unstructured childhood to life as a poet, Walton lacks the discipline and grounding in a scientific community that come from a regularized and institutional education. He needs that discipline and a place in a peer group to remind him of his own limitations and the importance of pursuing knowledge for its own sake (or, in Renaissance terms, to better understand God) rather than for personal aggrandizement. His belief that he is destined to find the open polar sea, like Victor's conviction that he will find the cure for all disease and even death, makes him subject to the weaknesses perpetuated by pride and immune to the cautions inherent in the institutionalized governance of scientific knowledge.

Victor and the Institutionalization of Scientific Knowledge Production

Victor, like Walton, pursues his scientific investigations outside the rules governing acceptable scientific knowledge production, which required community integration, peer review, and replicability. He does so, however, in one of the institutions instrumental in creating and enforcing these standards—the university. Anne Mellor, for example, has devoted several works to placing Frankenstein and his monster in relation to racial science and evolution, Humphry Davy's discoveries in chemistry, and Galvani's theory of animal electricity. In all of her work, she argues that *Frankenstein* exemplifies bad science according to the standards established during this period and the Creature serves to illustrate the dramatic costs of such bad practice.[11] This raises the important question: Why does Mary Shelley have Victor flout the emerging standards governing scientific practice and embrace a much older and apparently more dangerous approach to knowledge production?

Rather than merely an obvious warning about the dangers of unregulated scientific pursuit, Shelley offers readers an elegant historicization of the revolutions that had spun science from a dogged, individual pursuit for spiritual and natural truth—often undertaken despite social approbations and in secret—to a public, ritualized, and socially regulated form of knowledge production whose only applications were to the natural world. That transition occurred, as Steven Shapin convincingly argues, through the increasingly close alliance in the seventeenth century of gentlemanly identity with natural knowledge creation and scientific truth. He tackles the central conundrum of scientific design and experimentalism in the seventeenth century—and lasting through today—as one of a mixed relationship between autonomy and truth telling. In order to establish scientific authority, seventeenth-century gentlemen scientists rejected accepted knowledge and elevated the status of eyewitness testimony. But this shift required a shared acceptance of the erasure of the contributions made to scientific knowledge production by laboratory assistants, kitchen boys, and—as would be the case in Arctic explorations—sailors.

Shapin contends that this erasure reflects the trust placed in particular kinds of knowledge manufacturers: specifically, gentlemen embedded in a social and intellectual network that provides oversight for and value to the knowledge obtained in it. He also reinforces the importance of gentlemanly conduct for maintaining the social order and providing strength to bonds among gentlemen and between gentlemen and those from the lower social classes. When gentlemen behave according to the rules of civility, they gain authority and become trustworthy, allowing them to emerge as more authoritative and powerful, while any violation of their obligations undermines their social position and renders them dangerous to the social order.[12] As previously mentioned, Walton treads this line when he pushes his men to the brink of mutiny by endangering their lives so he can press into the Arctic and realize his dream of reaching the open polar sea. When he agrees to turn back, however, he reestablishes himself as a gentleman by honoring his obligations to those he leads and tacitly recognizes their greater knowledge of the sea and the Arctic. Their contributions to his understanding will, as Shapin contends, be erased in any formal discussions or printed versions of this adventure, as will the narrative of how close Walton came to losing his status as a gentleman and a truth teller. Walton's newfound expertise is only worth as much as his credibility, and his reliability depends upon his status as a gentleman. Should he sacrifice that, whatever he finds on his voyage will be meaningless, and thus knowledge pursued outside the rules defined by his social network is not worth the cost.

Kim Hammond provides additional support for this argument when she contends that the scientific critique in *Frankenstein* is subtler than other scholars have realized. She claims that the novel's scientific parable questions the Romantic ideals it seems to embrace and provides a positive approach to Enlightenment intellectual inquiry. Her work is most compelling, however, in forwarding the social relationships that surround—and legitimize—science in *Frankenstein*: "Shelley's launch of science fiction is an elegant historical landmark of the social changes of her time: a society committed primarily to the promises of the Enlightenment notion of progress epitomized by advances in science and technology and characterized by the apparent (modernist) separation of 'nature' and 'society.'"[13] At the same time, Hammond opens the door to some thought-provoking questions about the critical importance of scientific community in the novel and the framework it provides for thinking through larger questions about social relationships and changing social hierarchies in late eighteenth- and early nineteenth-century England. While the social strata occupied by characters in *Frankenstein* remains a crucial aspect of the novel, the importance Shelley places on community is equally essential to recognize the framework for understanding these relationships that necessarily encompasses the historical past it references. Placed in the context of revolutions, religious, intellectual, and class, *Frankenstein*'s scientific inquiries and the importance of particular texts, approaches, and projects become clearer indicators of the novel's broader critical commentary on the most significant questions of its time.

The importance of science as a creative force in *Frankenstein* is another fundamental area that has attracted academic attention. Some scholars trace the ways in which *Frankenstein* departs from similar technologically and scientifically positivist narratives published around the same time. Julia Douthwaite and Daniel Richter, for example, compare Shelley's novel to a 1790 story by François-Félix Nogaret, *Le miroir des évenémens actuels; ou, La belle au plus offrant: Histoire a deux visages* (The Looking Glass of Actuality; or, Beauty to the Highest Bidder: A Two-Faced Tale), which features a scientific contest to build society-helping automata. They argue that Nogaret's novel reflects the principles most important to post-Revolutionary France, especially the centrality of human invention and technology in civilized society, the human triumph over superstition and religion, and the increasing potential of human invention to mimic the original emergence of life.[14] While this well-known tale might well have provided Shelley with some of her ideas, the help the automata can offer is limited and socially responsible compared to the scientific experiments carried out by Victor Frankenstein.

During Victor's childhood, like Walton's, reading indelibly shapes his adult ambitions and defines his pursuit of natural philosophy. It also ill prepares him for scientific work in an eighteenth-century university such as Ingolstadt. Though he mentions attending school once, he does so only to explain how he met Henry Clerval, his devoted friend (1.1, 90). He spends the majority of his time pursuing his own interests, which include a Renaissance-based introduction to magic, alchemy, and natural philosophy, courtesy of a book by Heinrich Cornelius Agrippa that he discovers on a rainy day in a rented house.[15] He blames his father for his continued affinity for Renaissance natural philosophers, since he simply told Victor to read something more valuable rather than taking "the pains to explain to me that the principles of Agrippa had been entirely exploded, and that a modern system of science had been introduced, which possessed much greater powers than the ancient, because the powers of the latter were chimerical, while those of the former were real and practical" (1.1, 93). This strong endorsement of the modern scientific approach would certainly have set Victor on a different track, though the fact that he pursues his studies of Renaissance natural philosophy on the sly suggests that his interests might also be motivated by youthful rebellion as much as by personal interest (1.1, 93).

Before arriving at Ingolstadt, therefore, Victor receives his entire education in natural philosophy from solitary readings of Albertus Magnus, Paracelsus, and Agrippa, which results in his complete isolation from the eighteenth-century scientific community and its interests. Through these books, he develops both his obsession with the philosopher's stone, which promised great glory since it would allow him to banish death, and raising demons (1.1, (3–94). He exhibits a truly Renaissance reaction to his failure to make demons or spirits appear, recognizing that his failure results from "my own inexperience and mistakes, rather than a want of skill or fidelity in my instructors (1.1, 94)." The experiments he conducts on the natural world are an interesting overview of early modern science. Wolfson and Levao dismiss distillation as being alchemical, but it is also a foundational part of chemistry.[16] The latter use is evidently the one that interests Victor, since Paracelsus and Agrippa both write about distillation in alchemy, while Victor describes it, "and the wonderful effects of steam," as "processes of which my favorite authors were utterly ignorant" (1.1, 94)."

Victor also mentions Boyle's experiments with the air pump, which made the rounds of seventeenth-century drawing rooms and remained a staple of basic scientific education in the eighteenth century.[17] His education about electricity results from a lecture and demonstration by his father, who "constructed a small electrical machine, and exhibited a few experiments; he made also a kite, with a wire and string, which drew down that fluid from the clouds" (1.1, 96). Given the chance to attend a series of academic presentations on natural philosophy in Geneva, Victor misses all but the last, which "was entirely incomprehensible" (1.1, 97) and causes him to jettison his interest in all modern science in favor of ancient authors such as Pliny. By the time he enters university at Ingolstadt, Victor is fluent in Latin, Greek, German, and English and is a well-educated seventeenth-century natural philosopher. Unfortunately, the scientific community he encounters there has little patience for his dominant influences or for his scattered, undisciplined approach to studying the natural world; thus, the alienation he experiences in his early days at the university only entrenches his desire to attain glory through the solitary domination of death, to prove his superiority to those who mocked him.

Ironically, the only books that interest Victor are those by the Renaissance authors he repeatedly claims to have outgrown. When his professors offer him extensive lists of books to acquaint him with modern natural philosophy, he does "not feel much inclined to study the books." He attributes this to the ugliness of his professor and the weak promises of modern science, which only provide the tools to better understand the minute workings of nature, rather than the grand potential of Renaissance magic, which offers the keys to understanding the entire system governing the world (1.2, 103). He finds a more amenable mentor in Professor Waldman, who provides a way of understanding the true potential in modern chemistry by claiming that real advantage to mankind could be gained through it and likening their the achievements of those scientists who practiced it to those promised by Victor's Renaissance influences: "But these philosophers, whose hands seem only made to dabble in dirt, and their eyes to pore over the microscope or crucible, have indeed performed miracles. They penetrate into the recesses of nature, and shew how she works in her hiding places. They ascend into the heavens; they have discovered how the blood circulates, and the nature of the air we breathe. They have acquired new and almost unlimited powers; they can command the thunders of heaven, mimic the earthquake, and even mock the invisible world with its own shadows" (1.2, 104). These powerful words inspire Victor to study chemistry, so that he too might become a demigod and command the natural world. For two years, he remains part of the university, enjoys its discipline, and earns its faculty's respect. But when he feels that he has mastered all the knowledge he can learn from his professors, he sets off to identify what causes life through a series of entirely independent experiments with stolen body parts. Such actions, as discussed earlier, move him well outside the rules he has been taught that govern scientific experimentation and draw his imagination back to the promises made by the Renaissance authors who aroused his childhood passions.

A Brief Foray into Renaissance Natural Philosophy

For a modern reader, the following review of strange medieval and Renaissance authors might seem like the deluded maunderings of a historian gone mad, but it serves to illustrate some important characteristics that these authors have in common and that determine their place in Mary Shelley's novel. First, they were among the most notable natural philosophers who worked in Switzerland and contributed to its natural philosophical heritage. As a result, their works would make logical additions to a Swiss library such as the one Victor finds himself perusing on a rainy day during a family trip to the shore. Second, they were all connected through their ideas about the nature of the world and the importance of natural philosophy for understanding the way it worked. Third, they all championed independent and disciplined study of the natural world as a critical means for achieving insight into its workings and God's will. Fourth, they all held out, in varying degrees, the promise that a young man willing to dedicate his life to the study of nature could come to bend its forces to his will. Finally, their works were readily available in printed, vernacular languages for Victor's consumption, and they were paired up (often even bound) with falsely attributed treatises that promised even greater power over the natural world.

Victor Frankenstein first forms his understanding of nature and the means by which people could manipulate it by reading some of the most notable authors in late medieval and Renaissance natural philosophy, Albertus Magnus, Paracelsus, and Agrippa. Albertus Magnus (ca. 1200–1280) was a thirteenth-century Dominican philosopher and mathematician who studied natural philosophy, philosophy, and theology in Paris and, after a brief stint as bishop of Regensburg, spent the latter part of his life teaching and ministering in Cologne. Most notably, he reintroduced classical Greek authors, especially Aristotle, into the study of natural philosophy and mathematics. While Victor, as well as Mary

Shelley, likely read all or part of Albertus's *Opus*, which was a highly influential treatise in the field of mathematics, the book cited here as authored by Albertus is quite possibly the falsely attributed Renaissance book *The Secrets of Albertus Magnus*. Like other books in its genre, it offers a compendium of recipes for everything from quince tarts to the philosopher's stone, medical remedies, systems of sympathy and antipathy governing stones, beasts, plants, and other assorted curiosities.[18] Combined with Albertus's desire to pursue the secrets of the natural world for his own satisfaction, this pseudo-Albertus book provides a rich array of levers that would appeal to an eager young reader looking for ideas about the systems governing nature and a justification for his own curiosity. Although by the eighteenth century, science for its own sake was more widely accepted and the divide between religion and science far wider than it had been two centuries before, a respected authority such as Albertus declaring that scientific pursuits should be undertaken to satisfy one's desire to know about the world, not just for the greater glory of God, might have proven a welcome encouragement to young Victor.

Philippus Aureolus Theophrastus Bombastus von Hohenheim, more commonly known as Paracelsus (1493/4–1541), was a Swiss-born polymath whose studies in medicine, mining, and chemistry produced, among other things, a system of chemical medicine that provided, after his death, a worthy opponent to traditional humoral thought that grew in popularity from the sixteenth century through the eighteenth. He opposed traditional theories of health and disease, in which each body had its own unique constitution that, when out of balance, resulted in disease. He posited that diseases were separate entities that could be treated by chemical remedies derived from the three principles that comprised the whole world: salt, sulphur, and mercury. The vast majority of his works were published by his followers after his death, and though it is not clear which of his books Victor Frankenstein might have read, his interest in chemistry and the text's popularity suggest the *Archidoxis*, which was first published in German in 1569 and saw multiple publications in many vernacular European languages for the next several centuries.[19] Any of Paracelsus's books would, however, have presented a radically different approach to the study of nature that prized individual investigations over book learning and promised great power to a man willing to apply himself to learning the secrets of nature.

Heinrich Cornelius Agrippa von Nettesheim (1485–1535), a contemporary of Paracelsus, studied natural philosophy, magic, and theology and practiced as a physician in Cologne before serving in the courts of Francis I and Margaret of Austria. He remains best known for two works, *De incertitudine et vanitate scientiarum et artium atque excellentia verbi Dei declamatio* (1530/1531), a skeptical attack on the Church and all respected institutions and practitioners of science, law, the liberal arts, and medicine, and *De occulta philosophia libri tres* (1531/1533), his cosmology in which magic allows adepts to better apprehend the divine mind and perhaps even rejoin their original form and influence the natural world from within the divine realm.[20] It is likely the latter book, or perhaps even the falsely attributed *Fourth Book of Occult Philosophy*, that drew Victor Frankenstein's attention. Agrippa's claim that a true adept could pursue the study of nature back to the original idea illuminating the Creation and make use of celestial forces to create natural change promised great power to anyone willing to devote himself to the study of the natural world. It also contained information about many of the most dangerous and appealing forms of magic, including necromancy and the use of images and sounds to create visions and prophecies. Between promising to reveal the spark of life to those capable of devoting themselves to the study of natural philosophy, mathematics, and magic, Agrippa cautions his readers not to pursue magic for selfish ends as it would tarnish their souls and thus prevent them from achieving any meaningful magical work.[21] That said, Victor could be forgiven for eagerly paging through the five hundred thirty pages of this book in search of the truths Agrippa repeatedly promises and in eager anticipation of achieving great power.

These works inflame Victor's vivid imagination, rich as they are with details about the forces governing nature. They also convince him of his potential to improve nature beyond God's original plan, even though that kind of scientific pursuit had fallen out of fashion by the eighteenth century. He searches for the elixir of life because of the "glory that would attend the discovery, if I could banish disease from the human frame, and render man invulnerable to any but a violent death!" (I.I, 93–94) Frankenstein's dreams of fame as the just reward for his scientific endeavors prove an important point of separation from the authors who influence him. One of the central tenets of these Renaissance philosophers is that the honest pursuit of nature's secrets must be done solely for the glory of God, to better appreciate his plan, and never for personal aggrandizement or power. From a Renaissance perspective, Victor's dreams of making the elixir of life are perfectly acceptable, but unattainable for any student motivated by self-interest. The failure to keep God in the forefront of scientific investigations is among the fatal errors most frequently committed by natural philosophers, letting selfish goals eclipse their obligations to the divine plan. Such egocentric efforts must always end in failure, as their motivation comes from the basest elements of humanity rather than an intelligence enlightened by divine consideration. This failure is certainly Victor's error, but, within the context of the novel, the problem is less that he thinks he can transcend natural limits than that he intends to do so for selfish reasons rather than to better understand God.

By the eighteenth century, the separation between natural philosophy and theology was clearly defined and widely understood. While some scientists of this period praised their discipline for the insight it gave them into the beauty of the divine creation, they also maintained that it reminded them of their human limitations. During the Renaissance, however, no clear division between natural philosophy and theology existed. In fact, the pursuit of natural philosophy was, for the magi who influenced Victor, a critically important step to better understanding God. For all three authors, natural philosophy provided insight into the tools God left for man to manipulate his world, and all three also conceived of natural philosophy and magic as a means by which man could transcend the natural realm and assume nearly divine powers. All three also conceived of natural philosophy as a discipline that allowed man to better understand—and even support—God's plan, and as a result, the study of nature allowed adepts to attain a personal relationship with God not mediated by the clergy or under Church oversight. By the time Mary Shelley encountered these books and put them in her novel, however, they were often divorced from the religious and even intellectual contexts in which they were produced. All three authors were known, by that time, more for their rampant individualism and selfish intellectual excesses, and they were largely considered examples of the kind of misguided natural philosophy that had been replaced by the increasingly institutionalized science regulated by the Royal Society and the universities.

The novel places Frankenstein's background in natural philosophy and his convictions about its potential squarely within the intellectual framework of Renaissance philosophy, when magicians and thinkers such as Agrippa and Paracelsus created models of the world that mirrored their belief that unraveling nature's secrets would help them understand God. Theology and natural philosophy were inherently intertwined during this period, with Paracelsus, for example, developing a complete theory surrounding Mary that made her an intrinsic part of the Godhead, and Agrippa asserting that one could not understand the first without knowing the second, nor pursue magic without mastering both.[22] What the novel doesn't do, however, is cleanly articulate the divide that Renaissance natural philosophers such as Agrippa and Paracelsus used to govern their own inquiries and that was the foundation of occult thought: all inquiries into the divine must be undertaken in full humility and acceptance of eventual failure. Magical theology, to be considered valuable, must reflect the practitioner's acceptance of his own limitations and his inability to ever fully understand divine intention. His study of the world must reflect his faith and be in the service of honoring the divine through an attempt to better appreciate the parts of the divine plan he can grasp.[23] Pursuing a greater understanding of the power governing natural systems to increase your own power over them, as was the motivation for many magicians, directly disobeyed God's intention and challenged divine authority. It was heretical, dangerous, and deeply stupid. And, of course, divine commandments had been ignored many times before the Renaissance, even by God's own angels—not to mention by Victor Frankenstein and his progeny.

Frankenstein and the Angels

A significant divide regarding the religious themes in *Frankenstein* characterizes ongoing debates among Mary Shelley scholars. The first camp concludes that she was overtly irreligious based on the fact that her parents were atheists; after all, they note, she revered her iconoclastic father and her feminist mother—neither of whom expressed religious convictions—and ran away with Percy Shelley, an outspoken atheist kicked out of Oxford for expressing his antireligious views, when she was still a teenager and he was still married. Although she became more conventional in later life, the rebellious young Mary Shelley who penned the novel could not have behaved as she did, and consequently could not have written as she wrote, while under the sway of any religious orientation or traditional belief system. So, contends this group, *Frankenstein* contains very few religious references and has no overarching religious motivation. The second, and rather larger, camp of academic commentators maintains that the novel incorporates an overtly Christian framework, and various scholars propose multiple explanations for what it means. Their most convincing argument places *Frankenstein* in the context of Milton's poetic epic *Paradise Lost*, a sacred text to the Romantic writers, using Victor's self-identification with Lucifer's overreaching hubris and actual quotes from Milton as its most potent evidence.[24]

The novel, as often noted by scholars, is part of a larger discussion about the relationship between science and faith and the limits of human versus divine power; it also contains a debate about the relative powers of man and God, as well as the appropriate ways in which man can wield power over nature without doing damage to himself or others. While *Frankenstein* clearly contains theological elements, with Genesis its primary biblical referent, Milton is but one, and perhaps even not the primary, author to whom the parallel should be drawn. All of the Renaissance authors Shelley specifically cites as guides to understanding the price of disobedience to divine commands—Agrippa, Paracelsus, and Albertus Magnus—develop their angelologies from Genesis and devote significant portions of their work to the origins of the angels and their roles. Thus, exploring their systems of thought in relation to *Frankenstein* contains a valuable key to decoding Shelley's angelic understanding and identifying the particular group of rebel angels she uses as the basis for her novel.

Four significant themes evident throughout the novel support the conclusion that *Frankenstein* serves, in part, as an extended analogy of the story of the Nephilim. The first is the theme of the Arctic, discussed above as part of the scientific context of the early nineteenth century, but also expressed by the

Creature as a place of exile and eternal darkness. The second is the naming of Agrippa, Paracelsus, and Albertus Magnus as the most significant influences on Victor's thought, with the first two being named more frequently than the last. All these men believed that understanding the natural world required reading it alongside the Bible; and Paracelsus and Agrippa expressed significant interest in Genesis and the specific problem of how the world was created and peopled/creatured. Finally, both men wrote about angels and were certainly aware of the story of the Nephilim and the punishment handed down to those angels who strayed from God's plan. Thus, the writings of men specifically identified as strongly influencing Victor's thought in the text of Shelley's novel can offer insight and contextualization for a significant portion of the work.

The third theme to pursue in this line of investigation is the divided nature of the Creature as expressed by his extraordinary size, grotesque appearance, and preternatural sense of morality. The explanation that he is big because he was pieced together from human parts makes no sense, as noted in later chapters, although that does explain why he would be hideous. But taken together, these characteristics suggest a hybrid of angel and human and reflect the descriptions of the Anakim, giants produced by the coupling of male angels (Watchers) and human mothers. The fourth element in this contention is Victor himself, who has, as previous authors have demonstrated, all the hubris and pride of that greatest of all angelic rebels, Lucifer. Victor is certainly disobedient to divine intention, but if he has an angelic counterpart, it should be one of the Nephilim. He disobeys God by departing from his appointed role as a scientist, to watch and study the world (much as the Nephilim were sent to study humankind), and instead tries to adopt God's role in creation. These angels, created by God to be perfect and sexless, were uncorrupted by the need to reproduce, so their affairs with human women were entirely driven by their lust for beauty and sensation. It is true that the Nephilim were seduced by sexual desire, while Victor fell due to a lust for knowledge, but the comparison between the two is worth pursuing, especially since an analysis of the passages that have best supported the Frankenstein as Lucifer theory also provide ample evidence for the influence of the Nephilim story.

In order to understand the story of the Nephilim and its resonances in *Frankenstein*, we must return to Genesis, which contains the first mention of these angels in the Old Testament.

> Now it came about, when men began to multiply on the face of the land, and daughters were born to them, that the sons of God saw that the daughters of men were beautiful; and they took wives for themselves, whomever they chose. Then the LORD said, "My Spirit shall not strive with man forever, because he also is flesh; nevertheless his days shall be

one hundred and twenty years." The Nephilim were on the earth in those
days, and also afterward, when the sons of God came in to the daughters
of men, and they bore children to them. Those were the mighty men who
were of old, men of renown. (Genesis 6:1–4)

Legions of biblical scholars have devoted enormous amounts of time decoding this passage in the larger context of the Old and New Testaments, paying
particular attention to the phrase "sons of God" to more accurately determine
whether this indicates angels or men. The phrase is equally used to describe
godly men and angels. Therefore, it remains unclear whether this verse means
that the angels God chose to watch people had sex with women or that men
who believed in the Hebrew God, and were therefore called the sons of God, had
sex with women who were of another faith. If the latter interpretation is correct, however, it defies biblical logic that their children would become mightier
than the children born to parents who both worshipped the same god. Instead,
it suggests that the offspring of these unions were giants who perhaps lived
longer than other humans because they were, in fact, the product of relations
between angels and women. The book of Enoch contains clarification of the
Genesis verse: "And it came to pass when the children of men had multiplied
that in those days were born unto them beautiful and comely daughters. And
the angels, the children of heaven, saw them and lusted after them, and said
to one another, 'Come, let us choose wives from among the children of men
and beget us children'" (Enoch 6:1–2). This seems much clearer and supports
the idea that some of the angels sent by God to watch humankind became too
interested in the objects of their observation and consequently abandoned their
posts to pursue the human desire to have sex and children.

The results of these pairings were not beneficial for either the surrounding
countryside or the disobedient angels: "And they became pregnant, and they
bare great giants, whose height was three thousand ells, who consumed all the
acquisitions of men. And when men could no longer sustain them, the giants
turned against them and devoured mankind" (Enoch 7:2–4). The actions of these
giants parallel the Creature's with eerie familiarity. The Creature, too, tries to
live off the countryside and avoid people, but when that fails, and after being
rejected by the people he long admired, he turns violently destructive. The long
interlude he spends spying on the poor French family, fantasizing that their
enlightened natures will allow him to be included in their outcast state, best
illustrates this sad cycle of hope, despair and rage. When the Creature finally
reveals himself to the De Lacey family, they spurn him, despite his many kind-
nesses, because of his horrific appearance; eventually, an angry mob of terrified
farmers accuses him of every violent crime recently committed (he is responsible for one of them) and chases him from the area. His gigantic stature and vile

appearance draw their wrath and inflame their fears because they highlight his lack of humanity and immediately label him as alien and, quite literally, monstrous. Much as the horrific appearance of the giant offspring of the Watchers and their human lovers signaled their half-breed status and forced them first into ignominy and then into violence, the Creature is stigmatized as monstrous before his behavior actually deserves such an undesirable label.

The book of Jubilees (sometimes referred to as Lesser Genesis) details how irritated God was by the actions of his disobedient angels and their giant spawn: "And against the angels whom He had sent upon the earth, He was exceedingly wroth, and He gave commandment to root them out of all their dominion, and He bade us to bind them in the depths of the earth, and behold they are bound in the midst of them, and are (kept) separate. And against their sons went forth a command from before His face that they should be smitten with the sword, and be removed from under heaven." The passage continues, detailing the punishment the angelic Watchers received for disobeying God: "And their fathers were witnesses (of their destruction), and after this they were bound in the depths of the earth forever, until the day of the great condemnation, when judgment is executed on all those who have corrupted their ways and their works before the Lord" (*Jubilees* 5:6–7, 10). Victor, like the Watchers, is fated to spend the remainder of his days watching the havoc and destruction wreaked by his greatest mistake. He finishes the remainder of his life pursuing the Creature, following its bloody trail, and wallowing in grief for creating such a monster, but it never has the desired effect. He never masters the desire for renown that drives him to make the Creature in the first place, nor does he grasp the central message of Renaissance natural philosophy: the pursuit of knowledge must always be done in a measured way with appreciation for human limits and divine perfection.

Only his refusal to make the Creature a mate hints that Victor might have learned some hard lessons from his multiple tragedies, but Shelley emphasizes his complete inability to apprehend the first message by his death speech aboard Walton's trapped vessel. Broken down emotionally, and physically near to death, Frankenstein painfully rouses himself to passionately exhort Walton's mutinous crew to continue their futile journey into the Arctic, a potentially disastrous decision that would likely result in their deaths and destroy their scientific findings—all for personal honor and public glory. He also remains entirely unfazed by the probable loss of any samples they have collected, since the wreck of the ship and deaths of the crew members would doom those efforts and totally eclipse any scientific value of the trip. Despite all that has occurred in his benighted life, Victor beseeches the crew to venture forth on their expedition to locate and finally document the open polar sea for entirely self-centered reasons, to "be hailed as the benefactors of your species; your name adored" (3.7, 315).

Thus, even when faced with his own death earned for desiring glory and admiration above the disciplined pursuit of knowledge, Victor fails to apprehend why he spends hundreds of pages chasing his Creature to the ends of the earth. He describes to Walton both the passion and the pride that drove his investigations: "Even now I cannot recollect, without passion, my reveries while the work was incomplete. I trod heaven in my thoughts, now exulting in my powers, now burning with the idea of their effects" (3.7, 310). Previous commentators use this same speech to buttress their claims that *Frankenstein* is an allegory of *Paradise Lost*, since Victor compares himself directly to Lucifer in that narrative: "like the archangel who aspired to omnipotence, I am chained in an eternal hell" (3.7, 310). Certainly, like Lucifer, he overreaches; but like the Nephilim, he does so for desire and for the sake of natural knowledge, a gift the Nephilim gave to the women they married and that improved the lot of mankind—a goal Victor never manages to achieve. Consumed by the passion to know, even more than by the power to control and a refusal to submit, he winds up in chains for it. Lucifer (like Prometheus) also wore chains for his disobedience, but he was manacled in hellfire, while the Nephilim, like Frankenstein, were shackled in the cold and the dark.

If Victor was of the Nephilim, then the Creature was one of the Anakim, the giant offspring of the unholy union of angels and humans. The Creature's misery was no less awful than the one experienced by the giants described in the book of Jubilees. Horrible in appearance and spurned by the people he admires, he is driven from the warm harbors of civilized society by fear and anger. Suffering from this rejection, he directs his wrath toward his creator, much as the Anikim raged against the world that contained them, and both engaged in hideous acts of violence and destruction that their damned creators were doomed to watch. The Creature even leads Victor on a merry chase through northern Europe and into the Arctic, reveling in his creator's misery and terrifying people he encounters as they traverse the northern realms of ice. Unlike the Anikim, who died in the divinely sent Flood, the Creature survives to mourn the death of his creator. He sentences himself to death, however, and promises Walton he will commit suicide—ironically, by the very fire that consumed Lucifer and would truly be a miracle if conjured in the far north.

By situating *Frankenstein* tightly within the intellectual framework of early nineteenth-century science and simultaneously deriding the goals of Renaissance natural philosophy, Shelley joined her era's endeavor to separate its "science" from preceding efforts that lacked method and discipline and traversed too readily the boundaries between theology and natural philosophy and, of course, science and magic. For all of the monstrous accusations in *Frankenstein*, the only creatures it contains are man-made, and the novel rests solely in the realm of the natural, rather than the supernatural: it exists as part of our world, not of any other. The science it presents obeys the rules hammered out over the previous two centuries by the men of the Académie Royale and the Royal Society. By restating the importance of the boundaries between good and bad practice, it establishes the rules governing legitimate scientific practice and reifies the category of science at the expense of the richer intellectual engagements of the Renaissance. The enduring vision of Victor Frankenstein as the paradigmatic "mad scientist" emerges from implementing the more contemporary methodologies advocated by the accepted experimental approaches of his day.

From a twenty-first-century perspective, the ethical views toward people of other races and their property rights maintained by late eighteenth- and early nineteenth-century European governments do not inspire great admiration, but the public governance of how knowledge was obtained and the attention paid to creating an image of a moral scientist represent meaningful products of this effort. The rules governing scientific production during this period generated the ethical framework that would develop over the next century—perhaps most clearly with the set of rules governing human experimentation elucidated in Nuremberg and in response to the Tuskegee syphilis study—to define the regulations by which knowledge could be gained and at what point the human price to be paid was simply too high to be borne. Those rules continue to define how modern citizens characterize legitimate versus dangerous scientific pursuits. Peer review remains a staple of medical and scientific practice, and the importance of institutional oversight—whether from hospitals, professional agencies, or governments—has not declined. Lone heroes struggling late into the night inhabiting isolated laboratories outside the network of university/corporation/government that defines and regulates modern science are either the heroes of conspiracy-themed television—like the Lone Gunmen in *The X-Files* or Buffy and her friends in season 4 of *Buffy the Vampire Slayer*—or the dangerous maniacs who will stop at nothing to increase their own power, like Dr. Otto Octavius/Dr. Octopus in *Spider-Man* and the other mad scientists of countless movies and TV programs. Victor Frankenstein serves as an early example for why lone scientists pose a danger to themselves and the social fabric they abandoned when they chose to pursue natural knowledge outside the bounds of peer review and social oversight.

2

==================================

The Instruments of Life

Frankenstein's Medical History

> Both the new body and society are constructed from different elements
> from the present and the past; some living and contemporary, some
> industrial and mass-produced, others ancient and traditional.
>
> —Cecil Helman, *The Body of Frankenstein's Monster*

The Creature's appearance signals his monstrosity. It gestures toward his awkward straddling of the line between the natural pieces from which he was made and the unknown process by which he was animated. Walton describes the Creature as "gigantic in stature, yet uncouth and distorted in [his] proportions" with skin "in colour and apparent texture like that of a mummy." He exclaims, "Never did I behold a vision so horrible as his face, of such loathsome, yet appalling hideousness" (3.7, 319). The shock of seeing the vile nature of reanimated tissue—some of which had apparently been lying around for quite some time—stretched eight feet tall plunges Victor into a catatonic stupor. But looking like a monster is not the end of the story. The Creature enacts the role of monster as destroyer through multiple bloody murders woven into his committed experiment with creator-oriented sadism. His existential suffering at the hands of his creator's thoughtless exercise in power is written in the entrails and misery of his creator's beloved family and friends. On a quick review, the Creature's behavior does seem pretty horrifying, but the anguish he experiences reads as real and reaches a surprising level of humanity for a supposedly soulless, reanimated corpse. His responses and emotions provoke a crucial question: The Creature obviously has a body, however mutilated, and a mind, one clearly capable of reasoning and learning, but does he possess a soul? Did Victor, perhaps unwittingly, transfer a soul into that flesh pile when he endeavored to create a new species? The relationship between the body and the soul has remained a significant intellectual preoccupation and theological controversy for centuries, made slightly clearer by the Crucifixion but then complicated again by the Resurrection. While scholars and theologians never fully settled upon an authoritative definition of the soul, its characteristics have largely been accepted in Western thought: the soul is the combination of an individual's essence, his or her imagination, dreams, beliefs, and memories. The essential premise underlying these discussions was well established by the time Mary Shelley penned *Frankenstein*: the body could be damaged, even dismembered, and life extinguished without any damage done to the soul. The uncertainty remaining, however, was how long the soul stayed in or near the corpse, and whether it could remain attached to a piece of the body—perhaps the brain or the heart—if it was relocated to another being, as happened when Victor patched together the Creature. Thus, the prospect of an ensouled Creature is tantalizingly available in the text. He slowly recovers the memories of his early days, including Victor's rejection, dreams of acceptance by the De Lacey family and then by the mate he demands that Victor create, and develops a strong analogy between himself and the fallen angel Lucifer as described in Milton's *Paradise Lost*. His reactions to the injustices committed against him by his creator and the people he encounters throughout the novel reflect the dissolution of the lofty ideals he projected onto humanity, but their very presence suggests the existence of a soul. Finally, the Creature's display of rage and violence, much like his capacity for joy and love, demonstrates that he was ensouled; thus, his animation was not simply the electric rejuvenation of dead flesh but instead the creation of a new being equally worthy of respect as the humans who surround him.

Angels and Demons

The Creature's oversized reactions to injustice, unkindness, and even rage, much like his gigantic stature, render him a mirror that permits the reader a clearer vision of the society in which the novel is based, a distinctly premodern intellectual concoction of religion and science. That society had room for creatures we reject in modern discussions of science, particularly God, angels, and demons, and *Frankenstein* references all of these. The first and most frequent reference Victor makes to his Creature is, in fact, to call it a demon. (Mary Shelley spells the word "daemon," which is a Latinized version of the Greek *dimon*.) This word went through multiple meanings over the centuries, beginning as a relatively benign spirit and trending over time toward the malevolent. It has two potential meanings as used by Shelley in this context, and both will be examined during this chapter. The first is as a person's attendant spirit, or a preternatural being specifically linked to a person. The intimate bond between Victor and the Creature is clearly identified, since Victor made him, but this link might be even deeper than that between creator and creation. The intense passion Victor invested in his Creature's construction could have allowed some of his own soul to enter the Creature and, as a result, irreparably conjoined the two. The second meaning of "daemon" is the one we traditionally associate nowadays with "demon," a malignant spirit or an agent of demonic possession. This word was derived from "daemon," and the two were used interchangeably during Mary Shelley's era to describe a malevolent preternatural spirit.[1]

When Victor describes the Creature as a demon, he does so with the knowledge that these evil beings are fully capable of entering a body and taking it over. While most *Frankenstein* commentators dismiss these references as symbolic, they could equally be taken as factual. Demons were widely represented in early nineteenth-century popular culture and consistently appeared in more serious treatises as well. The very books that motivated Victor's project, including Agrippa's magnum opus, detail the ranks of demons and their constant desire to interfere with human life. Only forty years after the initial publication of *De occulta philosophia libri tres*, and supposedly using its author as a model for his protagonist, the playwright Christopher Marlowe shocked London theatergoers with his evocative depiction of a natural philosopher tempted by a demon to sell his soul for knowledge and earthly power. Like Agrippa's magical theology, Marlowe's Faustus was resurrected in the early nineteenth century, both reappearing in significant literary works in that period. Agrippa, of course, resurfaced in Shelley's *Frankenstein* and Faustus in Goethe's *Faust* (part 1, 1808; part 2, 1832). Because the temptations offered by science—power over the natural world, the ability to command things better left to God—were easily paired with demonic enticements, literary demons sang their siren songs alongside those appearing in natural philosophy, folklore, and theology.

The puzzle of how a demonic entity might have entered Frankenstein's Creature—and perhaps Frankenstein himself—has three possible solutions. First, Frankenstein could have entered into a willful bargain with a demonic entity that took his soul in exchange for the ability to create life. Second, Frankenstein's frantic quest to create life was so close to the line of acceptable human endeavor—and potentially sanity—that a demon, drawn to the manic energy and blurred lines between the natural and preternatural, could have entered Frankenstein's being without the creator's express permission because Frankenstein left the equivalent of a spiritual door open by engaging in such a dangerous project. Third, an atmospheric demon could have been drawn into the pile of body parts on the slab, partially because of the nonnatural aspects of bringing life to dead flesh and partially through the application of excessive amounts of natural forces such as electricity that destabilized the boundaries between the natural and the preternatural. All these possible scenarios rely on a set of early-modern expectations governing the ways demons behaved and their omnipresence in the world that seem slightly out of place in the early nineteenth century. But given that the early nineteenth century as written by Mary Shelley owes great debts to the Renaissance, especially its magical theologians, the presence of demons and their potential to interfere with human work is not particularly surprising.

Critically important to remember in thinking through this puzzle is the fact that the scene in which the Creature goes from a nonliving collection of sewn-together parts to a living being takes up three lines in the novel, and Frankenstein, in relating the event to Walton, repeatedly refuses to elucidate how he accomplished his great work. In an effort to protect Walton from traveling down a path similar to the one that shattered him, Victor remains adamant that he "will not lead you on, unguarded and ardent as I then was, to your destruction and infallible misery" (1.3, 109). Though readers remain in the dark about the mechanics of how Victor created life, this line to Walton might contain a reference to how Frankenstein wound up a dying wretch rather than a god among men. He chooses not to tempt Walton as he was seduced—perhaps by a demon—to accomplish the type of work that no man should attempt. His free will is sufficiently intact to preserve his sense of honor and to ensure that while he might wind up in hell, he will not be responsible for the destruction of another soul. He remains, at the end, capable of commanding his own will, even if he sold his soul for terrible knowledge and with unenviable results.

The potential for demons to enter Frankenstein's great work might be less difficult to believe if the notion of modern laboratory science is exchanged for Renaissance magical theology, which provides the intellectual framework for his scientific endeavors. Book 3 of Agrippa's *De occulta philosophia libri tres* clearly explains the omnipresence of demons in the world, outlining their role as an integral part in the ongoing struggle between good and evil. He delineates nine orders of demons paralleling the nine ranks of angels, ranging from those who challenge the authority of God and claim to be able to attain divine powers to liars, the inventors of wicked arts, revengers, imitators of miracles, corrupters of the elements, sowers of discord and war, accusers/inquisitors, and the tempters and ensnarers.[2] With all these demons to choose from, it seems quite possible that a suitable one could be found to satisfy each of the three possibilities by which a demon might have entered Frankenstein or the Creature. For the first instance, in which Frankenstein would have made a Faustian bargain, a demon from the final category seems a logical choice. Offering tremendous power—in fact, divine power—to the exhausted and frustrated Frankenstein, the demon would have gladly taken the scientist's soul in exchange. As in all such bargains, the mortal would reap more suffering than reward; he would live to regret his choice, either losing his direction in a sea of silly and superficial actions rather than striving only to acquire his desired end or, as Frankenstein did, observing his creation destroy everything he valued.

While the first option requires that the Creature actually come to life with demonic assistance, the second possibility introduced above invites a demon who could imitate miracles and appear to produce life from dead flesh in order to ensnare Victor. While this would have sacrificed the scientist's sanity as well as his soul, since the demon would have convinced him that his great work succeeded when it did not, some evidence in the text suggests that Victor's psychological state was already fragile. He describes to Walton his physical and mental state during his months of work, and he raises the possibility of preternatural assistance. "Unless I had been animated by an almost supernatural enthusiasm, my application to this study would have been irksome, and almost intolerable" (1.3, 108). Within the same paragraph, however, he casts doubt on the notion that he inhabited a world in which demons played any role, and he asserts his extreme rationality upon beginning his study of decay. "Darkness had no effect upon my fancy; and a church-yard was to me merely the receptacle of bodies deprived of life, which, from being the seat of beauty and strength, had become food for the worm" (1.3, 108). But months spent alone in churchyards and charnel houses take their toll, and his rational conclusions about the lack of preternatural agents in the world, much like his own human limits, are among the first of his educated preconceptions to be lost. He is struck, in the midst of the study of death and decay, with the secret of how to create life. To give him some credit, Victor did, albeit briefly, wonder why "I alone should be reserved to discover so astonishing a secret" (1.3, 108). Yet the great effort he had invested and the step-by-step nature of his process reassure him that his discovery results from legitimate scientific research rather than magic. And it is here that we see the hand of a demon guiding Victor: "The information I had obtained was of a nature rather to direct my endeavors. . . . I was like the Arabian who had been buried with the dead, and found a passage to life aided only by one glimmering, and seemingly ineffectual, light" (1.3, 109). The demon convinces Victor that he himself has the power to create life, and thus leads him along this fantasy until, as discussed later in the chapter, he is convinced that he has done so—and all the murders that ensue, he lays at the feet of an invented Creature, the product of his demonically influenced imagination or advancing mental illness.

The third possibility for demonic intervention in this story comes from a demon being drawn into the pile of flesh itself. This, of course, means that somewhere in that stitched-together meat puppet was a soul. As discussed in the next section of this chapter, an intellectual precedent exists for a soul to still be hanging around a newly deceased corpse. Agrippa offers an excellent rationale for why a demon would be intrigued by the opportunity to tangle with such a soul: "But all unanimously maintain that evil spirits do wander up and down in this inferior world, enraged against all."[3] The ranks of demons even offer a likely candidate for the job: headed by one of the seven dukes of hell, Asmodeus, these demons are devoted to revenge and, in some contexts, sexual perversion and lust. While the latter aspect of their demonic activities remains less relevant in this context, the first offers some interesting possibilities. The corpses that made up Victor's great work likely did not all die of old age in the midst of a loving family. Some might well have been the victims of a mortal crime, while others could have nursed serious grievances to the grave. Offered the chance to revenge itself upon those who wronged it in life, a soul clinging to the flesh it had until recently accompanied might well have fallen to a demon. The demon could, in turn, have brought the Creature to life; but, rather than pursuing the original object of the soul's revenge, it could have encouraged the soul to attach to the spark of life in the Creature and instead pursue revenge against the creator who dared to dream that he could imitate God and create life.

Victor actually seems to recognize the demonic energy motivating the Creature. For the rest of the novel, with the exception of the phrase "animated mummy" applied on the page following the quotes above, he refers to his repugnant creation as demon, monster, vampire, and fiend. In his meeting with the Creature after Henry's death, he announces their struggle to the death and hurls the following torrent of preternatural titles: "Abhorred monster! fiend that thou art! The tortures of hell are too mild a vengeance for thy crimes. Wretched devil!" (2.2, 170).

Textual evidence also supports the possibility that the Creature inherited a part of Victor's soul, rather than attracting a drifting demonic entity. Note that Victor refers to the Creature as his "own vampire," suggesting a personal tie that existed before the murderous rampage began. Given the considerable amount of personal investment required to force life into dead matter, the transfer of a piece of Victor into his creation is not unlikely. Magical work requires the practitioner's energy and will as necessary ingredients, and so, quite literally, part of the practitioner is always invested in the experiment. Black magic demands more of the practitioner's will because the desired act violates divine intention. Victor's work, though it did not result in the death or subordination of another creature—the traditional hallmarks of black magic—certainly violated divine intention and, perhaps worse, co-opted divine power. By reanimating dead flesh, Victor puts life back where it had been

Heinrich Cornelius Agrippa (1486–1535), whose work influenced the ideas and philosophy of Victor Frankenstein.

taken, and thus reverses the divine order, which mandates "a time to be born and a time to die." Eternal life after mortal existence is possible only through the appreciation of God's work and submission to his rules, and no biblical option exists for a second turn at life on earth. In order to accomplish this experiment, Victor necessarily invested a great deal of himself; his ambition, his intelligence, and his will all formed part of the energy that made dead matter return to life. The exchange of energies between Victor and his work during the process of assembling the parts and animating them plunged him into the throes of a passion that became an obsession and bleached him of all but this singular ambition: "I could not tear my thoughts from my employment, loathsome in itself, but which had taken an irresistible hold of my imagination" (1.3, 112). Victor's habitually lazy pursuit of academic goals, which caused him to miss countless lectures before he came to Ingolstadt and base his entire intellectual framework on a few books he read on a summer vacation, was replaced by a work ethic that sapped him of health and peace. He missed three-quarters of a year locked in his attic, and even as he nears his goal, his anxiety renders him sleepless and sick. "Every night I was oppressed by a slow fever, and I became nervous to a most painful degree; a disease that I regretted the more because I had hitherto enjoyed most excellent health, and had always boasted of the firmness of my nerves" (1.3, 113). This entire section of the text describes in painful detail Victor's alienation from his self and extreme immersion in his work. If his soul divided during his efforts to animate the Creature and part of it got transferred to his work, it would have taken some of his will and self with it, leaving him bound to his creation and inextricably entwined in its actions—quite literally a doppelgänger.

But was Victor's soul the only one inside the Creature? Two things open the possibility that multiple spirits helped to guide Creature's blighted path through the world. The first is the inconsistency of his behavior and thought. Scholars broadly accept the Creature as Victor's alter ego and locate the creator's inconsistencies in the Creature's actions. It is true that they share many traits and patterns, and this may be further evidence that the Creature is not Victor's alter ego but in fact shares Victor's soul. The Creature, however, does not always behave like a gentleman—traits that were believed to be inborn, not taught—but sometimes acts more like a brute and a criminal. Upon being rejected by the De Laceys, for example, he resolves to try to explain himself to the grandfather, hoping the man's blindness will allow him to appreciate the Creature's mind and prevent him from being terrified by his malformed body. Such a naïve plan suggests an incomplete understanding of the family dynamic on which he has been spying, since he knows the De Laceys rarely leave the grandfather alone for any length of time. Furthermore, it is inherently dishonest. He hopes the grandfather will be so impressed by his intellect that he will vouch for the Creature over the horrified remonstrations of his own family. Would Victor have done something this innocent and selfish? Certainly—he ignored his own family for nine months while playing with dead body parts, and he later plans to make a female Creature and release it upon the world to appease his existing monster. His gentlemanly status, too, is problematic, since he behaves more like an indulged child than a mature and responsible man of means. So perhaps the Creature's behavior really does simply mirror the weaknesses of his creator.

But even Victor's weak nature would not have reduced him to thuggery and violence upon rejection: Victor assembles body parts from a variety of sources, and some of them are likely from criminals, since only the bodies of murderers and those convicted of treason were legally provided for anatomical dissection in England at the time. So, perhaps, the Creature's criminal tendencies can be attributed to the spirits still attached to the flesh from which he was made, a possibility given the late eighteenth- and early nineteenth-century belief that aspects of the soul lingered in the body for some period after death.

The Creature's psychological state also reflects a volatile and ultimately disastrous mix of Victor's obsessive tendencies combined with something darker. Repeatedly, a violent and destructive rage overwhelms him. True, he is judged solely by his appearance and shunned by everyone he encounters, but the Creature's murders and vindictive actions cannot solely be attributed to social ostracism and seem substantially out of proportion to his experiences. An equally plausible response, for example, would have been to quietly start walking toward an uninhabited area and live on the edges of society, as he promises to do with a mate, or to end his own life, rather than committing multiple murders, arson, blackmail, and the protracted assassination of his creator through exposure and exhaustion. The Creature, while tormented, is also a tormentor, and his sadistic tendencies, rather than a rational response to the way he was treated, reflect an innate tendency to violence and cruelty.

Bodies and Souls

The relationship between the body and the soul, as mentioned earlier, was a profoundly vexing question for this period, and had been for several centuries; so, it is not surprising that it should form a central part of the novel. The history of medicine, especially anatomy, and the history of theology offer some useful tools to help sort through the relatively complex set of mind/body problems posed by *Frankenstein*. The two are often intertwined, but separating them offers some distance and perspective on this subject, which was as problematic and contentious when Mary Shelley was writing as it had long been and—for many—still is.

The fact that Victor made his Creature out of bits and pieces found in charnel houses and graves invites even the casual reader to wonder why he had
access to those body parts in the first place. As Ruth Richardson has established,
the illegal trade in body parts for anatomy labs posed a significant threat to
the eternal sleep of the grave. Starting in the late eighteenth century, anatomy
became an increasingly important part of medical education. This resulted from
several centuries of change that included Vesalius's publication of his revolutionary rejection of Galenic anatomical thought, *De fabrica*, and his resulting
elevation to the chairs of medicine and surgery of the medical faculty at Padua.
Vesalius's careful anatomical study and insistence that personal observation,
rather than accepted authoritative knowledge, should be the basis of knowledge production meshed with the increasing importance of examination in
medicine and natural philosophy that privileged observation and practice. It
still took several centuries, however, for medical education to move from the
Renaissance model, in which students watched a dissection in a large theater
while listening to a precept read from an anatomy text, to describe what they
were seeing.[4]

The practice of medicine had to change as well, slowly adjusting to the shift
in broader scientific thought that personal observation needed to be coupled
with knowledge of authoritative texts. This encouraged a slow transition away
from humoral medical practice, in which physicians were formally educated
scholars of medical literature and theory who rarely touched bodies—living
or dead—and relied upon patient narratives and outward symptoms to make
their diagnoses. They turned their attention to the mechanics of the body at the
same time that surgeons, previously regarded as uneducated craftsmen trained
through apprenticeship rather than in universities, began to enter the realm of
formal medical education. By the late eighteenth century, the period that provides the context for *Frankenstein*, the study of anatomy gained an even more
significant place within medicine as the result of a changing conception of the
relationship between disease and the body, in which the pursuit of a single
patient from illness through death and onto the autopsy slab allowed physicians
to develop an alliance of particular symptoms with the internal markers they
left. Increasingly, the practice of medicine required a comprehensive understanding of anatomy and physiology, and as the field changed, huge numbers of
corpses were needed to educate medical students and act as the basis for medical research. Private anatomy schools sprouted up to fill the gap students experienced in their formal medical education, providing them with the opportunity
to dissect and even practice surgical techniques. The need for corpses was not,
however, met with a ready supply.

Religious opposition to dissection coupled with a cultural acceptance of
particular practices for honoring and commemorating the dead added up to a

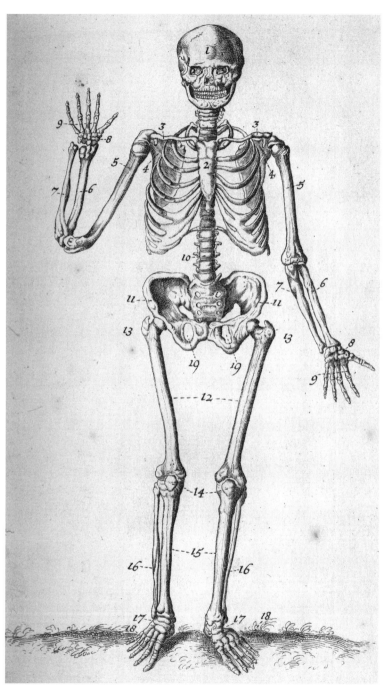

Drawings of the human skeleton were often used, in addition to hands-on dissections, by medical students learning anatomy.

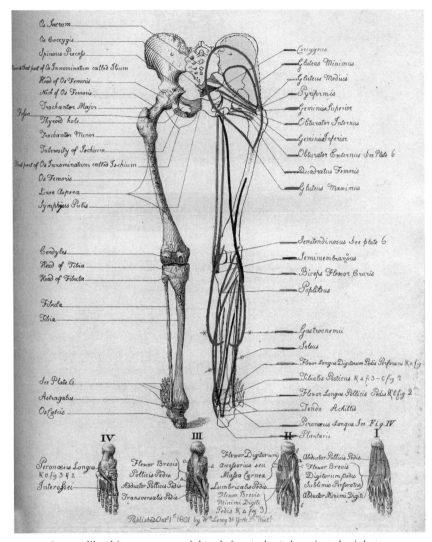

Images like this one were useful tools for students learning physiology.

singular lack of readily available bodies for anatomical study. In England, the
Murder Act of 1752, mandating that the bodies of all executed criminals be given
over for medical dissection as a means to extend their punishment beyond
death, attempted to address the shortage of cadavers and eliminate the desper-
ate measures to which some people would go to obtain study materials. Foucault has established the historical use of torture to demonstrate the primacy
of the king over the disobedient or traitorous subject through the destruction

of the corpse, particularly drawing and quartering, disemboweling, and post-mortem displaying of the dead body on the gibbet or the heads of traitors upon city walls.[5] While it is easy to see the literal might of the state carried out upon the weak flesh of the traitor, the act of abusing the corpse becomes even more powerful if by doing so the king denies the executed soul divine judgment. The extension of this power in the eighteenth century to physicians is remarkable. Now disobedient subjects would not simply become decomposing monuments to the king's power; in addition, their bodies would become fodder for the education of the kingdom's physicians, who would, in theory at least, help to make the kingdom itself stronger through the preservation of its loyal subjects.

But the Murder Act of 1752 also mandated that only the bodies of executed criminals be used for medical dissection, and even the relatively high execution rate of the late eighteenth century could not satisfy the crushing demand for bodies driven by private anatomy schools and medical institutions. Grave robbing became so common during the late eighteenth and early nineteenth centuries that those who could afford it hired watchers to guard their loved ones' graves to prevent fresh corpses from being stolen. Between the passage of the Murder Act in 1752 and of the Anatomy Act in 1832, which gave all unclaimed corpses in workhouses and hospitals for dissection—thus unfairly affecting poor citizens who were the most likely to die without family support—many students (and professors) engaged in criminal activity by buying stolen body parts from grave robbers. Why should Victor, whose privileged economic status guaranteed the funds to purchase any needed body parts, be different from his peers? Driven as he was to discover the very root of life itself and replicate it through his own creation, the law proved an easily ignored deterrent.

Several scholars have argued that the Creature reflects prevailing cultural anxieties about anatomical dissection and the cultural abhorrence of medical experimentation. Perhaps most radical among these, Tim Marshall has used the Anatomy Act as a retrospective lens through which to understand *Frankenstein*, concluding that the book was written and revised when grave robbing in the name of medical education became such an intense problem that the Anatomy Act, with its promise of a continuous and plentiful supply of legal research material, was the only acceptable answer. He contends that the novel reflects the public fear of grave robbing, which cheated people of eternal rest, and the need for bodies that generated grave robbers—and even murderers.[6] Retroactive historical reasoning may not be the best way to understand the relationship between this novel and the rising importance of anatomy in medicine, but it is hard to imagine that Mary Shelley was writing in a societal vacuum in which the threat of grave robbery did not exist. A more productive approach might be to frame the novel and its evident trepidation about the price of unchecked

scientific investigations within the extant public anxieties about medical experimentation upon the dead. All of this, however, raises the question of why people were so concerned that their bodies be permitted to molder undisturbed.

The answer lies, as Ruth Richardson explains, in the "prevailing belief in
the existence of a strong tie between body and personality/soul for an undefined
period of time after death."[7] Her claim gives two directions by which to understand this popular understanding of the relationship between the body and the
spirit, and both shed some useful light on dissection as a postmortem form
of punishment and the fears surrounding dissection for medical purposes—as
well as how these issues influence *Frankenstein*. First, if the spirit or personality remains in the body, then it can suffer the pain and humiliation of physical
disembodiment and thus extend the horrors of trial and execution beyond the
grave. Richardson also provides some useful insight into the potential damage
that could be done to a soul enclosed in a body not given the proper funerary rites. Perhaps the flashback to Antigone is overdone, but leaving a body
unshriven—even in late eighteenth- and early nineteenth-century England—
damned the spirit inside it. Christianity certainly provides the framework for
thinking about the purposes served by funerary rites, but as Richardson makes
clear, popular ideas about the purposes of formally mourning the dead reflect
no particular theological position but instead a loose conception that the soul
remained in or near the dead flesh and needed something to set it on its course
and perhaps improve its fate in the afterlife. Richardson concentrates on two
rites generally practiced at wakes and funerals: consuming food and drink in the
presence of the corpse so as to "consume" the sins the person committed during
life, and sin-eating, in which someone was paid to consume food or drink that
had been in contact with the corpse and thus take on the dead person's sins.
She contends that these rituals reflect the belief that what the living did could
affect the fate of the dead individual's soul.[8]

While Richardson connects only the first to an extended branch of the story
of the Eucharist, the second also seems logically connected to that Catholic tradition, though neither is perfectly matched to the original story in which the
Catholic faithful take communion to unite them with Christ through the consumption of his body and blood. The reality is that folk practice and theological
rules often have little in common. As a result, some scholars have dismissed
common beliefs and practices as "cultural debris" that held no coherent meaning, but Richardson's contention that these beliefs and practices reflect important cultural values, even if they lack theological consistency, appears more
likely.[9] The idea of consuming sins to lessen the amount of time the dead person would spend in purgatory certainly provides evidence for the idea that the
living could affect the state of the dead person's soul through their own actions.
It implies, too, that the soul hovered in or near the body for an unspecified

period after death, and thus could be harmed through improper treatment of the corpse. The development of funerary practice during the eighteenth century also demonstrates the cultural commitment to a proper way to treat a dead body to ensure the soul's passage into the afterlife and, as Richardson writes, "the protection of both the body and soul of the dead from evil or danger."[10]

The Creature is composed of so many body parts that it would be impossible to know how they were all treated between death and winding up in Frankenstein's attic. But even if each body received full funeral rites, the potential for souls still to be attached to fresh bodies was real. In essence, then, Victor's treatment of those body parts reflects the worst fears anyone of Shelley's period could have imagined about what could happen to their bodies and those of their loved ones after death. Medical students pawing through internal organs and playing catch with skulls would have been eminently preferable to having multiple bodies joined together into a single organism, then raised back to life by a megalomaniac doctoral student.

One of the fundamental beliefs underlying funerary practices during this period was that the corpse was neither fully dead nor fully alive for some period after the body's death. Some level of sentience remained in the corpse, resulting in its ability to react to the presence of others; murdered corpses would bleed in the presence of their murderers, and all corpses would indicate displeasure if an inaccurate will was read in their presence.[11] In fact, a body in *Frankenstein* does convey the truth about the manner of its murder, though not the identity of the murderer, and the way that the grieving family treats the corpse reveals a great deal about the relationship between the living and the dead. William, Victor's young brother, is the Creature's first victim. His father finds his body and writes to Victor that "I discovered my lovely boy, whom the night before I had seen blooming and active in health, stretched on the grass livid and motionless" (1.6, 134). This description could easily have described the body of a child struck down by a sudden and fatal illness; for example, a striking image that circulated during the nineteenth-century cholera epidemic was of a beautiful young woman in one panel and her emaciated corpse in the next, with the two drawn only twenty-four hours apart.[12] The sudden and seemingly capricious nature of death drove many parents to the same horrified discovery made by Victor's father, although the cause of William's death was soon revealed by his corpse: "The print of the murderer's finger was on his neck" (1.6, 134)." Elizabeth, despite being urged to avoid seeing her beloved cousin's body, insists on doing so, and upon seeing the marks on his neck declares herself his murderer (1.6, 134).

The long-established tradition of washing the dead body also demonstrates the conviction that what happened to a person's physical remains affected the eventual disposition of the soul. Cleaning the corpse not only made a more palatable body available for viewing at the wake and burial but also provided a form of soul cleansing that baptized the soul for its entrance into the afterlife. As Richardson ably notes, and historians of midwifery agree, the task of corpse washing was largely handled by women who were also responsible for the souls of women and children in childbirth and thus believed to be especially powerful in guarding the soul during liminal periods.[13] The soul (or souls) brought to life by Victor were given no such baptism, and it (or they) would be released back to the heavens unshriven. They also would have been brought into the world entirely without the hands of women, and this not only makes their animation unnatural but also deprives them of access to the spiritual power of the very people trusted to usher souls across the boundaries between life and death.

Finally, the importance of water in early modern popular magical thought should not be overlooked. Water—not holy water, but just the sort running in every stream—was broadly believed to be useful as a barrier to evil spirits and in cleansing departed souls.[14] The Creature's chosen end reflects the importance of the elements in ideas about the soul and demonic entities. By exiling himself to the Arctic, the Creature not only ensures that he will be alone for his final moments but also crosses a great deal of water to do so. His soul might have benefited from his lengthy journey, and any demonic entities left over in his soul (in a form of possession by the former owners of parts of him) might have been unable to cross the sea and thus been left behind. He also chooses to con-sign himself to a funeral pyre, where according to Christian theology, the fire would cleanse his soul and deliver it pure to God for judgment. The eighteenth century saw the end of the ardent witch burning that had consumed Europe for over a century, with the last witch burned in Scotland in 1727. Heretics had burned throughout Europe from the fifteenth century through the seventeenth, with the fire on earth acting like a parallel to the fire in hell, so that their souls would be cleansed during their deaths. Interestingly, burning was also the pun-ishment meted out to female murderers, traitors, and counterfeiters, since they could not be drawn and quartered as were men because it would involve public nudity. That practice ended with the Treason Act of 1790, which determined that condemned women would be hanged instead of burned, due to the inher-ent cruelty of the punishment and popular dismay over the smoke from the executioners' fires. All of these bodies burned, whether for the sake of their souls or to demonstrate the power of the state over the subject's body, rein-force the centrality of fire in eighteenth-century thinking about the soul and its fate. The Creature, by choosing the most painful death imaginable, guarantees the freedom of his soul(s) after his death.[15] Ironically enough, he also keeps his corpse out of the hands of the anatomists who would otherwise have had it, had he been found guilty of murder and hanged.

The connection between the soul and the body would fade after death, but the timing of that transition was difficult to determine, partially because time of death was hard to pin down (think of all those bell-pulls and corpse guards provided for buried bodies that might wake up and need to be quickly unburied) and partially because theology remained divided on the question. For Catholics, purgatory provided souls a place to serve their sentence before going to heaven, but it was erased in Protestant doctrine. Instead, two ideas took its place: either the soul's fate was decided upon death and was immediately sent on to heaven or hell from the body, or the soul and body remained united until Judgment Day, when they would be resurrected.[16] The latter was a significant part of the cultural understanding of the Resurrection. Richardson describes "an early nineteenth-century cartoon of the interior of a London anatomy museum on the Last Day of Judgment show[ing] a group of revivified headless and legless corpses, bewilderedly seeking their lost parts."[17] This demonstrates the anxiety surrounding proper treatment of the body and the potential disaster awaiting the deceased should funerary protocol be disrupted. Dissection, which destroyed the body and potentially separated parts permanently from each other, could sentence the soul to damnation because the parts would be unable to reunite for the Resurrection. All of this indicates the tremendous fear people experienced upon learning that a loved one's body had been snatched, since it was not just the corpse that would be damaged but the soul's eternal rest that would be destroyed. It also lends even more weight to the terrible punishment meted out by the Murder Act of 1752, which ensured that the executed person's soul, should its fate not have been determined at or near death, would never have the chance to be judged by God at the Resurrection.

Victor desperately aspires to be a scientist of his time and make a prodigious discovery that would guarantee him a place of respect among his peers and assure his fame for the ages. Yet he remains mired in the complicated spirituality of his time, a period where spirits walked, loud noises could frighten them away, and the fate of souls could be determined in the time that passed between death and proper burial. This dichotomy between the current scientific studies and the beliefs of earlier eras suggests that he was aware that the flesh he brought to life could well harbor the spirit that had originally inhabited it. Even so, "I dabbled among the unhallowed damps of the grave, or tortured the living animal to animate the lifeless clay. . . . The dissecting room and the slaughterhouse furnished many of my materials" (1.3, 111).

Earlier this chapter addressed the potential for multiple human personalities inhabiting the Creature, but this excerpt adds a new and disturbing twist. He is composed not only of pieces gleaned from different human bodies, some taken from dissecting rooms and therefore likely belonging to murderers and others stolen from graves and carrying more quotidian sins, but also of pieces taken from different (apparently quite large) animals. While those animals would not, under the rules of eighteenth-century spirituality, have been credited with souls, they would certainly have embodied specific characteristics linked to their breed that would have made bestial any living creature who inherited them. The amalgamation of these bits and pieces would have resulted in a true physical and spiritual chimera, which is nearly impossible to conceive since no specific details are provided to describe what dead individuals donated what parts. And what if they weren't all dead to start with? Among the most disturbing parts of this quote is the second half of the first clause, in which Victor confesses he "tortured the living animal to animate the lifeless clay."

In his early experiments, which are the only ones for which details are provided, Victor produces life in dead matter by transferring it from a living being, perhaps through the creation of extreme pain that would cause neurological excitement and a burst of energy from the living to the dead. At its most complicated and disturbing, then, the Creature might well have included portions of male and female human parts, a variety of fragments from dead animals, and perhaps a chunk or several from living animals of both sexes. If all of these brought some of their inherent characteristics into the new creature and the human parts brought their souls with them, the Creature would have been a very complex spiritual and physical creation indeed—perhaps even a being wracked by powerful but quite contradictory natures that he was powerless to harmonize or even to control. No wonder Victor couldn't stand the sight of him, nor anticipate the extraordinary demands his creation would place upon him as designer and giver of life.

The Mind

It is no surprise, then, that Victor went mad, or at least his friends and family believed him to be deranged. The entire novel can, in fact, be understood through the lens of nervous exhaustion, an increasingly common psychiatric diagnosis in the eighteenth and nineteenth centuries. This disorder, which most commonly afflicted upper-class people overly devoted to study, caused an imbalance in the nervous system that resulted in excessive melancholy, mood swings, and sometimes mania.[18] Victor's disproportionate devotion to his great project and later nervous collapse make a great deal of sense if seen as part of his fragile and excitable disposition. His lack of a center, however, cannot so easily be attributed to a nervous disorder. He slips through defining acts and relationships, first delineating himself and his interests through his relationships with Clerval and Elizabeth, then through his great work, and finally through his commitment to find and destroy the Creature. What remains most important to him is his potential contribution to human knowledge and passing on his experiences to anyone who will listen. But the cautionary tale you might expect from someone who has seen his entire life destroyed by the product of intellectual ambition does not come from his lips.

Even in his impassioned speeches to Walton about the critical importance of accepting human limitations and pursuing knowledge only through approved paths, he remains entranced with his own potential power, and the tantalizing dream of once again transcending human limits clearly dances before him. Pride is certainly a defining characteristic for Victor, who remains convinced of his own extraordinariness until his death. In speaking to Walton about the importance of limiting ambition, he manages to convey—again—how fantastic a creature he truly is, compares himself to God's favorite angel, and explains the depths of his suffering. It remains amazing that Walton doesn't drown him just to make him shut up, but instead listens with worshipful appreciation to his mentor's narrative of intellectual ambition gone—quite literally—to hell:

> When younger," said he, "I felt as if I were destined for some great enterprise. My feelings are profound; but I possessed a coolness of judgment that fitted me for illustrious achievements. This sentiment of the worth of my nature supported me, when others would have been oppressed; for I deemed it criminal to throw away in useless grief those talents that might be useful to my fellow-creatures. When I reflected on the work I had completed, no less a one than the creation of a sensitive and rational animal, I could not rank myself with the herd of common projectors. But this feeling, which supported me in the commencement of my career, now serves only to plunge me lower in the dust. All my speculations and hopes are as nothing; and, like the archangel who aspired to omnipotence, I am chained in an eternal hell." (3.7, 309–310)

Despite having created something that murdered everyone he cared about, landed him in prison, and drove him insane, Victor remains entirely convinced of his own greatness. This egomania, combined with his obsessive tendencies, makes him a perfect candidate for the asylum, and that is, of course, where he winds up after Elizabeth's death. His inconstancy does not escape the notice of those surrounding him. Walton describes him the following way:

> I never saw a more interesting creature: his eyes have generally an expression of wildness, and even madness; but there are moments when, if any one performs an act of kindness towards him, or does him any the most trifling service, his whole countenance is lighted up, as it were, with a

beam of benevolence and sweetness that I never saw equalled. But he
is generally melancholy and despairing; and sometimes he gnashes his
teeth, as if impatient of the weight of woes that oppresses him. (L4, 80)

Four times during the novel Victor is reduced to a trembling, terrified
wreck incapable of caring for himself. The first breakdown occurs after he views
the living Creature for the first time, and it takes weeks of Clerval's gentle ministrations to bring him back to his senses (1.4, 119–123). This episode includes
trembling, hallucinations, terror, raving, and excessive joy. Even under Henry's
careful ministrations, Victor takes several months to recover from his nervous
exhaustion, and its cause is evident throughout his recovery: "The form of the
monster on whom I had bestowed existence was for ever before my eyes, and I
raved incessantly concerning him. Doubtless my words surprised Henry; he at
first believed them to be the wanderings of my disturbed imagination; but the
pertinacity with which I returned to the same subject persuaded him that my
disorder indeed owed its origin to some uncommon and terrible event" (1.4,
122). Shelley never makes it clear whether Victor manages to convince Henry
that the Monster is, in fact, real. Instead, the Creature (real or imagined) provides Victor's psychological collapse with a focus on which his mind endlessly
deliberates and which renders him susceptible to future mental ruptures.

His second nervous collapse comes after Justine's execution for William's
murder. Failing to provide a convincing argument for Justine's innocence, Victor
watches her go to the gallows for him—or for his Creature—and then falls into
"remorse and the sense of guilt, which hurried me away into a hell of intense
tortures, such as no language can describe" (2.1, 157). Rendered sleepless, unable
to tolerate excessive human companionship or noise, and extremely nervous,
Victor obsesses about the Creature and fails to improve under the traditional
remedies of exposure to nature, quiet companionship, and gentle exercise. During this period of illness he encounters the Creature on a Swiss mountainside
and is so moved by the story of his early struggle to exist—and his promise
to leave Europe for some barren wasteland where he would shun all human
company—that he agrees to make a female companion (2.2–2.9, 169–231). Even
the most elementary understanding of mental disorder suggests that this return
to the original obsession cannot bode well for Victor's mental state, and several
chapters later, he is once again a nervous wreck.

This time the Creature has murdered Clerval, and Victor himself is a suspect in the crime. Rather than receiving the gentle care and thoughtful atten-
dance generally provided to wealthy men consumed by nervous exhaustion, he
is locked away in a prison cell for two months, wracked by his fevered ravings.
Even after he regains consciousness, deemed innocent of his friend's murder, and released to his father's far more benevolent care, Victor remains an

insomniac prone to ravings about the fiend who plagued his existence, killed his friends and family, and forced him to choose his loved ones' death over the destruction of the human race. His father despairs over his son's shattered mental state: "The conclusion of this speech convinced my father that my ideas were deranged, and he instantly changed the subject of our conversation, and endeavoured to alter the course of our thoughts" (3.5, 277). He does this by avoiding all discussion of Victor's obsession and Clerval's murder and then by reminding his son of his unfulfilled commitment to Elizabeth.

It is, of course, Elizabeth's murder that plunges Victor into his final nervous collapse. Even the townspeople think him mad after he claims he saw the Creature's face at the window while he was embracing his dead wife's corpse and shot at it, leading to a fruitless search for a missing fiend (3.6, 292). His father's death soon after Elizabeth's pushes Victor over the edge. This time, without his father and friends to protect and care for him, Victor spends several months in a madhouse.

> What then became of me? I know not; I lost sensation, and chains and darkness were the only objects that pressed upon me. Sometimes, indeed, I dreamt that I wandered in flowery meadows and pleasant vales with the friends of my youth; but awoke, and found myself in a dungeon. Melancholy followed, but by degrees I gained a clear conception of my miseries and situation, and was then released from my prison. For they had called me mad; and during many months, as I understood, a solitary cell had been my habitation. (3.6, 294)

It is not clear whether his final quest to destroy the Creature is also a hallucination born of this mental collapse. Did Victor's shattered mind invent Walton, his crew, and the last sighting of the Creature vanishing into the Arctic wastes? Perhaps he did actually travel thousands of miles after a fiend who alternately taunted and fed him to keep the chase alive, and perhaps Walton and his ship of sailors on the cusp of mutiny were real. But perhaps, like the Creature himself, they were the products of Victor's nervous exhaustion.

The negation of the Creature from the novel is, of course, the ultimate trick. So many scholars have already said that the Creature embodies Victor's (and humanity's) dark side that erasing him as a physical entity is, surprisingly, both logical and simple. The course of the novel doesn't change whether actual life was created or not, though of course the chain of artificial lives the novel spawned does. Entertaining the possibility that Victor is an exhausted scientist whose fragile grasp on reality snapped after too many nights in the lab is easy enough; but what to say about the pile of corpses amassed by the end? Who killed William, Clerval, and Elizabeth—and by proxy caused the deaths of Justine and Victor's father? Was it Victor? Upon viewing Clerval's corpse during his trial for his friend's murder, Victor exclaims, "Have my murderous machinations deprived you also, my dearest Henry, of life? Two I have already destroyed; other victims await their destiny: but you, Clerval, my friend, my benefactor—" (3.4, 267). Then he disintegrates into a series of convulsions and must be carried from the courtroom. Clearly this convinces everyone there he is guilty, and he spends the next several months under surveillance in full nervous collapse, alternately raving about how he must destroy the fiend pursuing him and shrieking in terror that it is trying to murder him. Even his protector, the magistrate Mr. Kirwin, spends those months ensuring his comfort but avoiding his company, since "he did not wish to be present at the agonies and miserable ravings of a murderer" (3.4, 269). In the end, however, Mr. Kirwin manages to convince the grand jury that Victor could not have killed his friend, since he had been on the Orkney Islands exactly when Clerval's still-warm body was found on the Irish coast (3.4, 273). A review of the text, however, reveals that the only being who could testify to Victor's location during the murder was, in fact, the Creature himself—and strangely, he did not appear in court. Plenty of opportunities exist for Victor to kill his friend, dump the body on an isolated beach, and sail away, returning later to relish the thrill of the corpse's discovery and the ensuing investigation. Perhaps, as he had done when he allowed Justine to die for a murder he—or his creation—committed, he planned to contribute to the investigation and help frame an innocent individual or, as he would do later, blame a creature only he could see.

It is not clear why no one suspects Victor of killing Elizabeth, since he is the most obvious suspect. Losing one family member to a violent death is unlucky, but a brother, a best friend, and a wife all within months of each other is simply implausible unless you consider that the person might be killing his closest companions himself. The final murder scene is as damning as they come. Victor is, after all, standing over his wife's strangled body with a loaded gun shooting at an empty window when the innkeeper and townsfolk enter. Though they join him in his hunt for the creature he describes, Victor understands it as a halfhearted effort conducted with "most of my companions believing it to have been a form conjured by my fancy" (3.6, 292). The novel makes it equally possible that Victor is a violent murderer whose fantasies of a scientific creation run amok provide him with the narrative he needs to explain his crimes, or that he created a being so vindictive that it murdered his family and friends when he failed to treat it in an appropriately nurturing manner. If Victor hallucinates the Creature, he has clearly left the relatively gentle diagnosis of neurasthenia and entered pathological psychosis. Nothing in the novel renders that impossible; in fact, mental breakdown from nervous exhaustion resulting from untempered, inappropriate scholarly zeal fits into the scientific context in which Shelley was writing better than it does into a universe of demons, shades, and wandering souls, which the world clearly wanted—but found difficult—to leave behind.

The value provided by considering the readings offered above, in which anatomy, souls, demons, and insanity play contributing roles, should not be overlooked just because it does not correspond with the majority of scholarly interpretations of *Frankenstein*. By taking the text at its words and engaging with the multiple intellectual, theological, and psychological contexts it proposes, the novel's world emerges as a complex and intriguing chimera of premodern and modern. Much like the Creature himself, it was made of pieces from a variety of sources. The bodies that donated parts include the folk traditions surrounding burial and shriving, biblical understandings of demonic activity, and the susceptibility of a sensitive mind to madness. These contributions are not, perhaps, as clearly part of the Frankenstein story as body stealing for anatomy labs, but in fact, the novel owes them a greater debt for providing some of the more compelling questions that continue to frame our ideas about the practice of science. When we engage in a scientific research project, how do we know that its conception stems from noble intentions rather than greed and ambition? When we pursue an experimental scientific undertaking into exhaustion, how do we know when to cease trusting our judgment and ask for help or simply stop? And finally, once we begin a narrative, how do we know when we slip into the story and lose our foothold in reality? These questions form the foundation for modern bioethics and provide the link between Victor's nightmarish landscape of demons, corpses, and sea ice and the modern labyrinth of responsible science exploration.

Bioethics

Whether the Creature is real or the product of Victor's deranged imagination does not detract from the important and very timely medical, anatomical, ethical, and spiritual themes resonating in the novel. The notion of when and how life begins and ends, the connection between the body and the soul, and even the relationship between mind and reality were highly relevant ones at the turn of the eighteenth century, when mortality rates remained high, life expectancy was low, and life could seemingly end without reason. The grounding of medicine in the physicality of the body and the increasing desire to identify disease according to the specific effects upon individual organs within the body coexisted with a need to better conceptualize the relationship between the immortal soul and the fragile corpse. The world of demons and restless souls did not disappear simply because the Enlightenment wished it would and offered in its place a rational, two-dimensional reality based in nature and the senses. Instead, the rich traditions of embodied spirituality perpetuated by Christian theology and vernacular ideas about spirits and souls continued alongside scientific trends, as they had done for centuries. *Frankenstein*'s value, then, lies not solely in its status as a warning against intellectual hubris and scientific progress, but also in its extraordinary ability to capture the many ideas—some apparently contradictory—that competed to make sense of the human condition at the turn of the nineteenth century. The questions the book raises continue to define contemporary medical ethics, as much as they did nineteenth-century thought.

In a collection of essays exploring organ transplantation, Leonard Barkan, an expert in antiquities and Renaissance literature, reminisces about an engaging after-dinner conversation with a group of interdisciplinary scholars from medicine, the physical sciences, and the humanities that followed a screening of James Whale's original *Frankenstein* (1931). All agreed "that everything in the story of the fabricated monster and in the way the film told that story was precisely relevant to organ transplant."[19] They were right: relocating body parts and organs from one being to another forms the medical basis of Shelley's novel and reappears in many of the contemporary renderings of her tale as well. Along with Shelley's original literary plot, however, a parallel and equally prevalent Frankensteinian narrative emerges over the decades: the reanimation of a deceased person, often one the reanimator knew in life. Victor Frankenstein's amalgamation of organs and body parts constructs a new, unique being without a history or memories, while the reanimation of corpses epitomizes the ardent human desire to keep a loved one alive. Both procedures raise fundamental questions that remain as pertinent to issues in our technological age as they were in Mary Shelley's day. As a result, *Frankenstein* has burrowed its way into our collective cultural consciousness and become "the governing myth of modern biology," a "mythic representation of what it means to be human" in Western culture that has become "a parable for our time [and] an enduring prophecy."[20]

Frankenstein blurs the boundaries between human and nonhuman, foregrounding a seemingly endless series of philosophical and practical debates about what society designates as natural and what it deems artificial. Words used to thrash out even a fragile consensus delineating the distinctions between persons and nonpersons, and the rights owed to each, contain encrusted layers of cultural resonances and emotional valances. What one person staunchly believes is normal and natural, another resolutely judges as unnatural or even unholy. Some would argue, for example, that any external intrusion into the biological process of procreation, a procedure evident in the majority of the Frankenstein narratives in every medium, should be considered unnatural, a philosophical position that classifies all the medical efforts that assist couples to have children as aberrant or perhaps even deviant. If so, then the products of those manipulations would not necessarily be afforded the status and rights generally granted to those beings society legally acknowledges as human. The outcomes of these cultural clashes have profound consequences, both for individuals and for marginalized groups: history provides abundant examples of various categories of people being denied personhood status—particularly racial, religious, or sexual-orientation minorities—as the first step in demonizing, then persecuting, and finally eradicating them.

Peter Cushing, the actor who played Dr. Frankenstein in the Hammer films, noted that he considered him "the forerunner" to Christiaan Barnard.[21] When Dr. Barnard, the South African cardiac surgeon, transplanted Denise Darvall's heart into the body of Louis Washkansky on December 3, 1967, it was heralded around the globe as a revolutionary procedure that would transform the medical landscape, and Barnard recognized its connection to Shelley: "I began by reporting the patient looked much better—even though he thought he was the new Frankenstein. Amid the laughter, Bossie noted Dr. Frankenstein was the man who created the monster—which meant I was the Frankenstein of Ward C-2. That led to more laughter."[22] It was also a moment when medical technology and scientific research merged with myth and metaphor: "Now for the first time one of the most important metaphors for personhood had been cut out, handled and cleaned, and then placed inside the body of another individual. In a few historic moments, the borders of one human body had been breached by the symbolic core of another. . . . The boundaries between Nature and Art, between physical reality and the language we use to signify it, were suddenly dissolved."[23] Certainly it was a shining moment for medical scientists, who reveled in Bernard's dazzling achievement and the status it bestowed on them—but only a relatively brief one. By 2013, a *Huffington Post* poll reported that only 36 percent of Americans had "a lot" of trust that the information they received from scientists was accurate and reliable; 51 percent said they had "only a little" confidence in such information, another 6 percent said they didn't trust it at all, and 78 percent believed that scientific studies were influenced by political ideology.[24]

A series of interlocking beliefs fuels these statistics: that science (e.g., global warming, immunization policies) functions as a catalyst for governmental regulations; that scientists are not impartial investigators; that commercial gain (or greed) propels pharmaceutical and other companies to subsidize and thereby influence the findings of medical science research; that scientists make mistakes and advocate policies that will harm or kill children; and that scientific conclusions (e.g., evolution, abortion) clash with strongly held doctrines of faith. For a combination of these and other reasons, a cultural backlash against scientific and medical authority, primarily among conservative and religious groups, has generated increasingly divergent attitudes toward the practice and results of scientific and medical explorations. Succinctly summarized: a sizable proportion of Americans currently believes that, rather than benefiting humanity, scientific medical research endangers our communal welfare and health—and *Frankenstein* is often their model and metaphor.

Mary Shelley cannot be held solely, or perhaps even chiefly, responsible for the contemporary fear of scientific expertise, medical research, and technical innovations. Such visceral mistrust stretches as far back as the Icarus myth and is as contemporary as fracking controversies. During her era, however, passionate debates raged over the defining characteristics of "good" science, and as argued in earlier chapters, Victor Frankenstein embodies the inherent flaws and lethal dangers of subjective, independent experimentation. But over time, the novel's complexities were disregarded, and the public awarded its central character a medical degree (Shelley never calls Victor a doctor), thereby converting the author's fictional inventions into malleable templates to express the perils of rampant scientific hubris and medical experimentation: Victor as the fanatical scientist, the Creature as the destructive product of his experiments, and the novel's other figures as societal victims of Victor's uncontrolled research.

Popular representations of the so-called mad scientist, commonly labeled as "Frankensteinian," certainly contribute to an atmosphere rife with suspicions about the motivations of scientists and medical researchers, as well as the outcomes and cultural ramifications of their investigations. The ongoing media mutations of the Frankenstein narrative personify communal anxiety, fueling the fires of skepticism, doubt, and fear. The misguided or deranged man of science thus becomes an amoral or malevolent figure who ignores conventional standards of ethical and socially acceptable behavior. Such conceptualizations illustrate that "when the fear of science is paramount—when science is conceived of as black magic rather than white—the evil has no attribution beyond that of the perverse will of an individual scientist."[25] In this sense, then, the research scientist becomes, at least potentially, a tragic hero, for the moral dimensions of his nature blended with the magnitude of his aspirations marks his spectacular plummet from the most sublime of heights. The person with the most knowledge has an obligation to use it wisely and for the betterment of humanity; any other purpose violates the fundamental ethical principles that should guide research and medical protocols.

Given the endurance and prominence of *Frankenstein* in Western culture, it should not be surprising that commentators respond with a knee-jerk reaction to something huge, pieced together, and potentially dangerous, often yoking "Franken-" with the specified subject, bringing us terms such as "Frankenstorm" and "Frankenfood." A less popular alternative conjoining hooks the last part of Victor's name with the object, such as "Cheneystein" and "McFrankenstein." Alternatively, "Frankenstein" can become part of a title, often of a book about biologically engineered creatures and the ethical questions they raise. These include *Frankenstein's Cat: Cuddling Up to Biotech's Brave New Beasts* (Emily

Anthes, 2013), *American Frankenstein: How The United States Created a Monster* (KS Cramer, 2010), *The Frankenstein Syndrome: Ethical and Social Issues in the Genetic Engineering of Animals* (Bernard Rollin, 1995), and *Frankenstein's Footsteps: Science, Genetics and Popular Culture* (Jon Turney, 1998). In short, "Frankenstein" has become shorthand for radical scientific experimentation with life and for ethically questionable experimentation.

A host of scholars have explored how *Frankenstein* provides the prototype of the "mad scientist," but few actually note the thin line that separates this compulsive figure from the dedicated researcher, the hero of modern medical research. In all likelihood, Francis Crick and James Watson, Marie Curie, Louis Pasteur, Niels Bohr, and Enrico Fermi all spent at least as many hours in their laboratories as Victor does in his "solitary chamber, or rather cell, at the top of the house" in Ingolstadt (1.3, 111). Was Jonas Salk "mad" when he volunteered himself and his entire family for the experimental polio vaccine trial? The same question applies to the immunologist David Pritchard (who injected fifty hookworms under his skin to test whether certain parasites improved immune responses), August Bier (who punctured his spine while testing spinal anesthesia), Sir Humphry Davy (who tested nitrous oxide on himself), Stubbins Ffirth (who poured black vomit into his open cuts and onto his eyeballs to determine whether yellow fever was contagious), Sir Henry Head (who severed his radial nerve to determine whether people who suffered nerve damage could recover sensation), Jack Barnes (who had jellyfish sting himself and his son to establish that the fish was the cause of Irukandji syndrome) or Giles Brindley (who injected his penis with a vasodilator, papaverine, and exhibited the results to hundreds of his colleagues in a lecture hall)? Indeed, the annals of medical history teem with science researchers who do things, often to themselves and their families, that would normally be considered quite insane—but are revered as valiant champions of humankind.

The difference, then, between "mad" and "heroic" appears to be located in the goal of the researcher, a tricky thing to determine given any scientist's compilation of competing motivations, and whether the outcome justifies the extreme actions taken to achieve it. Consider whether Victor would have been perceived as "mad" if the Creature had evolved into an immensely charming bandleader, a lovable role model for young children, or a skilled footballer who helped England win the World Cup. More to the point, every day in hospitals across the country, doctors perform biotechnical operations that mirror some of the "unhallowed arts" of Victor's "forbidden" procedures that "violate" natural developments: organs (particularly hearts and lungs) harvested from the dead and transplanted into the living, assisted reproductive technologies that make possible births without sexual intercourse, embryonic stem cell research, genetic manipulation, severed and artificial limbs attached onto living tissue, blood transfusions, electroshock conversion (defibrillation) of patients who have suffered cardiac arrest, ECMO machines that keep patients alive while their heart and lungs fail to function, plastic surgeries, and a growing array of life extension technologies (pacemakers, nanotechnology to repair aging cells, replacement of body parts, gene therapy, therapeutic cloning). While modern physicians have not realized Victor's dream—"to banish disease from the human frame"—they surely aspire to the same objective, as well as to prolong human life as long as possible.

Paul Root Wolpe aptly sums up the preponderance of critical opinion about the novel's significance beyond pop culture, noting how it has become "the base melody from which each artist creates his or her own improvisation": "It has become a signifier of a set of ideological stances toward science and technology and represents a set of cultural conversations around scientific and medical hubris, unfettered technological advances, transgressions of the proper limits of human intervention, and experiments without full knowledge or appreciation of implications and consequences."[26] Although Shelley's novel clearly functions as a text that explores common bioethical dilemmas in medical and scientific research, a rather ironic development in the tale's evolution has occurred. While Victor's image has been winnowed down almost solely to signifying a cautionary admonition about the misuse of scientific power, the character of his Creature has expanded to encompass an ever-increasing assortment of increasingly positive elements, as will be discussed in subsequent chapters.

Equally prominently in the evolution of the narrative, some modern readers identify the Creature not only as an abandoned child but also as a person with a disability, the embodiment of the stigmatized "Other" whose physical deformities will never conform to society's rigid standards of normality. Lennard Davis, for example, notes how often negative and evil characters in popular culture are depicted as physically grotesque, and how Victor Frankenstein recoils from "the frankly erotic agenda for the creature (the creation of a mate) as a contaminating danger to normal people."[27] Martha Stoddard Holmes typifies those scholars who foreground the novel's presentation of "what a baby with physical singularities, pronounced 'deformed' at birth, might experience growing up in a society that finds him or her monstrous or freakish"; thereby, she asserts, *Frankenstein* imparts "a memorable first-person account of the experience of being stigmatized and socially disabled by physical differences considered 'deformities.' "[28] Such readings encourage readers to sympathize with the abandoned Creature, while castigating his creator as a callous parental figure whose actions spawn his own tragedies.

Despite the fact that the Creature is supernaturally powerful and far more impervious to cold and pain than any of his human counterparts, his abnormality deprives him of the natural human connections that tie together members of everyday society, subjecting him to constant discrimination and ultimately rendering him a lonely, bitter, violent, and dangerous outcast. For critics like Stoddard, Victor's refusal to create a mate for the Creature is not evidence of a lesson learned but is instead the prejudicial decision of a "paternalistic figure of scientific/medical authority, in effect sterilizing his disabled child."[29] This "narrative prosthesis," a term coined by David Mitchell and Sharon Snyder to illustrate how writers often use a disabled character as a foil to demonstrate the normalcy of a work's other figures, "serves as a metaphorical signifier of social and individual collapse."[30] Some readers of the novel, such as Anne McDonald and Mark Mossman, write about their own physical disabilities and relate to the Creature in very personal terms, what Mossman calls a "sympathetic alignment."[31]

In a later chapter, we explore *Frankenstein*'s legacy in relation to current representations of cyborgs and robots. Here, however, we can note how robots and robotic machines, as well as myriad manifestations of artificial intelligence, are now a commonly accepted part of our everyday lives, but one need not board a rocket ship to view cyborgs. Our daily world already abounds with cyborgs generated by modern medical procedures, one of the latest examples being a prosthetic hand that can be controlled by the mind and linked directly to the nervous system, which allows it to be controlled like a natural appendage.[32] Such dramatic instances of humans and machines merging into new configurations will undoubtedly continue to emerge as researchers develop more and more sophisticated ways to enlarge restricted human intellectual and physical capacities. But more mundane examples proliferate as well, such as a generation of baby boomers slowly being outfitted with metal knees, plastic hips, and other assorted devices that fuse their flesh with nonorganic materials. We are, to put the matter simply, evolving into a cyborg culture that as it continues to develop will certainly allow our biological bodies to undergo a transitional reformation of prosthetics and, along with it, new formulations of what it means to be human.

Despite its predictable association with fear of the new and the unknown, something related to *Frankenstein* occasionally appears in a good light. Dr. Jean Rosenbaum, the inventor of the pacemaker, freely admits that his inspiration for this widely used invention "comes from the *Frankenstein* movie." When he was a child, Rosenbaum's mother took him to see the 1931 film; he was thrilled and particularly fascinated by the special effects in Frankenstein's laboratory. In 1951, as a freshman medical student, he witnessed the untimely death of a young woman whose heart stopped beating, a disturbing event that almost caused him to drop out. That night, Rosenbaum had a vivid dream about Frankenstein's Creature being hoisted into the lightning storm and the electricity that brings him to life. Inspired by this vivid dream, Rosenbaum wondered if a small jolt of electric current could be mechanically produced to stimulate a damaged heart—a muscle that functions by electricity—causing it to beat regularly again and revive a patient. He put together a portable machine to perform this function, but, after testing the results successfully on animals and freshly arrived DOAs, his superiors still deemed the process too dangerous for use on a living human being. Frustrated during this two-year waiting period, Rosenbaum (nicknamed the "Black Vulture" by his colleagues) felt like he was Dr. Frankenstein and the timorous medical community the frightened town mob. Finally, he was given a chance to demonstrate how the machine would work on a patient whose heart had stopped for three minutes; the rest is medical history. "The pacemaker came from the *Frankenstein* movie," says Rosenbaum.[33] A more recent example of the "positive" *Frankenstein* allusion appears in the July 25, 2013, headline in the *Huffington Post*'s Lifestyle section: "Frankenstein's Dream: Electricity Could Be Used to Regrow Limbs." But such articles are exceptions rather than the norm.

To some degree, any new scientific theory, technological invention, or medical breakthrough inevitably changes the ways people think, behave, and interact with others, causing alterations in our daily lives and belief systems that engender doubts and anxieties. Whatever its flaws, ongoing iterations, and unanticipated mutations in popular culture, Shelley's narrative has become a primary text for a host of these issues in the contemporary world and an indispensable part of serious (and some not so serious) discussions about the role of science, medicine, and technology in our culture. As such, *Frankenstein* has arguably become more relevant in the twenty-first century than it was in the nineteenth. As Paul Wolpe observes, the fundamental issues raised in *Frankenstein* "have become, if anything, more immediate and trenchant as the power to alter our nature has actually emerged. . . . The power and longevity of the novel is due to the primordial nature of its social and ethical insights about science."[34] At its core, then, the novel explores the increasingly blurry boundaries and distinctions between what we label human and nonhuman, and the natural and the unnatural, and examines the interconnected relationships between social responsibility and scientific/medical research. For the essayist Rebecca Solnit, the novel is "a masterpiece that would dwarf all the works of the Romantic poets in the directness of its impact on the collective imagination" and that ultimately becomes "part of the necessary furnishings of the imagination and shorthand for an aspect of the human condition."[35] Certainly, researchers have unleashed forces, both natural and human made, that can easily range out of control: nuclear power, organ transplantation, genetics (research, therapy, and manipulation), modifications of the human body, reproductive technologies, cloning, ectogenesis, artificial intelligence, the cyber world and space exploration—just to cite some clear examples. All these technological feats should give us pause to contemplate the ramifications of scientific endeavors made in the name of humankind, yet having the potential to destroy it. As a result, Mary Shelley's novel raises fundamental questions that strike at the very heart of our culture, become central to our values, and speak to the very survival of our species.

Shelley might also have been prescient in foreseeing the formalization of the inchoate universities of her time into streamlined academic complexes where knowledge production would increasingly be defined by the rules and expectations of the academic communities themselves. While we have certainly created a huge quantity of scholarship since 1818—a surprisingly large amount of which is actually about *Frankenstein*—we have also shied away, in most cases, from dealing with the very questions that so enticed Victor. Apart from a few physicists who admit to seeing a pattern behind the universe they study, most of us are reluctant to systematically engage with the idea of a coherent world in which the visible and the invisible, the natural and the sublime, are united. Physicians are largely just as reluctant to link natural and divine knowledge, even when they have had the rare privilege of holding a beating heart or witnessing the symmetry of the spinal cord. The modern scientific world, governed as it is by a devotedly secularized form of logic, does not want to talk about God. We have replaced theological responsibility, in which Renaissance scholars believed themselves to be pursuing knowledge to better understand the divine plan, with humanist thought, in which we strive to find new information to better the human condition. But the ways in which we do that have not always been particularly humanist, and this problem ties Victor Frankenstein to our modern conversations about the how and why of science and medicine.

Those hallmarks of modern bioethics, Mengele's experiments on concentration camp inmates and the Tuskegee syphilis study, bring to mind the suffering that can be generated by unmonitored scientific experimentation. The cardinal rule of medical practice, that the physician must first do no harm, had no impact on the people who conducted those experiments. The suffering of their subjects cannot even be chalked up—as though this were acceptable—to the pursuit of knowledge; in the latter case, certainly, we needed no further documentation of the progress of untreated syphilis, and in the former the subjects were never viewed as human beings. Like the Creature, brought into being as a result of scientific inquiry and then dumped, the subjects of unethical medical experimentation have rarely been provided the care and support they deserve. And like the Creature, they were not asked if they were willing to sacrifice their lives so that others might benefit—or not. Perhaps someone did ask, though; Mary Shelley gave her "patient" a voice, tinged with romantic fantasy as it was, and he clearly said he would have preferred never to be created and, having no choice in that matter, demanded to be treated as an equal.

The Creature's voice speaks clearly from the shadows to say that those who bear the burden of undisciplined, ungoverned scientific experimentation do not give their consent. He speaks for the millions of people who have been and may yet be tormented in some way when, to satisfy our desire to know more, we practice science on those who cannot defend themselves—the weak, the poor, the young, the incarcerated, the disenfranchised, those from unpopular minority groups, and even the dead. In this way, the Creature is immensely human, and he calls upon us to exercise those oft-sleeping angels of our better natures to recognize the human in those we deem alien and to meet them with kindness, rather than hiding a desire to destroy difference inside the more culturally acceptable desire to understand it.

3

==

A More Horrid Contrast

From the Page to the Stage

> Because you are designed to want something that will hurt you. And
> you cannot help wanting it. You cannot stop wanting it. It is your design.
> And when you finally find it, this thing will burn you up. This thing will
> destroy you.
>
> —Daniel H. Wilson, *Robopocalypse*

None of those huddled around the fire telling ghost stories in Byron's elegant villa could possibly have imagined the success young Mary Shelley's story would have in the nineteenth-century world. Neither could they have envisioned that the title of her book would become a perennial catchword encapsulating modern society's fears of misguided scientific experimentation and the possibility of technological advancements going horribly awry. For thirty years of the nineteenth century, *Frankenstein* would reign as the most popular novel in the English-speaking world; it would eventually be translated into at least twenty-nine foreign languages and has remained in print from the day of its publication till the present. Indeed, Mary's novel provided her with much more popular acclaim in her own lifetime than the public accorded Percy Shelley in his, and for over twenty-five years she was regarded as a major novelist who had been married to a minor poet; the revenues from just the first edition of *Frankenstein* in 1818 equaled more than the sum of Percy's lifetime publications, and the royalties from the 1831 reprinting ran into the thousands.

The Page

The second half of Shelley's title, *The Modern Prometheus* (originally intended to be the book's full title), blends the novel's narrative with the Greek myth of Prometheus, the Titan who defies the Olympian gods by stealing fire and providing it to mankind, thus forging a pathway to civilization. (In Ovid's version

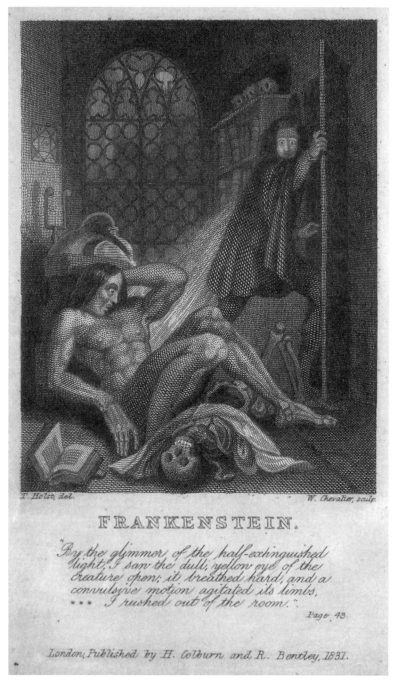

FRANKENSTEIN.

"By the glimmer of the half-extinguished
light, I saw the dull, yellow eye of the
creature open: it breathed hard, and a
convulsive motion agitated its limbs.
... I rushed out of the room.".

Page. 43.

London, Published by H. Colburn and R. Bentley, 1831.

Cover of the 1831 printing of *Frankenstein*, the first with pictures—here the moment
the Creature becomes conscious—illustrated by Theodor von Holst (1810–1844).

of the myth, Prometheus actually creates the human race.) For his disobedient act, Zeus sentences Prometheus to an endless cycle of agony by chaining him to a rock in the Caucasus Mountains where an eagle eats his liver, which then regenerates overnight, only to be eaten by the bird again the next day. Artists as far back as the classical era, such as Aeschylus, were attracted to the pain and glory of the Prometheus narrative, but his revolutionary act of defiance was sacrosanct to the rebellious poets of the Romantic age. Both Byron ("Prometheus," 1816) and Percy Shelley (*Prometheus Unbound*, 1820) saw the Titan's story as encapsulating the spirit of their turbulent age and his saga as a model for insurrection against entrenched and oppressive institutions, such as the church and the monarchy. Yet, as Harold Bloom and others have noted, even the earliest iterations of the Prometheus myth contains negative elements, and his gift of fire estranges mankind from the gods.

Logically, the Promethean figure in *Frankenstein* would be Victor. The novel views his bold but ultimately destructive experimentation in creating life, followed by his severe punishment at the hands of his creation, ambiguously, at times allowing the Creature to attain intellectual and emotional heights that Victor never reaches. Much traditional *Frankenstein* criticism emphasizes the theory that Victor transgressed God's moral and natural laws by creating life from dead matter, thereby violating the sanctioned boundaries for human exploration of the unknown and assuming a creative power only God should wield. However, a close reading of the novel reveals that this perception of events represents a simplistic view of the work at best, and at worst a total misreading. Mary Shelley refuses to make definitive and rigid value judgments in *Frankenstein*, allowing both the creator and his creation to state their cases with equal eloquence and forcing the reader to evaluate each figure's actions and moral reasoning. That is not to say that judgments cannot be rendered. Although the Creature's agency is more limited than Victor's, both characters understand the fundamental difference and possess the ability to choose between the ethical and the unethical, but they consistently make hasty and flawed decisions, often based on frayed emotions rather than careful thought, that destroy others and ultimately themselves.

On a cultural level, the novel juxtaposes the tensions between the man of genius and his world, and between a creator and his creation, never assigning total good or evil to either one. The novelist Joyce Carol Oates offers an aggressively modern reading, one at odds with some contentions in our earlier chapters, when she claims that Shelley's universe "is emptied of God and of theistic assumptions of 'good' and 'evil.' Hence, its modernity."[1] To understand the method by which Shelley carefully develops the seemingly opposing sides of her fictive world—society versus the genius, creator versus creation—one must first recognize something that seems very basic, but that most commentators fail to mention: Victor Frankenstein's experiment appears to be spectacularly successful. He literally does the miraculous by turning dead matter into a living organism, but the consequences resulting from his actions are far from his lofty expectations of gratitude and fame. Whatever deaths may occur in the rest of the novel, whatever grief his research occasions, nothing should blind us to his truly brilliant achievement: he finds "the cause of generation and life," which allows him "to bestow animation upon lifeless matter" (1.3, 109). In doing so, however, he demolishes his family and best friend, sacrifices his fiancée, and relinquishes his sanity for much of the novel.

The zealous aspirations and personal ambitions of dedicated scientists, explorers, and artists to discover something original and produce something significant, to "go where no man has gone before," are neither inherently evil nor fundamentally immoral; rather, such majestic yearnings remain the origins and driving impetus of many famous breakthroughs. Victor states his initial motivation, a natural outgrowth of his mother's death from scarlet fever and "the bitterness of grief" that followed this "most irreparable evil" (I. 2,99), as quite altruistic: "to banish disease from the human frame, and render man invulnerable to any but a violent death" (1.3, 109). But in isolation as he pursues this ambitious goal, his compassionate vision quickly degenerates into egotistical reveries as he dreams of a new species that "would bless me as its creator and source; many happy and excellent natures would owe their being to me. No father could claim the gratitude of his child so completely as I should deserve theirs" (1.3, 110). The failure to integrate his grandiose objectives with his social obligations turns Victor's philanthropic dream into a violent nightmare and his story into a paradigmatic cautionary tale for the ages. Ignoring the model provided by his own "tender" mother and father (1.1, 88), Victor's reckless ambition and then his refusal to take parental responsibility for his "offspring" seal his fate and that of those he most loves. Even at the end of his life, Victor offers excuses for his failure as a parent: "I created a rational creature, and was bound towards him, to assure, as far as was in my power, his happiness and well-being. This was my duty; but there was another still paramount to that. My duties towards my fellow creatures" (3.7, 317). Even an inspired act of luminous creation must be recognized as only the first step in an ongoing and evolving process that necessarily demands accountability for whatever—or whomever—one delivers into the world.

Frankenstein's isolation, as noted earlier, is a major reason for the tragedies that result from his "filthy" research, which uses materials from "charnel houses" to expose "the tremendous secrets of the human frame" (1.3, 111). As was established in chapters 1 and 2, Victor relies solely upon himself and rejects the institutional support and overview of the university faculty. As a result, he becomes totally preoccupied with how the outcomes of his labors will affect

Mary Shelley, author of *Frankenstein.*

him while completely ignoring how they might drastically transform the world beyond the narrow boundaries of his attic. By virtue of this self-imposed seclusion, his experiment spins outside of any moral constraints, and Victor degenerates from a humane research scientist into a deranged addict compelled to obtain his objective at any cost. Crucially, he rejects the characters embodying the most humanizing forces in the novel: masculine friendship personified by Henry Clerval and feminine love incarnated by Elizabeth. Discarding the only potential salvation offered in the novel, a union with a like spirit on either the sexual or fraternal level, Victor's solitude inevitably leads to blind egoism that dooms his family and closest friends. The title of Delmore Schwartz's short story "In Dreams Begin Responsibility" aptly encapsulates what Frankenstein never comprehends until he refuses to create a mate for the Creature.[2] Such a reading no doubt reverberates in contemporary eras traumatized by disasters "deliberately created by man's ingenuity."[3]

Shelley had a strong foundation for combining intellectual goals with human interaction, for both of her male models—her father, William Godwin, and her husband, Percy Shelley—stressed the need for even men of genius to integrate their personal quest for knowledge with the social concerns of the outside world. In his *Enquiry concerning Political Justice,* Godwin wrote: "No being can be either virtuous, or vicious, who has no opportunity of influencing the happiness of others. . . . Even knowledge, and the enlargement of intellect, are poor, when unmixed with sentiments of benevolence and sympathy . . . and science and abstraction will soon become cold unless they derive new attractions from ideas of society."[4] Percy Shelley's long poem "Alastor," published a scant six months before Mary began *Frankenstein*, contains an even more profound vision of the relationship between one who "seek[s] strange truths in undiscovered lands" and the society he rejects. The poet in "Alastor," much like Victor Frankenstein, makes his bed "in charnels and on coffins" as he obstinately searches for "what we are." Although Percy Shelley expresses deep admiration for the doomed protagonist of his work, he makes his position clear in the preface: "The intellectual faculties, the imagination, the functions of sense, have their respective requisitions on the sympathy of corresponding powers in other human beings. . . . Those who love not their fellow-beings live unfruitful lives and prepare for their old age a miserable grave."[5] Perhaps overstating his case when mired in the muddy gloom of his near-death despair, Victor's warning to young Walton echoes the admonitions of Godwin and Percy Shelley: "If the study to which you apply yourself has a tendency to weaken your affections, and to destroy your taste for those simple pleasures in which no alloy can possibly mix, then that study is certainly unlawful, that is to say, not befitting the human mind" (1.3, 112).

Given these sentiments, *Frankenstein* exemplifies what Harold Bloom labels "the internalization of Quest-Romance," a turning away from an outward union of man with nature and a turning inward toward an internalization of the imagination that becomes overly self-conscious and destructive of the social self. Such a shift from external connections to internal solipsism characterizes much of the literature written during the Romantic age, as well as many movies featuring the "mad scientist" fanatically experimenting in his laboratory. Bloom notes that as the Romantic authors struggled to widen their consciousnesses to intensify their intellectual insights, they simultaneously narrowed themselves to an acute overpreoccupation with the self. As a prime example of this perceptual and emotional shift from the many to the one, Frankenstein mistakenly substitutes cold abstractions for the warmth of human affection and love. *As a consequence Shelley's novel*, like many other great works of the Romantic age, cries out for a secure union of mutually sympathetic beings that transcends personal fixations: Walton, Elizabeth, Alphonse and Caroline Frankenstein, Henry, Safie, the De Laceys (who initially offer examples of mutual respect and affection), the Creature, and even Victor at times all long for the healing warmth available only through companionship and love.

If Frankenstein deserves punishment for his actions, therefore, it is not for desiring to "know what it feels like to be God"[6] or to "penetrate into the recesses of nature, and shew how she works in her hiding places" (1.2, 104), but rather for ignoring his fundamental obligations to the social order, abandoning the restorative powers of friendship and love, and refusing to engage in a relationship that puts the needs of others—even his Creature—before his own. *Frankenstein* places a high value on these very human, some might say conventional or even mundane, responsibilities to others, conceptualizing them as beneficial constraints on any intellectual quest—no matter how worthy. But Shelley offers a more nuanced concept than an either/or choice. Nowhere does *Frankenstein* unambiguously preach that Promethean figures must exchange their glorious dreams that exceed the ordinary imagination for the more temperate and commonplace pleasures of hearth and home. Instead, it yearns to find a viable compromise between the two: a complementary enrichment of one by the other, rather than a destructive competition in which one must vanquish the other. To fail to achieve this reconciliation transforms the scientist from a socially concerned citizen into a morally indifferent researcher, perhaps even into a sociopathic renegade. Victor spends most of the novel deluding himself or justifying his actions, finally attempting a doomed effort to remedy the wrongs for which he is responsible by exterminating what he has brought to life.

But Victor's blindness extends beyond his severely flawed research methodology. Initially, he fails to comprehend what John Milton so eloquently illustrates in his magisterial epic of good and evil, and of the glory and failure of creation, *Paradise Lost* (1667). The defiant literary artists of the early half of the nineteenth century never embraced the vengeful God of Milton's epic, but instead celebrated the audacity of his archenemy, the mutinous Satan. From their perspective, Milton's unconquerable Satan—with his "courage never to submit or yield" (1.108) and his brazen declaration that it was "better to reign in hell than serve in heaven" (1.263)—emerged an equal to the heroic Prometheus. God's explicit command for Adam and Eve not to eat the forbidden fruit from the Tree of Knowledge was, for the Romantics, another example of an institutionalized tyrannical power designed to keep mankind chained in ignorance. For the Romantic writers, Milton's sacred poem proved a far more powerful inspiration than the Bible itself, which they identified as a key component of the pervasive hegemonic repression that defined and sustained the rigid social boundaries of polite society.

Mary Shelley was reading Milton as she wrote her novel, and *Frankenstein* contains an intricate web of allusions to *Paradise Lost*, as noted by many scholars. Not only is it one of the crucial texts by which the Creature educates himself, but Shelley also directly quotes lines from Milton's epic. In addition, the Creature compares himself both to Adam ("united by no link to any other being in existence" and to Satan ("the fitter emblem of my condition"), leaving Victor to fill the role of God as "Cursed creator" (2.7, 209–210). On the summit of Montanvert, where Victor again confronts his "offspring," the Creature conflates these figures; he declares, "I ought to be thy Adam; but I am rather the fallen angel, whom thou divest from joy for no misdeed" (2.2, 171) and, eventually, demands that his creator fashion an "Eve" to share his persecuted life. At their core, then, the Prometheus myth, *Paradise Lost* and the Book of Genesis all provide Shelley's novel with the same trio of truths: that punishment inevitably follows disobedience, that creation always entails pain, and that sorrow is always part of gaining knowledge.

Within its vast Miltonic framework and direct allusions to the Bible, therefore, *Frankenstein* entwines knowledge and sorrow, as illustrated by Adam and Eve's tragic fate after eating the sacred fruit from the Tree of Knowledge. As Milton warns, knowledge "is as food, and needs no less / Her Temperance over Appetite, to know / In measure what the mind may well contain, / Oppresses else with Surfeit, and soon turns / wisdom to Folly, as Nourishment to Wind" (7.126–130). Victor comes to realize that "dangerous is the acquirement of knowledge" (1.3, 109). Both creator and Creature eventually grasp that their "sorrow only increased with knowledge" (2.5, 199) and that such pursuits make them wretched outcasts. While it puts no limitations on the quest for knowledge, the novel questions whether the individual of genius can accede to the natural demands of society, thus avoiding the risk of dissipating his/her wisdom in an unproductive void of sterile solipsism and perpetual alienation, while still progressing along the path toward greater knowledge. Exploring what price must be paid to gain knowledge, the novel reaches its highest tension point and, not coincidentally, speaks most directly to our own age of rapid technological leaps and transformative inventions.

But why does Victor reject the Monster, abandoning his parental obligations and setting off the chain of events that will destroy himself and everyone dear to him? In the very act of the Monster's "birth," Victor successfully breaks through the "ideal bounds" of life and death to "pour a torrent of light into our dark world," but he immediately witnesses the ever-widening gap between his original vision and the deformed reality that stands before him with "agitated limbs." Because the "minuteness of the parts formed a great hindrance to [his] speed," the researcher resolves to make the Creature of gigantic stature (1.3, 110). If Victor had been more skilled at plastic surgery and fashioned a being with a pleasant appearance, not only might his breakthrough have been hailed, but also the tragedies that followed might have been forestalled—and consequently presented a far less powerful work of fiction. Instead, once Victor beholds his Creature's "dull, yellow . . . watery eyes, . . . shrivelled complexion, and straight black lips, . . . the beauty of the dream vanishe[s]," and the creator, "unable to endure the aspect of his being," is filled with a "breathless horror and disgust" that compels him to flee the room (1.4, 114, 116).

The dream vanishes, but the discarded Creature remains, a love-starved thing called to life by a creator who now rejects and abandons him. Such a misshapen and hideously twisted being seems doomed to remain a miserable outsider, forever cast out by a callous society that judges an individual's worth by external appearances. Shelley epitomizes the Creature's fate when he saves a young girl from drowning and is first shot, then quickly subjected to the ignominy of a child who merely sees him and begins screaming, "Monster! ugly wretch! You wish to eat me, and tear me to pieces—You are an ogre" (2.8, 224). At this point, the Creature faces hatred solely on the basis of his outward form, which Victor has designed and produced. (In some of the later movies based on Shelley's novel, the artificial being created is strikingly beautiful, but still excluded by a fearful society.) The Monster's initial crime, therefore, is his physical repulsiveness, something over which he has neither a part in nor can control. Indeed, at one point, the Monster rises to a level of moral understanding unsurpassed by any other figure in the novel, lecturing his maker on the responsibilities of creation: "Yet you, my creator, detest and spurn me, thy creature, to whom thou art bound by ties only dissoluble by the annihilation of one of us. You propose to kill me. How dare you sport thus with life? Do your duty towards me, and I will do mine towards you and the rest of mankind" (2.2, 170). Thus, the Monster's drive to revenge and murder results from his intense desire to obtain what Victor so carelessly rejects: friendship and love.

Seeing that he cannot any expect parental tenderness and affection from his creator, the Creature demands the next best thing: "I am alone, and miserable; man will not associate with me; but one as deformed and horrible as myself would not deny herself to me" (2.8, 226). Whether or not Frankenstein errs by denying the Creature a female counterpart remains open to discussion, but his very refusal provides evidence of moral growth. Previously, Victor gave no heed to the consequences of inspired actions, but here he considers the potential ramifications of a second creation. He worries that a female counterpart "might become ten thousand times more malignant than her mate, and delight, for its own sake, in murder and wretchedness." Even if the pair departs for some isolated location (he considers them going to the "new world") could they give birth to "a race of devils" that would threaten mankind? Tormented that he might "inflict this course upon everlasting generations" and "that future ages might curse [him] as their pest," Victor resolves never to "create another like yourself, equal in deformity and wickedness," and in so doing calls down the vengeful wrath of the Creature (3.3, 254–56), who pursues Victor in a destructive rage, murdering his creator's best friend and then his wife, while causing the death of Victor's father and others along the way. Driven past his psychological and physical limits and failing fast, Victor at the last imparts his words of wisdom about the importance of limiting scientific experimentation and his final quest to Walton. The Romantic experimentalist earnestly accepts the job of killing the Creature, and then encounters him grieving over his creator's corpse. Their talk decides Walton's path of action. He rounds up his crew to return home and watches the Creature, who vows never again to see humankind, disappear into the black night to "ascend [his] funeral pyre" and have his ashes "swept into the sea by the winds" (2.7, 324). Although the novel ends with Frankenstein's offspring leaping onto his ice-raft and being "borne away by the waves, and lost in darkness and distance" (2.7, 324), its cultural resonance was just beginning.

The Stage

When Mary Shelley returned to England five days before her twenty-sixth birthday and a year after the death of her husband, she was shocked to discover that "lo & behold! I found myself famous!"[7] She soon realized that her sudden celebrity did not result solely from the success of her novel—first published anonymously (1818) in three volumes with a modest printing (five hundred copies) by the small London company Lackington, Hughes, Harding, Mavor, & Jones. Instead, her fame developed largely as a consequence of the public's embrace of Richard Brinsley Peake's dramatic production *Presumption; or, The Fate of Frankenstein* (1823). Because the law provided her with no copyright protections, Shelley exerted no authorial control and received no royalties from this or any of the subsequent plays inspired by her writing. Yet she did benefit from their growing fame. The popularity of Peake's production triggered a second, two-volume reprinting of *Frankenstein* in 1823 supervised by her father and published by G. and W. B. Whittaker, which finally identified Mary Wollstonecraft Shelley as its author for the first time, although she excises her father's last name and replaces it with her mother's.

One hundred and thirteen years separate the initial publication of Mary Shelley's *Frankenstein* and the release of James Whale's film, and a century elapsed between the appearance of the 1831 version of the novel on bookshelves and the arrival of the 1931 movie in theaters. But the creator and his Creature never vanished from the public scene during the years between the novel's first printing and its classic screen adaptation. They remained a dynamic part of the cultural maelstrom, as various authors integrated and purged elements from her novel to construct their plays. This parade of stage performances exposed Shelley's characters to an even wider, and quite different, audience than did the ongoing marketing of her literary work. In his history of *Frankenstein* dramatizations, Steven Earl Forry lists twenty-two plays—mostly staged in England or France—written prior to the original *Frankenstein* movie in that stretch from 1823 to 1930, and a total of ninety-six as of 1990.[8] The pre-Whale productions provide a crucial, generally ignored transition between the editions of the book and the production of the film.

As noted in the section that follows, the drastic streamlining of Shelley's plot and characters to conform to the time, conditions, and dramatic requirements of a theatrical performance, as well as the accretion and deletion of characters and narrative developments, substantially altered Shelley's original vision in the popular imagination. Several major revisions present in these early stage adaptations proved enduring and remain part of the common conception of *Frankenstein* to this day: eliminating Walton's Arctic voyage to compress the action; rendering the plot as linear rather than revealing it through a series of subjective flashbacks; portraying Frankenstein as a mature scientist rather than a naïve youth, with little mention of his formative boyhood experiences; making the Creature unable to speak, and thus more animalistic; having a vengeful mob hunt down the Creature; adding an assistant/servant for Frankenstein; and presenting the simultaneous deaths of both the scientist and his creation via a final confrontation.

On August 29, 1823, Mary Shelley, her father, and Jane Williams, the widow of Edward Williams (Percy Shelley's companion in the boating accident that took both their lives), attended a performance of Peake's *Presumption*, a month and a day into its initial run at the English Opera House. The drama featured Thomas Potter Cooke as the Creature, a role that brought him as much fame in his time as Boris Karloff attained after his groundbreaking appearance in Whale's movie. Cooke, who had starred as Lord Ruthven in the 1820 stage adaptation of Polidori's *The Vampyre*, painted his face green and yellow, his body blue, and his lips black, disheveled his long stringy hair, and wore a toga-like costume. The actor ultimately assumed the role of the Creature some 365 times and earned Shelley's praise: "Cooke played ——'s [the Monster, as in the movie and the book, was given no name] part extremely well; his seeking, as it were, for support; his trying to grasp at the sounds he heard; all, indeed, he does was well imagined and executed. I was much amused, and it appeared to excite a breathless eagerness in the audience."[9] Cooke's Creature never spoke, but instead communicated through a series of guttural sounds and gestures, a tactic often used in subsequent plays and movies.

Peake's adaptation and its companion, the self-parody *Another Piece of Presumption* (1823), were among the first of several versions of Shelley's tale on the boards before the publication of her final edition of the novel in 1831, such as Henry M. Milner's *Frankenstein; or, The Demon of Switzerland* (1823); *Humgumption; or, Dr. Frankenstein and the Hobgoblin of Hoxton* (1823); and *Presumption and the Blue Demon* (1823). Within three years of Peake's first production, fourteen other English and French plays employing Frankensteinian themes appeared onstage, including Milner's *The Man and the Monster; or, The Fate of Frankenstein* (1826) and John Kerr's *The Monster and the Magician; or, The Fate of Frankenstein* (1826).[10] In Paris, Jean-Toussaint Merle and Beraud Antony's *Le monstre et le magicien* (1826) ran for an astounding ninety-four performances, inspiring six comic versions, two burlesques, and three productions that Forry labels as "classical extravaganzas."[11] The theatergoing public's appetite for a spectrum of plays about Frankenstein and his Creature proved insatiable during this period, whether such productions took the form of serious melodramas, burlesques, or even musical comedies. The last Frankensteinian stage play of the nineteenth century, Richard Butler and Henry Chance Newton's musical burlesque *Franken-stein; or, The Vampire's Victim* (1887), united characters inspired by Shelley and Polidori for the first time, drew large audiences, and ran for 106 performances.

Despite their often substantial deviations from the novel, the astounding success of these ongoing stage presentations entrenched *Frankenstein* firmly in the public's consciousness and played a pivotal role in the printing of a third version, containing a preface by the author, that appeared in 1831 and ran into the thousands. Winnowing down Shelley's philosophical writing to appeal to a more conservative and less highly educated audience, these plays usually substitute conventional moral lessons about overweening hubris, as Peake's title suggests, moral transgressions, and contrition for the novel's probing intellectual questions. They also furnish audiences with far more simplified characterizations of the "mad scientist" and his brutish creation, portraits that lack Shelley's poignant, ambiguous complexity. Yet they play a crucial role in the evolution of the Frankenstein narrative.

Reading Peake's play after Shelley's novel feels like revisiting a once-familiar room now made strange by the rearrangement of its furniture. Songs appear throughout the production: solos by Clerval, Felix, and Agatha; duets between Fritz and his wife (Madame Nonon), Fritz and Agatha, and Safie and Felix; and a chorus of Gypsies. Clerval falls in love with Elizabeth, who is Victor's sister, while Victor loves Agatha De Lacey, Felix's sister, whose rejection has driven him to embark on his scientific quest. The Monster—rarely called a Creature—kills Agatha, and at the end of the play, created and creator perish together under an avalanche triggered by Victor's attempt to shoot the Monster. The introduction of Fritz, who in films becomes Frankenstein's physically deformed assistant, here fulfills a mostly comic role as a frightened servant who never participates in his master's experiments and loves his cow more than his wife. Because Peake's audience never witnesses the birth of the Monster, Fritz becomes their conduit, reporting that Victor may be "raising the devil," equating Frankenstein with Faust, and repeating his employer's frantic exclamation, "It is animated—it rises—walks!"

Despite all of these transformations, Peake's essential portrait of Frankenstein's grandiose hubris remains similar to Shelley's conception of the megalomaniacal scientist who justifies unorthodox research protocols by his "astounding results." He regales Clerval with the "enticements of science" and nature's "strange, undreamed-of mysteries" that have culminated in his "grand, unheard of wonder" in pursuit of his goal: "The vital principle! The cause of life! Like Prometheus of old, have I daringly attempted the formation—the

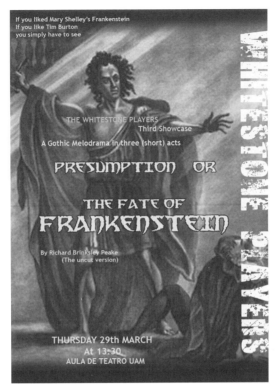

If you liked Mary Shelley's Frankenstein
If you like Tim Burton
you simply have to see

THE WHITESTONE PLAYERS
Third Showcase

A Gothic Melodrama in three (short) acts

PRESUMPTION   OR

THE FATE OF
FRANKENSTEIN

By Richard Brinksley Peake
(The uncut version)

THURSDAY 29th MARCH
At 13:30
AULA DE TEATRO UAM

An advertisement for a revival of *Presumption; or, The Fate of Frankenstein* at the University of Madrid showing how the Creature (T. P. Cooke) was presented.

animation of a Being." Peake puts some of Shelley's language in Frankenstein's mouth when he first beholds the consummation of his experiments:

> I saw the dull yellow eye of the creature open, it breathed hard, and a convulsive motion agitated its limbs. . . . Ah, horror! His cadaverous skin scarcely covered the work of muscles and arteries beneath, his hair lustrous, black, and flowing—his teeth of pearly whiteness—but these luxuriances only form more horrible contrasts with the deformities of the monster. . . . The dreadful spectre of a human form—no mortal could withstand the horror of that countenance—a mummy embued with animation could not be so hideous as the wretch I have endowed with life! (1.3)

Frankenstein's dream vanishes, as in the novel, and "breathless horror and disgust" fill his heart. Later, wounded by Felix's shotgun, the Monster grovels at

Victor's feet imploring him for protection (according to the stage directions), but Frankenstein attempts to stab him with a knife. Proclaiming that his kindly feelings toward the human race have been met "by abhorrence and violence," the Monster declares that these sentiments "are now all converted into hate and vengeance" as he burns down the De Laceys' cottage. He revenges himself by killing Victor's younger brother and his beloved, as in the novel.

Notwithstanding Peake's efforts to make *Frankenstein* more palatable to general audiences, a group called the London Society for the Prevention of Vice organized a leaflet campaign urging theatergoers to boycott his blasphemous production, "pregnant with mischief" and "dangerous doctrines,"[12] and instigated a highly publicized controversy whose notoriety no doubt contributed to the play's overwhelming crowds. Many charges of immorality and public outbursts leveled against Peake's play, according to Forry, were inspired by animosity toward the radical political and social positions espoused by the circle of family and friends surrounding Mary Shelley—who had nothing to do with the production—including Godwin, Wollstonecraft, Byron, and Percy Shelley. Most of the negative reviews included references to their revolutionary viewpoints that brazenly defied contemporary moral standards. As such, *Presumption* was lumped together with an entire set of attitudes it did not necessarily espouse or even contain. Such accusations dogged the production as it toured outside of London as well, but it still continued to be one of the most popular plays of its era, being revived three times in Covent Garden and twice at the English Opera House.

The first of the comic stage productions, *Frank-in-Steam; or, The Modern Promise to Pay*, debuted at the Olympic Theater on December 23, 1824. More a parody of Peake's *Presumption* than of Shelley's novel, the play sets its action within London and its suburbs during 1824. A debt-ridden Frank-in-steam, about to be married to Penelope De Lacey, receives the welcome news that his major creditor, Mr. Snatch, "drank himself to death in despair of catching me." Nonetheless, he foolishly reanimates his foe, proclaiming: "It lives—it snores—it cries!" The rest of this short work consists of the Monster chasing his creator and Frankinsteam escaping time after time. Finally, a boiler explosion blows up Snatch, followed by a chorus singing of Frankinsteam's victory: "Now from every danger free." Like Peake's play, *Frank-in-Steam* incorporates songs, and Fritz, while still comic, expands into a major character. In one clever segment, Frankinsteam and Fritz even speak to each other in matching rhymes.

Henry M. Milner's 1826 play *Frankenstein; or, The Man and the Monster!* debuted on July 3 at London's Royal Coburg Theater. Billed as "A Peculiar Romantic, Melo-Dramatic Pantomimic Spectacle, in Two Acts," it declared that the action was "founded principally on Mrs. Shelley's singular work . . . and partly on the French Piece, *Le Monstre et le Magicien*." Milner sets his plot in and around the estate of the Prince del Piombino near the foot of Mount Etna, Europe's highest and most active volcano, which rises above the city of Catania on the island of Sicily. Unlike previous dramas, Milner's play features royal characters wearing fancy costumes such as a green tunic richly embroidered with silver and a crimson sash (the Prince), or white (Julio) and pink (Rosaura) embroidered satin; Frankenstein sports a black velvet vest, and a gray tunic slashed with white. Despite these splashes of color, however, Milner's play strikes more dramatic and somber notes than Peake's. This version of Shelley's narrative contains a new backstory for Frankenstein. In the "fumes of his diabolical preparations . . . the dreams of his mad ambitions, all his human feelings are lost and annihilated." To gain the money necessary to continue his experiments, he deserts his German wife, Emmeline, and his child "to poverty and want" while seemingly willing to marry the Prince's sister, Rosaura. At the same time, his manservant, Strutt, falls in love with Lisetta, the daughter of the Prince's dyspeptic attendant, Quadro. At the beginning of the play, Strutt praises his master as an "illustrious genius," a profound philosopher," and the greatest man who ever lived," and he remains steadfastly loyal to Frankenstein, despite being charged as an accessory to murder.

Milner's play allows both the creator and his Creature to fill their allotted roles within the action. Frankenstein believes that his accomplishment will bring him: "The brightest joy that e'er was yet attained by mortal man.—What monarch's power, what general's valour, or what hero's fame, can rank with that of Frankenstein? . . . How vain, how worthless, is the noblest fame compared to mine! Frankenstein shall be the first of men!" As expected, of course, the "terrible reality" of the Creature's ugliness forever punctures this flamboyant egotism, and Frankenstein hurls a string of insults at his Creature throughout the drama, branding him "hideous," a "wretch," an "infuriated monster," "a form of horror," a "dreadful monster," "a loathsome mass of animated putrefaction," "hellish," the "wretched product of my ill-directed efforts," and a "demon of cruelty." He tries to kill him several times, attempting to run him though with his sword and, when that fails, to strangle him. The villagers struggle to bind the Monster to a rock, but he escapes to do more damage. O. Smith played the Monster, again unnamed, whose vengeful anger leads to heinous crimes: he strangles Julio, the Prince's son, throws a villager off the mountain top, threatens to hurl a young child off a cliff, and sets Emmeline's father's forest cottage ablaze with people inside it. Ultimately, the Monster chooses his own death: he jumps off the summit of Mount Etna and into a fiery lava pit after stabbing Frankenstein to death.

No stage productions based on *Frankenstein* appeared between Paul Dickey and Charles Goddard's 1915 farce *The Last Laugh* and Peggy Webling's *Frankenstein: An Adventure in the Macabre*. The most documented transitional bridge

The playwright Peggy Webling (1871–1949), who adapted *Frankenstein* to the stage for Hamilton Deane.

between the literary texts and screen versions of Mary Shelley's novel begins with Webling's play, which premiered at the Empire Theater in Preston, England, on December 7, 1927. It featured the veteran actor/director Hamilton Deane, who, after his repertory company successfully toured Europe in an adaptation of Bram Stoker's *Dracula*, commissioned his friend Webling to write a new drama based on Shelley's work. Assuming the role of the blood-sucking Count and the deformed Creature on alternate evenings, Deane's popular double bill of the bat and the brute toured England for two years, with Deane presenting audiences with a more sympathetic Monster than previous productions. Forry points out that Webling's play accentuated the doppelgänger theme between creator and creation. It was, for example, the first production to refer to the Creature as Frankenstein, and both creator and creation wore identical costumes.[13]

Webling's Creature speaks but remains hideously ugly, and Deane's appearance, a refabrication of Cooke's earlier incarnation in *Presumption*, featured "'a strange mixture of blue, green, and red [makeup]—with thick red lips,' . . . a tangled fright wig, and . . . lifts in his boots to exaggerate his six-foot-one inch height."[14] This Frankenstein anoints his creation as a member of the family, and Victor Moritz (her Clerval figure) observes, "He is strangely like yourself in gesture and movements."[15] The playwright changed various aspects of her play from its premiere in Preston to its opening in London's West End in February 1930, particularly the ending, in which the Creature rips out Frankenstein's throat and is then destroyed by a dramatic lightning bolt. Webling rechristens Victor as Henry and introduces the character of Dr. Waldman as the rational man of science, alterations Whale keeps in his movie. She also heightens the intimate bond between Emily (Victor's fiancée in the play) and the Creature, as shown in this speech: "There was some call from his body to mine that I cannot deny. It was as if one heart, torn asunder, throbbed in his breast and in my own. Our blood ran in the same swift current. He is part of you and part of myself, and we are all one."[16] Forry asserts that Webling's play strikes different notes from previous stage adaptations due to the "general disillusion following World War I and preceding the Great Depression," concluding that her version "must be viewed in terms of an age frightened by a spectre of its own creation" and that her work "presages the most popular modern theme associated with the novel: society's ability to destroy itself."[17]

Enter Horace Liveright. The cofounder of the Modern Library publishing company and a prominent theatrical producer, Liveright staged a highly profitable version of Hamilton Deane's *Dracula* on Broadway in 1927 staring Bela Lugosi (the Count) and Edward Van Sloan (Van Helsing)—roles they reprised in Tod Browning's 1931 film for Universal Pictures. To make *Dracula* more appealing to American audiences, Liveright hired the playwright (later scriptwriter) John L. Balderston to revise Deane's script. This collaboration eventually led the three men to bring *Frankenstein* to the United States: Deane convinced Liveright and Balderston that an outcome equally as lucrative as their *Dracula* endeavor would result from an American staging of his other repertory hit, Webling's *Frankenstein: An Adventure in the Macabre*, with Balderston again contributing any necessary revisions. In March 1929, Balderston signed an agreement to adapt Webling's play, sharing copyright credit and royalties with her. Having scant respect for her work, Balderston radically overhauled Webling's material, almost never consulting with his English counterpart. Ultimately, Balderston's revision of Webling's play failed to materialize on any American stage due to Liveright's inability to raise sufficient funds to produce it. Deep in debt from business failures and ravished by alcoholism, Liveright sold his option in the *Frankenstein* play to Universal, leaving one of the men most responsible for transporting it across the Atlantic with very little to show for his efforts. Liveright died of pneumonia in 1933 at the age of forty-nine.

Balderston and Webling fared a bit better. They sold the screen rights to their combined play for $20,000 plus 1 percent of the worldwide box office gross to Universal, which, as Frederick Wiebel suggests, likely did not want a *Frankenstein* play running on Broadway simultaneously with the movie's release.[18] Universal's president, Carl Laemmle Jr., eagerly sought a horror story that

The playwright and scriptwriter John Balderston (1889–1954), whose adaptation of Peggy Webling's play was bought by Universal as the basis for the studio's *Frankenstein* movie.

could duplicate his company's lucrative success with *Dracula* and believed *Frankenstein* was the vehicle to achieve his financial objective. He was right: costing around $125,000 to produce, *Frankenstein* eventually cleared over $12 million in profits for Universal, and the *New York Times* named it one of the best films of 1931. Once Laemmle secured the rights, as many scholars have noted, at least three scriptwriters (Robert Florey, Garrett Ford, and James Whale), two actors (Lugosi and Karloff), two final scenes (Frankenstein dies/Frankenstein lives), two directors (Robert Florey and James Whale), and one fabulous makeup man (Jack Pierce) added their own touches to the narrative, jettisoning many of the more stolid segments of the Balderston/Webling drama. Universal's scriptwriters and directors never remained slavishly faithful either to Shelley's novel or to Balderston/Webling's version in their screen adaptation, but the studio finally paid Balderston/Webling an additional $100,000 in a 1951 out-of-court settlement that ensured Universal's rights to all *Frankenstein* sequels as well as the original film.

Although it remains unclear which, if any, of the earlier Frankenstein plays Balderston consulted, he obviously read Shelley's novel and incorporated key elements from her original conception that many prior stage adaptations had eliminated, such as the appearance of Baron Frankenstein and the absence of a laboratory assistant. He returns the characters to Shelley's locations (Ingoldstadt becomes Goldstadt) around 1800 and includes snippets of Frankenstein's childhood related by other characters, including his boyhood friend Victor Moritz, his fiancée Amelia Lavenza, and his father. Crucially for modern audiences, Balderston's version grants science entry into the creation scene: although he pours the contents of a small bottle that contains "the Elixir of life" down the cadaver's throat, Henry, according to the stage directions, "attaches wires of galvanic battery to arm, [and the] machine fizzes and gives off queer lights, and sends out sparks (1.1). Earlier, he talks of using "ultra violet rays" that are "life-giving, even life-creating" (1.1)—another nod to scientific advancements. This stage modification, for the first time, also contains the Monster's troubling demand for a female companion, an important element in Shelley's novel. Upon seeing Amelia, the Creature "gazes hungrily" at her and commands Frankenstein to provide him with a "wo-man," asserting, "I am YOUR master now" (1.2). Balderston's version, therefore, restores at least some facets that enliven Shelley's original story.

The script, simply called *Frankenstein*, differs substantially from the novel and other stage productions by fusing religion and science in the figure of Dr. Waldman, who is both an anatomy professor and a priest. Throughout the action, however, Waldman behaves far more like a man of God than a man of science, repeatedly challenging his former pupil about theological issues, preaching traditional Christian doctrines, and engaging in religious dialogues. As early as the fourth page, he warns Frankenstein that it is not "for the layman to probe these mysteries (the physical process of decay in dead mater and the nature of the vital force that infuses life into matter) too deeply. We know that life comes from God, from God alone. It is presumption to think the human mind was ever intended to fathom these supreme mysteries. . . . We must remember that we can deal only with matter, not with spirit, which is the breath of God" (1.1). Such stringent admonitions continue unabated throughout the play. Once Frankenstein unveils his creation, Waldman accompanies these reprimands with demands for repentance and absolution. "You have made yourself equal with God," he tells Frankenstein. "That was the sin of the fallen angel!" (1.2). After a traumatized Frankenstein finally admits his sin of pride—by "usurping the prerogative of God . . . I tried to make myself his equal"—Waldman offers at least partial comfort: "After sin comes repentance, and punishment, and I hope expiation" (1.1).

At crucial points in the Balderston drama, Frankenstein and Waldman consider whether or not the Creature has a soul. This long history of this philosophical/theological controversy, as discussed in chapter 2, defines his status as either human or nonhuman and, in turn, determines the morality or immorality of their actions toward him. Frankenstein recounts that earlier he revived a dead young man using his galvanic battery, as he had done previously with a frog and a dog, but reburied him because he did not want to "restore" but rather desired to "create" life (1.1). Stunned by this tale, Waldman instructs Frankenstein that when a person dies his soul goes to heaven, to hell, or to purgatory; then he poses the play's fundamental question: "Suppose you succeed now. Your corpse moves and breathes. It seems a man. But can Man exist without soul? Is it then a Man? What is it?" (1.1). This same quandary erupts again when Frankenstein resolves to kill his Creature, but he and Waldman switch their previous theological positions. "I've mocked God by giving life when I cannot give a soul," declares Frankenstein, adding as his rationale for the murder: "It is not human, it's a beast and can be killed without sin" (1.2). Now, however, Waldman defends the Creature's humanity, noting that "there is a Mind there" and that because the Creature feels emotional pain he must have a soul—"the part of man God calls back to himself after a man dies" (1.1, 3.1). Such lofty philosophical considerations of ensoulment, as discussed previously, are almost totally eliminated in Whale's movie.

Balderston presents Frankenstein as far nastier and more cruel than seen in previous versions. He resembles Simon Legree more than Louis Pasteur. The creator locks his Creature in a dark little cellar beneath his bedroom, while keeping him chained, drugged, and tortured; he treats him like an animal and whips him when he disobeys—"a beaten cur obeys his master" (1.2). As in many previous productions, Frankenstein hurls invectives at him, calling him names such as "devil," "satanic secret," "slave dog," "worse than a corpse," "vile creature," and "filthy mess who moves and talks." Maintaining the tradition of the stage melo-dramas, Balderston's Creature appears far more brutish than Shelley's figure. The stage directions describe his entrance in this manner: "Frankenstein sham-bles in; half-clothed in coarse rags, matted hair, slightly stumbling, walks half-crouching, like an ape, shielding his bloodshot eyes." When Waldman allows sunlight into the room, he "backs out like a scared animal," then "holds up his hands like a savage in prayer to the sun, muttering gibberish" (1.2). Later, he attempts to rape Amelia and accidentally drowns Katrina, the only person who treats him with kindness.

Despite his disdain for Webling's writing, Balderston preserves elements from her version, some of which she incorporated from earlier dramas. For example, he maintains Webling's change of Frankenstein's first name from Vic-tor to Henry and her substitution of Victor Moritz for Clerval. More crucially, he expands her doppelgänger theme by having the creator give the Creature his family name: Frankenstein. Waldman tells Henry that the Creature is "linked to you more strongly than a son to a father. . . . It is a part of yourself," and Fran-kenstein agrees: "He's part of me and I hate myself" (1.2). Amelia concurs that the Creature looks like Frankenstein, and since the Creature is part of Henry, his near-rape of Amelia takes on added density. Near the climax of the play, Frankenstein tells the Creature, "You are part me. I know how God felt when he made man and man turned into a filthy mess. He must have hated us and yet . . . we were his responsibility" (2.1). Echoes of this line appear in Whale's film when a hysterical Frankenstein declares: "Now I know what it feels like to be God!"

While perpetuating some of the components he found in Webling's play, Balderston also adds some elements of his own that Whale, in turn, retains in his production. For example, in the Balderston version Frankenstein cuts down a thief from the gibbet to use in his experiments, and the distraught Creature accidentally drowns an innocent victim, although a grown woman instead of a child like Little Maria. The fact that, in both cases, he expresses sorrow for these inadvertent deaths demonstrates his human emotions. In Balderston's creation scene, the Creature first moves his right hand, a gesture that becomes a repeated trope in many of the Frankenstein movies. Balderston portrays the delicate relationship between Frankenstein's best friend and his fiancée quite overtly, with Victor declaring his love for Amelia and the two ending up together at the play's conclusion; Whale offers viewers a more subtle but clear connec-tion between these characters. Finally, the whole relationship of the Creature to light and to fire becomes a dominant visual motif in Whale's film as well as in Balderston's drama.

Shelley's *Frankenstein* possesses all the raw materials for an exciting theatri-cal production. Playwrights from its first publication to its most recent staging have realized that the novel's larger-than-life characters are adventurous and memorable, its narrative crammed with narrow escapes and grisly deaths, its subject matter risky and taboo, and its themes significant—all components for successful dramas. The creation scene, in particular, offers opportunities for stunning pyrotechnics, and the Monster's deformities have inspired the imaginations of makeup artists for decades. But, most of all, the cultural third rails *Frankenstein* touches keep it pulsating with life. Jeanne Tiehen contends that the novel spawned so many stage and film reinterpretations because segments of society always fear progress: the adaptations have "created a myth that we culturally understand and embrace . . . [and that] reflects social anxieties and mirrors a hope for returning to normative conditions through the demise or punishment of the creature and Dr. Frankenstein."[19] The stage productions of Shelley's complicated novel convert it into a series of morality plays that rebuke the creator's hubris and castigate his creation's actions, a fitting resolution for conservative theater audiences. Frankenstein becomes more the mad doctor and the Creature more the brutish killer. In these plays, both succumb to conventional middle-class standards and serve as object lessons rather than characters yoked together by conflicting motivations and unbreakable bonds of love and hate.

Converting any novel into a play, and even more so into a film, becomes an act of transplantation more than transcription transforming written text into visual images. Language that succeeds on the page often falls flat when spoken by actors on the stage or in moving pictures on the screen because they supplant the reader's imagination with a set of specific recreations that may or may not correspond to an audience member's private vision of the tale. The monstrous creatures we conjure up while reading a work of literature can be far more terrifying than their concrete regenerations on the stage or the screen—and more personally threatening since they spring from our darkest imaginings, deepest fears, and hidden desires. Different eras of history find particular images horrifying, so a monster that terrifies one generation may bore the next generation or even more likely elicit laughter. So it is with *Frankenstein*, both on the stage and on the screen, as we explore in subsequent chapters.

4

==

It's Still Alive

The Universal and Hammer Movie Cycles

Whoever fights monsters should see to it that in the process he does not become a monster. And when you look into the abyss, the abyss looks back into you.

—Friedrich Nietzsche, *Beyond Good and Evil*

"That body is not dead; it has never lived. I created it. I made it with my own hands," exults Frankenstein in the 1931 movie. Despite such flamboyant boasting, many commentators still equate the creation of new life with the reanimation of dead bodies. Let's be clear. Shelley's Frankenstein and many of his movie successors collect parts from different, unidentified corpses buried in graves and hanging on gallows; then, they fuse these organs and appendages together to beget a new living being rather than a regenerated cadaver, a biomechatronic cyborg, or an automated robot. While these reenergized organisms, half human/half mechanical cyborgs, and motorized robots all represent important offshoots of the Frankenstein family tree, this chapter focuses on the intricate connections between the various film characters specifically named Frankenstein and the composite creatures they construct. These other "monsters" remain derivative rather than strictly imitative of Frankenstein's corporeal amalgamation, making only cameo appearances in this chapter and waiting impatiently in the wings for their time in the spotlight.

Although some debate exists about the role of the supernatural in Shelley's book, as noted in our previous chapters, the overwhelming majority of the movie Frankensteins bestow life upon their creatures purely by scientific methods, thereby making the basic narrative as germane to the rapid technological transformations of twenty-first-century life as it was to the shifting scientific paradigms of the nineteenth century. As a result, one of the recurring narrative arcs that yokes these films together and leads back to Shelley's novel remains the tragedies that ensue when socially normative beings interact with artificially created life forms. This dynamic insertion of the "Other" into the daily world of the common activates the dramatic confrontation between the known and the unknown, the natural and the manufactured, which is the major source of the dramatic tension that has made these narratives compelling over the decades. The resulting clash between the definable and the indefinable disrupts conventional social organizations, arouses xenophobic hysteria, and motivates savage actions, unavoidably ending with ruinous outcomes both for protagonists and the society that surrounds them.

Silent Screams

The earliest use of the name "Frankenstein" in a movie title, *The Frankenstein Trestle* (1899), records a train crossing a 520-foot bridge spanning the 2,555-foot-high Frankenstein Cliffs (named for Godfrey Nicholas Frankenstein [1820–1873], a German immigrant and landscape painter born in Darmstadt near Burg Frankenstein) located in Crawford Notch State Park, New Hampshire. It is part of the thirty-mile stretch of the P&O railway line between Portland and Fabyan constructed in 1875 and has nothing to do with Shelley's novel. More directly for our purposes, Stephen Jones's *The Frankenstein Scrapbook* lists forty-one silent films with Frankensteinian themes, including Fritz Lang's Art Deco science fiction film *Metropolis* (a dystopian tale of income inequality, a mad scientist/inventor, and a seductive/deadly robot) and several versions of the golem story (1914, 1916, 1920) about a rabbi who summons an artificial entity into being to protect his people. It also includes a now lost 1920 Italian silent, *Il mostro di Frankenstein* (*The Monster of Frankenstein*) and *Life without Soul* (1915)—a loose adaptation of Shelley's novel.

Many of the silent movies incorporating Frankensteinian narratives and themes function as psychologically soothing, wish-fulfillment fantasies, rather than the gloomy and menacing nightmares of later eras. In these early movies, reanimated figures often return from the grave to right some obvious wrong (*The Return of Maurice Donnelly*, 1915; *The Face at the Window*, 1920) or plague those who harmed or cheated them in life (*The Devil to Pay*, 1920' *Legally Dead*, 1923). This large cluster featuring revenge themes envisions reanimated beings righting the scales of justice and allowing truth to best falsehood—even from beyond the grave. Other silent productions permit a scientist/father to revive a dead child cruelly snatched from him, thus utilizing modern scientific methods to rectify a heartbreaking act of fate (*Without a Soul*, 1916). Given the wrongs perpetrated on them in life, these reanimated beings garner far more viewer sympathy than the manufactured monsters that frequently appear innately evil and indiscriminately murderous in later films. Both of these narratives common during the silent era—the return of a justifiably vengeful figure and the reanimation of a loved one—connect with similar plot elements that appear repeatedly in many later Frankenstein-themed films as well.

To accomplish the rebirths that necessarily characterize such movies, early filmmakers depict a variety of bizarre operations, most recurrently transplants involving animal parts (*The Monkey Man*, 1908; *The Secret Room*, 1915)—again a scenario that haunts our contemporary imagination. Such narratives register an uncomfortable acknowledgment of Darwin's theories, but they also presage the famous Baby Fae xenotransplant (1984) in which an infant with hypoplastic left heart syndrome received a baboon's heart. Another grouping incorporates surgeries that produce dramatic changes in a person's basic personality, such as transforming a criminal into a law-abiding citizen (*The Surgeon's Experiment*, 1914; *Esther Redeemed*, 1915; *Doctor Maxwell's Experiment*, 1913); in *The Love Doctor* (1917), a doctor takes brain cells from a women who loves him and inserts them into the brain of a woman who spurned him. More metaphysical operations also appear on the silent silver screen, such as personality (*The Secret Room*, 1915) and soul (*The Monster*, 1925) transplants that move their narratives beyond primarily corporeal issues. These films probe, in halting steps, whether something created rather than naturally born can possibly have a soul: the unanimous answer in the silent era is no. But even couched in semireligious terms, this fundamental question about the personhood status of created beings lies at the heart of every Frankenstein narrative from Mary Shelley onward and becomes an even greater moral dilemma in an age replete with human-looking robots and cyborgs.

One high point during this early era, *The Magician* (1926), based on a 1908 W. Somerset Maugham novel and helmed by the well-respected director Rex Ingram, influenced both James Whale's 1931 *Frankenstein* and his sequel, *Bride of Frankenstein* (1935), particularly in the castle scenes. Yet, as in the golem films, magic—not to mention the "heart blood" of a virgin "maiden of fair skin"—is necessary to produce artificial life (a homunculus), not nature's lightning bolts and the science of electricity. The heroine, Margaret Dauncey (Alice Terry), a sculptor, falls in love with the handsome and brilliant young American surgeon Arthur Burdon (Ivan Petrovich), who performs an operation that saves her from permanent paralysis following a severe work injury; but she is also desired by a Parisian medical student, Oliver Haddo (Paul Wegener—based on the British occultist Aleister Crowley), whose obsessive quest to create life leads him deep into the dark arts. On the day of her wedding to Burdon, Haddo hypnotizes Margaret, kidnaps her, and marries her "in name only." He then whisks her off to Monte Carlo and finally takes her to his laboratory in Nice, where he plans to cut out her heart for his experiment. Burdon bursts into "the Sorcerer's" laboratory, situated in a towering castle atop a mountain and "gleaming through the storm like two evil eyes," to find the crazed surgeon, assisted by his dwarf servant, ready to slice open the terrified Margaret's chest as she lies bound and gagged on his operating table. The men fight, the villainous Haddo stumbles backward, his lab coat catches fire, and he goes up in flames. The blaze destroys both his formula for creating life and his entire laboratory. Ending in flames became a central image for the Frankenstein films, which developed the theme from the Creature's Arctic funeral pyre—imagined, though never seen—in the novel.

On the silent film branches of the Frankenstein family tree, the most important early production is the Edison Studio's 1910 version, released on March 18 and directed by James Searle Dawley. Any discussion of this one-reel, fifteen-minute adaptation must begin by paying homage to the sustained work of Frederick C. Wiebel Jr., whose herculean efforts to find, restore, screen, and distribute this "lost" print have bequeathed an invaluable contribution to all those engaged in researching the Frankenstein narratives. On a personal note, Fred has been incredibly gracious and helpful during our various discussions, and, although the following interpretation of the film sometimes stands at odds with his reading, we are indebted to his work for the majority of the authoritative historical information about this movie. Such a short film, by its very nature, necessarily eliminates huge swaths from Shelley's novel, and this admittedly "liberal adaptation" of her narrative includes only a bare-bones outline: Frankenstein (Augustus Phillips) setting off to college, creating the Monster (Charles Ogle) two years later, comforting his frightened fiancée (Mary Fuller), confronting his creation, and eliminating the Creature. Yet for Wiebel, whose book provides extensive biographical information about the main actors and director, discovering this rendition, "was like finding the Rosetta stone of the progenitor of the most popular series of monster movies that ever escaped Hollywood, spawning the term 'Horror film.'"[1]

The film's severely truncated sketch of the original story borrows some conventions popularized in the various stage productions that preceded it, including the mute Creature, a more limited role for Frankenstein's assistant, and a highlighting of the doppelgänger motif. As in most of the variations, Frankenstein begins his quest with reasonable intentions—"to create the most perfect human being that the world has yet known"—but he clearly lacks the initially altruistic goals of Shelley's character, being inspired more by unbridled ego than any desire for social good; a combination of the dark arts, unnamed chemicals (not body parts from previous owners), and "the evil in Frankenstein's mind" brands the resulting Creature a malevolent embodiment of his maker's basest instincts. Thus the creation scene, as in many of the previous stage adaptations, partakes of magical elements more than of lightning/electricity, and a cauldron (duplicated in Cranach's later film) rather than a slab lifted into a storm serves as the Creature's birthing site. In the film's final sequence, he enters the room and stares into the mirror, eventually disappearing but leaving his image trapped within the mirror. Frankenstein enters and stares into the same mirror,

Charles Ogle as the Creature in Edison's silent version of *Frankenstein* (1910).

only to see the Monster reflected back to him; however, that disturbing image soon fades and is replaced by Frankenstein's actual form. His positive traits triumph over his evil nature, making it possible for him to embrace his bride and domestic tranquility at the film's conclusion—similar to the added coda in Whale's version.

The emphasis on the Jekyll-and-Hyde dichotomy within Frankenstein's character signals a shift away from religious interpretations and toward a more psychologically oriented reading of the narrative. Totally absent, however, are the novel's complicated interplays between science and religion, nature and nurture, and human and artificial beings. Dawley's film does maintain the tension between solo scientific experimentation and domestic stability, and the semierotic relationship between creator and creation. In fact, the Creature flies into a jealous rage when Frankenstein affectionately embraces his fiancée. Equally important, the Creature never murders anyone, although he demonstrates more than sufficient strength to kill Frankenstein. Yet his sinister appearance still threatens and repels the other characters in the movie. Wiebel hypothesizes that Ogle would likely have seen illustrations of Cooke's physical depiction of the Monster in Peake's play and based his makeup on that model, although his representation in the Edison film clearly partakes of the grotesque more than earlier versions, resembling a link between simian and human.

As is often the case with early silent films, Dawley situates his camera in the same locked position an audience member might occupy while watching a live theatrical production, never breaching the proscenium-arch perspective with camera movements, different angles, or a variety of diverse shots. This aesthetic choice establishes a picture-frame-like construction. Within its fixed parameters, the performers, dressed in nineteenth-century garb, enter, exit, and move around in front of the stationary camera as if acting on a stage, whether in the library dominated by the huge mirror, the laboratory complete with skulls and a full-sized skeleton, or Frankenstein's small bedroom with its desk and bookshelves. Despite the stolid nature of Dawley's visuals, Wiebel argues that his main contribution to cinema history "is in the way that he used actors" and by doing so "legitimized movie acting in the eyes of the theatrical players with his attention to details in the staging of scenes, blocking and their enactments, refining and adapting their craft for the film medium." Technically, Dawley was among the first directors to employ process shots (in which live action is filmed in front of a screen upon which a previously filmed image is projected) and utilize arc lamps to simulate sunlight on his sets. Wiebel believes that the look of Whale's film and Jack Pierce's conception of the Monster were influenced by the Edison *Frankenstein*, which was still in circulation during the early 1930s, although in a 1967 interview Boris Karloff claims never to have seen the earlier movie, and no direct evidence exists to support this contention.[2]

The Mad Doctor

As the previous section demonstrates, darkened movie theaters provide hospitable dwelling places for man-made monsters—and their creators as well. From the earliest flickering one-reelers to our contemporary IMAX screens, the mad scientist who obsessively engages in hazardous research projects that potentially could either save or destroy humankind has remained a resilient film character, fascinating and frightening generations of audiences. Cinematic representations of mad scientists, argues Christopher Frayling, suffer from the same problems as literary ones: a "gap between specialized knowledge and public understanding lies at the root of most fictional cinematic representations of the scientist."³ Endowed with godlike intelligence coupled with a compulsive curiosity and overweening hubris, these characters habitually descend into a neurotic absorption that dooms their results. Their audacious but imprudent quests veer into arcane realms of knowledge far beyond the understanding of mere mortal beings, leading them into perilous realms of experimentation where more cautious men fear to tread.

Inevitably, the serpent of pride tempts these explorers to consume fruit from the tree of knowledge—called by Satan in *Paradise Lost* the "Mother of Science" (9.680)—that provides enlightenment but also lures them down the path to their destruction. Among the most (in)famous of these early cinematic scientists who contour the mad doctor stereotype in the twenties and thirties are Dr. Jekyll (*Dr. Jekyll and Mr. Hyde*, 1920), Dr. Caligari (*The Cabinet of Dr. Caligari*, 1920), C. A. Rotwang (*Metropolis*, 1927), Dr. Moreau (*Island of Lost Souls*, 1932), and Dr. Jack Griffin (*The Invisible Man*, 1933). Given the seemingly incalculable number of these highly negative portraits, one cannot help but note the irony that a commercial film industry so utterly dependent on scientific and technological advancements for its very existence and continued survival seems committed to rendering predominately dire warnings about the dangers of such pursuits in the figure of the cinematic scientist.

A parallel, although smaller, track of films counterbalances these negative portrayals with dedicated scientists who function as stalwart bulwarks protecting humanity from destructive natural disasters and virulent diseases. Examples in biopics drawn from history include Louis Pasteur (*The Story of Louis Pasteur*, 1936), Dr. Paul Ehrlich (*Dr. Ehrlich's Magic Bullet*, 1940), Marie Curie (*Madame Curie*, 1943), and Dr. Corydon M. Wassell (*The Story of Dr. Wassell*, 1944); among the fictional characters are Dr. Leonara Orantes, Dr. Erin Mears, and Dr. Ellis Cheever (*Contagion*, 2011), Dr. Eve Saks (*Dallas Buyers Club*, 2013), and Dr. Emma Brookner (*The Normal Heart*, 2014). In these movies, heroic researchers tirelessly engage in experimentation (mostly medical) to eradicate threats to the health of individuals and the body politic. Such dedicated scientists, as embodiments of enlightenment and knowledge, often risk their lives by fighting against the unknown, the lethal, and the evil forces that endanger human survival. They use their learning judiciously, not to probe too deeply into mysteries beyond their control but rather to rid the world of the disease and ignorance that threaten either personal or communal destruction.

While intense scientists impelled by varying degrees of altruism and megalomania make intriguing characters within provocative dramas, their boundless ambitions and pretentious utterances furnish equally fertile grounds for parody and satire, as evident in figures such as Dr. Emmett "Doc" Brown (*Back to the Future*, 1985), Dr. Peter Venkman (*Ghostbusters*, 1984), and Dr. Mephesto (in the TV series *South Park*). Even Walt Disney and Warner Bros. pillaged the lexicon of the deranged scientist, producing a number of animated films containing mad doctors interacting with Mickey Mouse, Daffy Duck, Porky Pig, Elmer Fudd, and Bugs Bunny.[4] Such works temper social anxieties about the course of scientific investigations by highlighting humor rather than horror, thus allowing viewers to confront their fears in a safe environment and, to a certain extent, dispel them with laughter.

One name tops almost every list of noteworthy mad scientists: Victor Frankenstein. Published in 2001, *The Frankenstein Film Sourcebook* sets the number of "Frankenstein Films"—those in which a creature (usually nameless) confronts his/her/its existence and creator—at two hundred, while Frayling doubles that figure to four hundred derivatives. In his cultural history of monsters and mad scientists, Andrew Tudor designates *Frankenstein* as the prototype for one of the three core narratives in the horror genre, the "Knowledge Narrative." (The other two are the "Invasion Narrative," typified by *Dracula* [1931], and the "Metamorphosis Narrative," as in *Night of the Living Dead* [1970].)[5] In one subset of the Knowledge Narrative structure, the archetypal mad scientist creates or literally becomes the threat to the social order by releasing a severely disruptive element into his placid surroundings, usually an unforeseen and deadly life form called into being by medical experiments conducted in dangerous realms. Once unleashed, these unruly entities terrorize the scientist's orderly world and destroy innocent bystanders. In another subset of Tudor's Knowledge Narrative, laboratory accidents, rather than the researchers, bring unintentional mutations into being, so the scientists only indirectly set the ensuing disasters into motion, as seen in *The Incredible Shrinking Man* (1957), *Attack of the 50 Foot Woman* (1958), and *Jurassic Park* (1993). But they still cannot shirk at least a portion of moral responsibility for the tragedies that result from their imprudent experiments.

Not surprisingly, therefore, the *Frankenstein*-inspired brood of films usually focuses on medical quests to create life, reanimate the dead, or drastically alter the living—all in the name of scientific advancement or species improvement. Spurred by the fanatical pursuit of an ambitious scientific goal, fervent ambition, and unbridled hubris, scientists like Victor Frankenstein and his cinematic descendants forsake human contact to compulsively pursue their questionable projects and ultimately descend into a solipsistic frenzy that endangers their lives and everyone else's. The web of victims widens far beyond the tight circle of the scientist's family and friends, ensnaring a range of guiltless people who accidentally become collateral damage. These researchers lose sight of their responsibilities to those outside their cloistered laboratories, forgetting that the outcomes of their investigations will profoundly affect the surrounding community and realizing this painful truth only after dead bodies begin to accumulate.

The Aesthetics of Frankenstein Films

Scholars of the horror/monster genre like Stephen Prince note that in these films, unlike most others, "offscreen space" dominates the visual constructions, and directors employ "shot compositions that convey the sense that something bad or evil or sinister lies waiting just beyond the borders of the frame."[6] This titillating anticipation of what horrible thing might happen next is a fundamental part of the horror/monster movie's appeal and an integral part of the Frankenstein movies, particularly as we anxiously wait for the Creature to be revealed. The traditional horror/monster film juxtaposes what is known and what is unknown, what is rational and what is irrational, what is seen and what is unseen, what is real and what is unreal, a dramatic strategy that forces viewers to share the restrictive point of view of the Creature's potential victims; thus, we inescapably identify with the victims rather than with the perpetrator of the violence, making us, at least while sitting in the dark theater, as susceptible to danger as the characters on the screen.

Equally as important as point of view in the classical horror/monster movies, and manifest in both the Universal and Hammer Frankensteins, are the atmospheric sets, fitting backgrounds for the lethal action that predictably transpires. Dark, remote, isolated, and eerie locations permeate the genre, such as gloomy old houses, spooky graveyards, foreboding castles, underground caves, cobwebbed cellars, ancient crypts, and sinister laboratories. Early films, such as the Universal Frankenstein series, were often set in exotic foreign lands, but as the genre developed, monsters appeared in the most common and deceptively safe of American locations—the community and the home, as illustrated in the Hammer movies. Many of these conventions come from one of the roots of the monster/horror movie, the Gothic novel. As the genre became increasingly violent, more gruesome elements, such as severed limbs and gory deaths, became standard conventions and seemingly endless rivers of blood and more blood pour into these movies.

The visuals in horror/monster movies tend to be more excessive, more distorted, than those found in most other genres—part of the lineage inherited from the German Expressionist movement, as discussed below. Close-ups and extreme close-ups, oblique camera angles, shafts of light and dark, and high- and low-angle shots all disturb our notions of traditional visual compositions and, as a result, contribute to the menace and tension so crucial in this genre and to the lasting appeal of the Frankenstein films over the decades. Like Frankenstein's Creature, the monster in many horror/monster movies is larger and, at least initially, more powerful than the common folk it threatens, thus increasing the viewer's sense of vulnerability; we become children in need of a protecting parent, a brave hero, or a magic talisman to escape and survive. Equally important are the sound elements in horror/monster movies, a familiar catalog of screams, screeches, squeaky doors, creaky floorboards, claps of thunder—and silence, one of the most effective conventions of the genre, which ramps up the anxiety of the viewer as we wait for the mayhem that surely will develop.

The Frankenstein Film Family: An Evolutionary Genealogy

Unlike the novel's discarded Creature, the unruly characters inhabiting the various branches of the Frankenstein family tree can legitimately claim a mother, Mary Wollstonecraft Shelley. Her "anxious invocations" called forth a "ghastly image" that haunted her "midnight pillow" and gave birth to a sprawling brood of texts that trace their lineage, sometimes through twisted paths, back to her novel. Her characters, narrative, perceptions, and concepts inspired a swelling horde of men and monsters, fathers and brothers, sisters and cousins, children and stepchildren, some as recognizable descendants and others as more remote offspring. Technological innovations nourished the Frankenstein family tree; across a sweeping terrain of movies, TV shows, video games, and Internet sites, swarms of characters with links to a nineteenth-century teenager's imagination colonized every conceivable medium with countless iterations of the basic narrative. Take, for example, the writer/director Josh Whedon's comments about his *Avengers: Age of Ultron* (2015): "It's our new Frankenstein myth. . . . We create something in our own image and the thing turns on us. It has that pain of 'Well, why was I made? I want to kill Daddy.'"[7] To put it simply, then, all imaginative works containing a man-made creation running rampant, threatening to devastate society, and finally destroying its creator share kinship within the Frankenstein family tree and trace their heritage back to Mama Mary.

Frankenstein's Children: Adaptations

Had it not been for the movies, observes Stephen King in *Danse Macabre*, Mary Shelley's "modest gothic tale" probably would have remained the province of earnest English majors, rather than morphing into an immensely popular cultural archetype.[8] According to IMDB, some 200 titles with the word "Frankenstein" embedded within them currently exist. This list includes 169 titles with the words "Frankenstein and Monster," 46 titles with the words "Frankenstein and Doctor," and 133 titles with a "reference to Frankenstein" noted. Obviously, the productions of movies about the man and his creation have an extensive history, stretching from silent films to *Victor Frankenstein* (with Daniel Radcliffe as Igor and James McAvoy as Victor, 2015), and forward into forthcoming productions such as *This Dark Endeavor: The Apprenticeship of Victor Frankenstein* (directed by Matt Reeves), *The Casebook of Victor Frankenstein* (directed by Timur Bekmambetov), *Frankenstein Created Bikers* (directed by James Bickert), and the director Guillermo del Toro's planned adaptation—not to mention ongoing TV programs (*Penny Dreadful*) and video games for children (Island of Dr. Frankenstein) and adults (Frankenstein: Through the Eyes of the Monster). Rest assured we are not going to drag reluctant readers through all these Frankenstein films, a group rife with hidden treasures, cult favorites, earnest adaptations, and shoddy exploitations. For those desirous of exploring the history and ever-expanding body of "Frankenfilms," the following compendia will skillfully guide you through its arteries: Gregory William Mank's *It's Alive! The Classic Cinema Saga of Frankenstein* (1981), Stephen Jones's *The Frankenstein Scrapbook* (1994), Gary J. and Susan Svehla's *We Belong Dead: Frankenstein on Film* (1997), and Caroline Joan S. Picart, Frank Smoot, and Jayne Blodgett's *The Frankenstein Film Sourcebook* (2001). Whatever young Mary Shelley discovered, as she writes in her 1831 introduction, during that "wet, ungenial summer" in Switzerland clearly struck a deeply responsive chord in her own day that continues to reverberate on modern screens.

A Note on German Expressionism

The director James Whale repeatedly screened many German Expressionist films (particularly *The Cabinet of Dr. Caligari*, *The Golem* [1920 version], *Metropolis*, and *Nosferatu*) while preparing to shoot *Frankenstein*, and their impact permeates his visual approach to the narrative, evident in the distorted set designs, canted camera angles, and chiaroscuro lighting. It is therefore useful to understand the hallmarks of this dramatic filmmaking style that profoundly influenced the visual design of many early horror/monster movies—as well as film noir crime/detective movies—and that continues to play a significant role in a wide spectrum of modern productions as well. This movement, which focused on the murky and disturbing facets of the human psyche, rose out of the ashes of a German culture deeply scarred by the country's humiliating defeat in World War I and the widespread poverty and social chaos that followed in the wake of its surrender to the Allies in 1918. Reflecting this postwar disorder, social confusion, and physical dislocation, German Expressionist films reject the neatly balanced frames prevalent in Hollywood movies; instead, they feature off-centered, unbalanced depictions of eerie nightmarish landscapes swarming with sinister acts of horror, physically deformed creatures, depravity, paranoia, madness, and death. Some commentators interpret these German monster/horror movies as reflecting post–World War I revulsion at the destruction caused by the military conflict, the mutilated creatures inhabiting them denoting the maimed soldiers who limped home to confront what remained of their country.

Responding to these conditions, a talented group of German filmmakers during the early 1920s devised a series of movies with an appearance and a thematic outlook quite different from the invisible editing structure and typical happy ending that characterize mainstream American cinema. Innovative directors—such as Fritz Lang (*Dr. Mabuse: The Gambler*, 1922; *Metropolis*, 1927), Robert Wiene (*The Cabinet of Dr. Caligari*, 1920), and F. W. Murnau (*Nosferatu*, 1922)—inspired by postwar avant-garde painting and theater movements sought to counter Hollywood's dominant realistic aesthetic with stylized visual distortions and off-kilter set designs that communicated their characters' disturbed emotional and aberrant psychological states. Although setting their movies in fantastical, often hostile worlds, these German directors worked on carefully controlled sound stages, employing oblique camera angles, painted backdrops, and irregular shapes that disrupted and disturbed the normal expectations of viewers. Chiaroscuro lighting, one of the defining features of the German Expressionist movement, created sharp, dramatic contrasts between bright and dark areas, catching and losing characters engulfed by their bizarre surroundings composed of looming shadows and huge silhouettes, slanted walls and curved buildings, offset doors and protruding windows, twisting streets and narrow alleys, polished mirrors and reflecting surfaces, exaggerated shapes, and theatrical makeup. All these unconventional elements meshed to fabricate an ominous atmosphere, dragging the viewer into precarious, frightening, and dangerous worlds.

Although German Expressionism began as a radical alternative to mainstream narrative cinema, it eventually became a vital part of American filmmaking and was adopted by many talented Hollywood directors, including John Huston, Alfred Hitchcock, and Orson Welles. Eventually, Hollywood lured many of the prominent filmmakers and technicians who pioneered German Expressionism to make movies within the studio system they once sought to undermine—and later offered opportunities for German artists fleeing Hitler's oppression. Whale's *Frankenstein* and *Bride of Frankenstein* exhibit the pervasive influence of German Expression on his visual imagination, particularly in the architecture of Frankenstein's castle and laboratory with their huge walls and irregular staircases, the skewed elements that dominate the opening graveyard sequence, the omnipresence of shadows and silhouettes, particularly of Fritz and the Creature, and the ominous chiaroscuro lighting through which all the characters move.

The Universal Film Production Cycle

The first great series of Frankenstein films was the Universal Pictures cycle (1931–1948) that includes *Frankenstein* (1931), *Bride of Frankenstein* (1935), *Son of*

Frankenstein (1939), *The Ghost of Frankenstein* (1942), *Frankenstein Meets the Wolf Man* (1943), *House of Frankenstein* (1944), *House of Dracula* (1945), and finally *Abbott and Costello Meet Frankenstein* (1948). The Creature also makes cameo appearances in *Hellzapoppin'* (1941) and *Abbott and Costello Meet Dr. Jekyll and Mr. Hyde* (1953). As mentioned in an earlier chapter, Carl Laemmle Jr., the president of Universal, bought the rights to the Webling/Balderston theatrical revision of Shelley's novel in hopes of duplicating the box office success of *Dracula* (1931). Like Frankenstein, Webling and Balderston stitched together parts sliced from older stage productions and appended a few new elements to fashion their drama, a process replicated by Universal's screenwriters and directors, who freely embellished Shelley's novel and Webling/Balderston's version in their screen adaptation. Laemmle's risky gamble paid off handsomely, as Universal eventually cleared over $12 million in profits from *Frankenstein*, a picture that cost somewhere around $125,000 to produce, and the popular sequels kept the often debt-ridden studio afloat during dire financial times. Embodied in Boris Karloff's iconic figure and haunting performance, Frankenstein's hulking, groaning, gesturing creation emerges as a distant cousin of Shelley's literate figure. But Karloff's acting skills craft a compelling portrait of a vulnerable, frightened, and even congenial mute, an awkward and lonely victim of society's cruel intolerance. The film catapulted Karloff from minor roles to overnight stardom, and he affectionately christened the Monster "my best friend."[9]

Most critics agree that Universal's versions of *Frankenstein* and *Dracula* laid the groundwork for the modern horror/monster genre, with the man-made creature and the vampire remaining popular cultural icons to this day. Before *Dracula* and *Frankenstein* appeared on the screen, however, Universal's horror/monster films, such as *The Hunchback of Notre Dame* (1923) and *The Phantom of the Opera* (1925), already featured sympathetic monsters, and this pattern continued throughout the cycle. Tormented monsters in *The Invisible Man* (1933), *The Mummy* (1932), and *The Wolf Man* (1941) exist as hunted pariahs outside the boundaries of conventional society; as such, they evoke at least slivers of understanding and even compassion from audiences—none more than Frankenstein's lumbering, childlike Creature. While these Universal films may have shocked audiences in the thirties, they seem tame by today's violent standards, offering viewers eerie atmospheres and offscreen violence rather than overt gore and visual brutality.

The fearful period of national anxiety that gripped America during the years of the Great Depression and World War II found an apt representation on the screen in *Frankenstein* and Universal's other monster movies. While newsreels and war films made during and after World War II "did not show the carnage, the horror film did picture it in the physical mutilations appearing in Universal's huge run of *Frankenstein* sequels."[10] Christine Gerblinger and other commentators see Whale's monster movies through a prism of "the two cataclysmic social crises of the time: the Great War and the post-war years leading up to the Great Depression." For Gerblinger, Whale's vision is "a sutured amalgamation of traumas inflicted by subjecting the body to modern warfare," and his Creature is rendered as "a returning and mutilated soldier, in turn a Forgotten Man and the disposed citizen of a depressed economy."[11] James Whale was intimately familiar with death and the carnage of war. An officer in the British Army's Worcestershire Regiment who fought in the trenches during World War I, he was taken prisoner during the Flanders Campaign (1917) and spent two years in a German prisoner of war camp.

Critics like Gerblinger argue that Frankenstein's creation, dressed in workman's clothing, represents the disfigured veterans and homeless tramps wandering around the countryside in the postwar era.

James Twitchell observes that Universal's monsters of the thirties and forties evoked figures derived from childhood horrors that often cling to adults throughout their lives, including "haunted houses, deformed hunchbacks, underground phantoms, werewolves, scarfaces, mad doctors, flour-white zombies, miniature freaks and overgrown apes, vampires, and monsters-with-no-names."[12] In addition, the Universal film monsters know and interact with each other. They inhabit the same fictional and timeless universe, allowing them to make guest appearances in each other's movies, and the actors portraying them like Karloff, Lugosi, Frye, Carradine and Chaney form a stock company of sorts. *House of Frankenstein*, for example, features a deranged scientist (Boris Karloff), Count Dracula (John Carradine), Frankenstein's Monster (Glenn Strange), and the Wolf Man (Lon Chaney Jr.). The tradition continues into the twenty-first century with the modern monster mash *Van Helsing* (2004), which contains Dracula (Richard Roxburgh), Frankenstein's Monster (Shuler Hensley), Igor (Kevin J. O'Connor), and Victor Frankenstein (Samuel West)—not to mention Dr. Jekyll (Stephen Fisher) and Mr. Hyde (Robbie Coltrane).

Frankenstein (1931)

James Whale's variations on the Frankenstein narrative offer an instructive example about the fundamental aspects of the literature-to-film relationship during the process of adaptation. Try to recall the last great novel that also made a great film. Few exist because potent works of literature used as what Julie Grossman labels as "home texts" usually result in weak films, whereas great films are most often based on mediocre books.[13] The best film adaptations transmit the spirit rather than the letter of their original source; in fact, the transfer of that essence from the page to the screen often demands violating the letter of the work. No film can precisely duplicate a work of fiction. Put at its simplest level, written language is fundamentally different from visual language: the former can delve deeply inside a character's mind, while the latter (other than often clumsy voice-overs) essentially depends upon and can primarily depict external actions. In large measure, then, the strength and complexity of powerful literary works typically result from their author's compelling use of language, a dexterous facility with words that are either eliminated or seem pretentious when spoken in a movie. The director Lewis Milestone accurately stated the situation when he observed: "If you want to produce a rose, you will not take the flower and put it into the earth. This would not result in another rose. Instead, you will take the seed and stick it into the soil. From it will grow a rose. It's the same with film adaptation."[14]

Critics who insist that a film version of a literary work remain strictly faithful to the words on the page predictably characterize adaptations as less complex than their source materials because such productions only recreate the husk of literary pieces or fail to encompass all the events and complexities of the characters Such an approach, however, ignores the myriad strengths of visual language. It is precisely in terms of his visual constructions, particularly figures, motifs, and sophisticated mise-en-scène compositions, that Whale communicates many of the essential tension points never fully resolved in Shelley's novel. Recognizing the disparities between the textual and the visual narratives, some commentators adamantly maintain "it is in those instances where the [Frankenstein] movies deviate from the source novel that the artistry of Universal . . . comes to the forefront."[15] The following discussion of Whale's two influential Frankenstein films rarely ventures very far beyond what viewers see on the screen. Their production background, while interesting, has often been covered, and readers can easily access the reams of scholarly and popular writing about the genesis and gestation of these classic movies, particularly in comprehensive works by Caroline Joan S. Picart, Gregory William Mank, Donald F. Glut, Robert Horton, Gary J. and Susan Svehla, David J. Skal, and Susan Tyler Hitchcock (and Carol Adams for fun) as well as numerous online sites.

Although James Whale directed twenty-one features, his reputation, perhaps unfairly, rests on just four Universal horror movies, most prominently *Frankenstein* and *Bride of Frankenstein* (the other two being *The Old Dark House* [1932] and *The Invisible Man* [1933]). He did, however, work across a spectrum of genres, among them the war film (*Journey's End*, 1930), melodrama (*Waterloo Bridge*, 1931; *The Impatient Maiden*, 1932), musical (*Show Boat*, 1936), biopic (*The Great Garrick*, 1937), historical drama (*The Man in the Iron Mask*, 1939), adventure saga (*Green Hell*, 1940), comedy (*Remember Last Night?*, 1935), crime drama (*Wives under Suspicion*, 1938), and romance (*Port of Seven Seas*, 1938). Yet Whale's other films have been overshadowed by his flamboyant life as an openly gay man (depicted in *Gods and Monsters*, 1998) living with his partner, the producer

David Lewis, from 1930 to 1951, far before such relationships were accepted, or even safe. As David Lugowski argues, Whale's fluid and lengthy camera tracking shots (aptly demonstrated in the opening scene of *Frankenstein*), his "obsessive use of mirrors or mirroring devices to establish doubling . . . extremes (or extreme shifts) of mood or lighting . . . [and] gay-coded characters" (such as in *Bride of Frankenstein*) reveal the stylistic excellence of a gifted yet underrated director usually, and wrongly, consigned to the lower circles of film history.[16]

Whale's initial Frankenstein film profoundly influenced successive generations of filmmakers and even now captivates the imagination of contemporary movie lovers. Rick Worland summarizes the critical consensus when he states that Whale's production "originated much of the prevalent iconography" of the subsequent Frankenstein movies and has become not only "the most famous horror film of all time but one of the landmarks of Hollywood cinema . . . the definitive screen version that every subsequent retelling has had to confront."[17] His screen adaptation beautifully translates the tragic majesty of Mary Shelley's novel from the page to the screen, transforming nineteenth-century language into early twentieth-century imagery. Whale weaves an intricate pattern of light and dark, both natural and man-made, throughout the film, never subverting the movie's contextual unity for a strained or baroque effect. Perhaps the novel itself inspired Whale's figure patterns, most specifically the "dazzling" lightning during a "most violent and terrible thunder-storm" that utterly shatters a mighty oak, rendering it a "blasted stump" composed of "thin ribbands of wood" (1.1, 94–95). This remarkable display of destructive natural forces delights Shelley's fifteen-year old Victor, inspiring him to harness the incredible power of electricity during his experiments. After several tragedies result from his actions, Victor comes to view himself as a "spectacle of wrecked humanity," expressed in a figure that harkens directly back to this formative childhood moment: "But I am a blasted tree; the bolt has entered my soul" (3.2, 247). Whether their source is Shelley's novel or Whale's love of German Expressionism, dramatic light/dark configurations dominate the visual style of the film, symbolically reinforcing the juxtaposed realms of danger and security, of private ambition and social connections, of knowledge and ignorance.

Frankenstein begins with an atypical scene for a horror movie: a warning delivered directly to the audience. A man dressed in a tuxedo, complete with a jaunty boutonnière, steps from behind a heavy curtain to greet us with a genial "Howyado." Although this dapper gentleman never identifies himself, astute viewers might recognize him as Edward Van Sloan, or at least as the character actor who recently played Dr. Van Helsing in the very popular *Dracula* movie (and will play Dr. Waldman in this film). Van Sloan clasps his hands in front of him as if preparing to recite a poem, but instead offers us "a friendly warning." As the camera slowly glides toward him, ending with a medium shot, he cautions that we are about to watch "one of the strangest tales ever told," one that may thrill, shock, or even horrify us. Van Sloan ends with his tongue buried deeply in his cheek, telling those who willingly subject their "nerves to such a strain" that they have been warned. His statement, of course, is designed to entice viewers, not urge them toward the exits. To further assure paying customers that gory thrills awaited them inside, some owners stationed ambulances outside their theaters and prominently displayed medical devices in their lobbies during screenings of *Frankenstein.*

This distinctive opening provides some intriguing clues about how the film will approach Shelley's materials. Van Sloan's speech characterizes Frankenstein as "a man of science" who failed by not "reckoning upon God," thus seeming to align the subsequent narrative along a religious rather than an ethical spectrum. His speech portends that the movie will focus on Frankenstein sacrilegiously challenging God rather than ignoring his own moral and social responsibilities, as highlighted in Shelley's novel. Starting with a blatantly theatrical setting and a direct address to an invisible audience disrupts the illusion of a fourth wall and clearly identifies what follows as an artificial construct, thus explicitly denying any semblance of realistic depiction. While such a Brechtian approach often distances the viewer of a play, here it frees the audience to indulge in—and enjoy—the mayhem that will occur. This device, however, was not Whale's idea. Universal's studio executives inserted this opening (an earlier draft written by John Huston) weeks after the movie was completed, specifically designing it to condemn Victor's blasphemous arrogance and thereby appeasing Catholic Church authorities who objected to the film's subject matter.[18]

After the credits roll ("The Monster" is identified only with a question mark instead of an actor's name) against a creepy backdrop of a sinister face surrounded by rotating eyes, set to original music written by Bernhard Kaun (the only music until the end credits), the film begins with a close-up of a pair of hands hauling up a rope and the sound of a Latin prayer. The following sequence, which appears neither in Shelley's novel nor in any of the plays derived from it, exemplifies Whale's fluid visual style. The camera starts a long pan rightward through a graveyard, while the soundtrack consists of weeping voices and a tolling bell. It continues moving smoothly past a young boy with a scarf around his neck, two sobbing old women dressed in black, an old man comforting the second woman, a middle-aged man stifling a yawn, a priest holding a banner and a Bible, another man staring sadly into the grave, a large tilted cross, another priest holding a scepter topped with a glass container enclosing the ringing bell, another mourner, a slanted skeleton, and the Grim Reaper with clasped hands leaning on a sword, then continuing onward toward some trees and a fence. The camera finally rests on a wide-eyed, ghoulish face (later identified as Fritz [Dwight Frye]) trapped between the posts of an iron fence that stick up and resemble two horns growing out of his head. From youth to old age, the figure shows, death remains a constant companion, continuously watching and finally enfolding us.

Immediately, a more aristocratic, well-dressed man standing directly behind the hunchbacked Fritz yanks him down. Whale then cuts to a close-up of this man, later identified as Henry (Victor in the novel) Frankenstein (Colin Clive), with the iron fence posts sticking up like horns attached to his head as well. Whale's camera then shifts leftward, back past the Grim Reaper, and follows the funeral procession trudging out of the cemetery. At this point an old gravedigger, hat in hand, waits for the mourners to leave, removes his jacket, rubs his hands together, and buries the coffin. We hear the desolate sound of dirt hitting the wood, dull and hollow in the cemetery's stillness. Finishing his chore, the gravedigger searches his pockets for a pipe and some matches. Lighting up in the night, he gives viewers the first of numerous images of fire surrounded by darkness, or darkness penetrated by light, which the film offers as its central visual motif. Here, however, the fire is small and under control, harnessed to provide aid, pleasure, and comfort. As Frankenstein and Fritz sneak toward the gravesite, Whale conjoins them in the frame with the tilted cross, the Grim Reaper, and a new figure: Christ on the cross. The image, then, portends how death, resurrection, and religion will pursue them throughout this movie's twisted world.

The two men remove their jackets and begin to unearth the coffin. One revealing moment occurs when Henry, standing in front of the cross, quite literally throws dirt in the face of the Grim Reaper, foreshadowing his quest to bury death forever, a dangerous obsession that results in unwanted life and even more deaths. "He's just resting, waiting for a new life to come," explains Henry, gently patting the coffin before they remove it from the grave. As they leave the graveyard, trundling the coffin along on a wheelbarrow, Henry and Fritz encounter the swaying corpse of a convict hanging on a gibbet—a foreshadowing of Fritz's own hanging death. Here, the film's second fire/light image appears, a lantern similar to the gravedigger's match in that it represents how the tremendous forces of natural light and energy can be controlled to aid rather than damage humankind. The lantern that Fritz and later Henry carry slices out patches of light in the shadowy night so that Fritz can cut down the convict whose brain will complete their experiment; but, as revealed later, the man's broken neck renders his brain useless.

Up to this point, the entire film possesses a dark, nightmarish quality illuminated only by tiny snatches of light. The next scene, however, thrusts us into the brightly lit surgical theater of the Goldstadt Medical College, a room dominated by high-powered lights positioned over an operating table and

the commanding presence of Dr. Waldman (Edward Van Sloan), almost glowing in his white lab coat. In this institutionalized center of learning, students
and professors jointly share their medical studies, not crouching in shadows
or laboring in isolation but rather connected with each other in a common
quest to gain scientific knowledge and to defeat disease. In fact, several shots
illustrate the predominance and power of the lights in the frame, particularly
when Whale positions low-angle shots beneath the feet of the cadaver, making
the ring of lights on the wheel-like fixture seem like a protective circle. When
Fritz creeps into the deserted medical school, his enlarged shadow slithering
along the walls in a classic German Expressionistic image, the bright lights have
been extinguished. A creature of darkness and of night, a twisted Caliban figure who later will mercilessly whip Frankenstein's creation, Fritz embodies the
cycle of the abused becoming the abuser. Sent to steal Frankenstein a normal
brain from the medical school, the careless Fritz drops the perfect specimen
and instead brings back the abnormal brain of a brutal, violent murderer. This
pivotal mistake results in Frankenstein implanting the malformed brain of the
typical criminal rather than a natural brain into his Creature, a new plot component found in none of the previous Frankenstein narratives. This noteworthy
addition, one integrated into many subsequent Frankenstein films, shifts the
reason for the Creature's homicidal actions from a lack of nurture, as in Shelley's
novel, to biological causes, a criminal brain that makes his killings inevitable,
echoing the nineteenth-century conviction, as shown in chapter 2, that criminal behavior rested in the body and could be transmitted through inheritance
and transplantation.

     Whale matches the fade-out on the now dark and empty medical school
with a fade-in on a close-up of Henry's photographic portrait illuminated by
candlelight, quickly followed by close-ups of a maid and of Victor Moritz (Henry
Clerval in the novel [John Boles]), whom she is admitting into the Frankenstein parlor. The glow of candles casts light throughout the luxurious room: on
the piano, on chandeliers, over Elizabeth's (Mae Clark) shoulder as she reads
Henry's letter to Victor, who clearly yearns for a romantic relationship with
Elizabeth but remains loyal to his friend Henry. Troubled by the letter, Moritz
and Elizabeth visit Dr. Waldman, Frankenstein's sympathetic tutor at medical school, who warns them of the "mad dream" and "insane ambition" that
have driven Henry from his formal studies into the shadowy realms of human
experimentation. Large bookcases stuffed with scholarly volumes and, on one
shelf, human skulls surround the trio, while a microscope, symbolic of scientific
research, sits prominently on Waldman's desk. Overhead, a gleaming electric
light bathes the trio in brightness. In this setting, Whale pictorializes Mary Shelley's idea that the study of human life and death need not be evil, and when
carried out under the proper conditions—lighted, in the open, and surrounded

by colleagues and friends, as discussed in our earlier chapters—can contribute to the betterment of mankind.

It would be possible, of course, to continue listing and interpreting all the various sources of light in the film, but this opening description should provide sufficient insight into the feeling and metaphoric associations of the film's images. Three major sources of light exist: the untamed natural forces, such as lightning, the sun, and the moon; the light made subservient to man, such as lamps, candles, and matches; and the light that exists somewhere in between, like torches, that can either illuminate or destroy. As mentioned earlier, the director's use of chiaroscuro lighting produces a bold pattern of low-key and high-contrast lighting that results in dramatic visual effects. Throughout the entire film, therefore, Whale makes us aware that light in various contexts presents a mixture of meanings. Like the knowledge it comes to symbolize in the film, light is a double-edged sword capable of great harm or great good. Again, it is not a matter of rejecting fire (light), but of realizing its potential for both evil and value, as illustrated in one of the movie's key scenes.

Fritz's parody of the porter scene in *Macbeth*, accompanied by a lantern, sets the stage for one of the most famous sequences in movie history: the pyrotechnic creation scene, far more elaborately depicted than in Shelley's one general paragraph (1.4, 114) or in the theatrical adaptations that followed it. It starts in the gloomy and secluded tower (it was originally slated to transpire in the same windmill where the last scene between Frankenstein and the Monster occurs) lit by a fierce lightning storm, foreshadowing that light/knowledge is no longer under human restraint. Frankenstein sends up his being's body like some ancient votive offering to the powerfully creative forces in the universe as symbolized by the lightning. The buzzing, sizzling, flashing, sputtering lights in the laboratory initially seem under his control, but this assumption proves to be merely a treacherous illusion shared by most of the cinema's mad scientists. The naïve and potentially harmful fallacy that experimenters can safely manipulate their research and tame technology recurs as a prominent theme in all the Frankenstein narratives over the decades, signaling a general mistrust of both scientific investigations and the researchers who conduct them.

Frayling notes that Frankenstein's laboratory is a mixture of materials from 1816 and 1931, including "incomprehensible dials, a huge Voltaic battery, a Wimshurst machine, lightning-arc generators, piles of Bakelite bric-à-brac and leiden jars and an adjustable metal hospital bed"—all inspired by Rotwang's lab in *Metropolis*.[19] Whale believed that the creation scene was the high spot in the film, stating, "If the audience did not believe the thing had been really made, they would not be bothered with what it was supposed to do afterward."[20] Frankenstein's outlandish bursts of hubris in these scenes—such as when he exults, "The brain of a dead man is waiting to live again in a body I made with my own

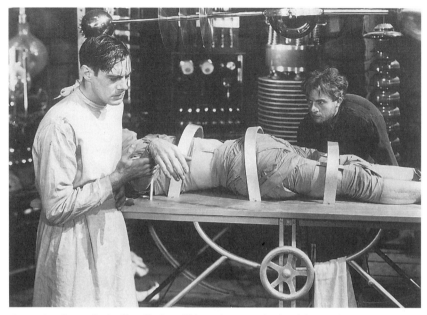

Henry Frankenstein (Colin Clive) and his assistant, Fritz (Dwight Frye), test his unborn Creature (Boris Karloff) for signs of life in *Frankenstein* (1931).

hands," and even more famously, "In the name of God. Now I know what it feels like to be God" (the latter deleted in some early screenings)—establish his motivations as egotistical and starkly dissimilar from Waldman's more altruistic goals and the formal training given students at Goldstadt. As noted in earlier chapters, Frankenstein's isolation—morally, physically, and intellectually—from the community of learned men contributes to his ultimate downfall and death.

Like Mary Shelley, Whale refuses simply to censure Frankenstein as a luna- tic, making him an incredibly vulnerable figure embodied by Colin Clive and giving him the most dramatic speech in the entire film:

> Have you never wanted to do anything that was dangerous? Where should we be if nobody tried to find out what lies beyond? Have you never wanted to look beyond the clouds and the stars or to know what causes the trees to bud and what changes the darkness into light? But if you talk like that, people call you crazy. But if I could discover just one of those things, what eternity is, for example, I wouldn't care if they did think I was crazy.

This daring aspiration to decipher nature's profound mysteries, even at the risk of being disparaged and labeled as deranged by polite society, provides Henry with an aura of audacious grandeur. But how does he try to accomplish his dream? First, he secludes himself from the positive forces of love, friendship, and familial affection and replaces them with Fritz (a character not present in the book), who represents some sort of middle stage between human being and monster. Although a friend (Moritz), a loved one (Elizabeth), and a father figure (Waldman) witness the actual "birth," none of these people influence the process that culminates in this climactic moment. As in the novel, Frankenstein's dream becomes an obsession; his focus remains not on the Creature he never deigns to describe with a personal pronoun, however, but instead on his unparalleled ability to animate dead matter, echoed in the oft-repeated phrase "It's alive! It's alive!"

Frankenstein's cruel rejection of his creation in the film, as in the novel, motivates the remainder of the action. When informed that he mistakenly inserted a criminal brain, Frankenstein puts out his cigarette (tamed fire) and tells Waldman the Creature is "only a few days old" and has been kept in complete darkness, adding confidently, "Wait till I bring him into the light." And in the poignant scene that follows he does just that, but in a manner that forever seals his fate. First, Frankenstein hears the Creature's heavy footfalls. He reaches up and turns out the lamp (man-made light) and carefully watches as the Monster appears in one of the greatest reveals in film history. The door opens and the Creature, bathed in darkness, backs into the room, turning slightly to his left and showing the famous steel bolt (exterior electrodes) stuck through his neck. The light catches him as he continues turning to his left, as Whale unveils him in closer and closer shots. He starts with a medium profile shot, then a full-front medium shot that changes to a close-up that exposes the Creature's flattened head, scarred forehead, leaden eyes, and sunken cheeks. Whale cuts to an extreme close-up from the middle of the Creature's forehead to the tip of his chin, one half of his face hidden in darkness. Then, finally, he shifts to a full figure shot framing the stitched-together Creature in the doorway. It must have been a breathtaking moment for audiences in 1931 who had never envisaged the now-ubiquitous image of Karloff as the Creature.

Frankenstein beckons his creation "to come in" and seats him in the plain wooden chair, reaches over for a chain that slides back the hatch in the ceiling, and permits the sunlight to enter the sparse, inhospitable room. The Monster glances upward toward this thrilling new sensation, stands, looks directly up into the sun, and slowly reaches out his oversized arms to embrace its warmth and light. In the touching moment that follows Frankenstein locking out the sunlight—a fitting visual metaphor for his depriving the Creature of emotional warmth and intellectual light—this mute being tenderly holds out his hands like a supplicant, silently begging for more light, more knowledge, more love. But Frankenstein refuses, and when Fritz slams into the room with his brightly burning torch, the volatile flame that can illuminate or set ablaze, the Monster reacts in terror: too much light, too fast. Frankenstein's refusal of natural light

The iconic Creature (Boris Karloff) in *Frankenstein* (1931).

and Fritz's harsh imposition of man-made fire frighten and enrage the Monster, causing him to be shackled in the dark cellar while Fritz tormented him despite his anguished cries.

From this point until the film's conclusion, Frankenstein refuses to accept responsibility for the results of his experiments. Telling Fritz to "come away . . . just leave it alone," he abandons the being to his demented assistant's sadism, although it is never explained why he hates the hapless Creature. Ultimately, the Creature wreaks his revenge, breaking free and hanging the brutish Fritz, the first of his murders. After the Creature nearly chokes him to death, Henry allows Dr. Waldman to deal with the disastrous results of his research; that failure of nerve results in the Creature's second killing, although murdering Waldman can be considered an act of self-defense, as the doctor was about to dissect the Creature. Unaware of Waldman's demise or the Creature's escape, Henry and Elizabeth sitting lovingly on the patio of his father's house, a beautifully composed and sumptuously decorated mise-en-scène whose lustrous imagery dramatically contrasts with the shadowy and foreboding isolation of the tower laboratory. But Henry's hiatus from terror lasts for only a fleeting moment. Hearing his father toast to "a son of the House of Frankenstein," he recognizes the irony: the House of Frankenstein already has a "son," one who will soon make his presence felt throughout the countryside.

Henry finds a modicum of moral courage only after this "son" inadvertently drowns an innocent young girl, Little Maria (Marilyn Harris), and attacks his intended bride, his rival for affection and love, asserting ethical leadership by directing a search party to find the Creature in the night. "I made him with these hands," he tells Victor, "and with these hands I will destroy him." The mob of torch-bearing villagers, a convention that reappears in many Frankenstein movies, sets off in three directions, with Victor leading those assigned to the mountains. There, alone and protected only by a sole torch that the Monster, now without fear, knocks to the ground, Henry confronts his creation amid the mountains of Universal's sound stage; after being knocked unconscious, he awakens in the windmill for one last battle. This confrontation between a creator who has lost control of his creation has since become a predictable component of Frankensteinian movies, emphasizing the cruel irony that human beings are often responsible for their own destruction by virtue of how they misuse their intelligence.

Here yet again, Whale's visual sensibility enhances the clash between the Creature and his maker around the large gear apparatus that turns the windmill. Whale shoots each in an identical pose through the mechanism, visually emphasizing that much of the Creature resides in Frankenstein, and much of Frankenstein lives in the Creature. The shot further underlines the inevitability of their fates being forever linked together, whirling round and round each other in an endless cycle of anger, horror, anguish, and murder. Whale emphasizes their shared entrapment and identity when the burgomaster points to the windmill's platform where the creator and his creation are grappling and screams, "There he is. There's the Monster." But which one is the true monster?

Two actions occur then that conclude the film's consistent image patterns of circular shapes composed within chiaroscuro lighting. The Monster throws Frankenstein from the top of the windmill. He catches on one of the blades (which have been moving clockwise), changes its direction (counterclockwise) for a moment, then falls seemingly lifeless to the ground, while the wheel returns to its original rotation. The angry townspeople plunge their torches into the windmill, trapping the now-pathetic monster in the blaze. Finally, after a huge beam falls on him, the Creature perishes in agony (in the original version) amid the fire he has both sought and avoided throughout the film. For the Creature, light is both death and enlightenment. As in the novel, the more knowledge he gains, the more despair he feels; the more torture he receives, the more crazed he becomes. Originally, both Frankenstein and the Creature were slated to perish at the end of the movie, but preview audiences objected, and Universal added a short coda—written by Whale—that allowed Henry (played by a different actor) to recover and join Elizabeth in a conventional happy ending.

Bride of Frankenstein (1935)

James Whale never wanted to make a sequel to *Frankenstein*, despite the fact that, as studio executives kept reminding him, it was the blockbuster movie of the year and had filled Universal's nearly empty coffers with much-needed cash. He contracted to do so only after Carl Laemmle Jr. reluctantly allowed him to direct films outside the horror/monster genre as well—such as *The Impatient Maiden* (1932), *By Candlelight* (1933), and *One More River* (1934). Before returning to Shelley's world, however, he did revisit the horror/monster genre with *The Old Dark House*, again staring Karloff, and *The Invisible Man*, about another obsessed doctor whose brilliance destroys him. Whale also demanded and received far more input into the earlier stages of the sequel's process and retained almost complete control as the production evolved. Such influence, and a substantially bigger budget, allowed the director to suggest various plot points to the scriptwriters, including writing an opening prologue, allowing Elsa Lanchester to play both Mary Shelley and the Bride, and having Pretorius show Frankenstein his little homunculi. Whale also envisioned Frankenstein as a far more sympathetic figure than in the earlier movie, with the arch Dr. Pretorius replacing him as a less ambiguous villain.

Cinema historians such as Rick Worland, who views *Bride of Frankenstein* as Universal's "horror masterpiece," Christopher Bram, who claims "it's one of the great American films, right up there with *Citizen Kane* and *Sunset Boulevard*," and Bob Madison, who labels it "the most complex and most brilliantly achieved and conceived horror film ever made," all agree with the horror film director Joe Dante's equally effusive praise: "It's an old cliché in Hollywood that a sequel is never as good as the original. But director James Whale set conventional wisdom squarely on its head with *Bride of Frankenstein*, the crowning achievement of Universal's golden age of classic horror. Never before had a studio lavished so much imagination, production values, and acting talent on a so-called monster movie. But *Bride of Frankenstein* truly transcended its genre."[21] Such grandiose claims, while appreciated by Whale fans, often ignore the director's adroit mixture of horror and humor in his second venture into Frankenland, a mixture that makes the film as much a camp tour de force as a horror movie—whether or not it was Whale's conscious intention to add this layer. In this sense, it exemplifies one of Susan Sontag's most famous definitions in her 1964 *Partisan Review* essay: "Camp sees everything in quotation marks. It's not a lamp, but a 'lamp'; not a woman, but a 'woman.' To perceive Camp in objects and persons is to understand Being-as-Playing-a-Role. It is the farthest extension, in sensibility, of the metaphor of life as theater."[22] While later commentators disagree with some of Sontag's assertions, most concur that campy works of art serve up generous helpings of playfulness, exaggeration, stylization, and theatricality, all elements on full display throughout this movie. Indeed, at times *Bride of Frankenstein* pokes fun at its famous forefather, most evidently in the wry figure who dominates the movie, Dr. Pretorius (Ernest Thesiger), a far less ethical and more insidious scientist than Frankenstein because he lacks any hint of a social conscience to stem his rampaging ambition.

The title sequence announces the new world order. Due to the overwhelming popularity of the earlier movie, Karloff attained star status, and befitting his new fame and stature, his last name appears, all in capital letters, above the title. Now the question mark that had obscured his identity in the earlier movie sits across from the character tantalizingly described as "The Monster's Mate." What next transpires, at least to present-day eyes, seems to parody posh English costume/historical dramas. Lord Byron (Gavin Gordon) and Percy Bysshe Shelley (Douglas Walton) question Mary—identified as Mary Wollstonecraft Shelley but historically still Mary Godwin at this point in her life—about her as yet unpublished tale. The principals, dressed in silken finery and moving decorously about an opulent drawing room warmed by a blazing fire, watch the fierce lightning storm ranging outside their windows. The *r*'s roll effortlessly off Byron's tongue like a cascading waterfall as he wonders how such a "bland and lovely brow could have conceived a Frankenstein," confusing—as will succeeding generations—the nameless monster and his creator. Mary, pausing from her needlepoint, claims that her purpose was "to write a moral lesson of the punishment that befell a moral man who dared to emulate God"—a line meant to appease Joseph Breen and his fellow censors at the Production Code Administration (PCA). To the surprise of the two poets, she reveals that more transpired after that tale, at least once the box office receipts had been counted at Universal Studios. And, following what must undoubtedly be one of the campiest prologues in movie history, we are back where the previous Frankenstein film ended.

Almost every element from the opening to the closing credits in *Bride of Frankenstein* is more exaggerated than in *Frankenstein*. Even the number of deaths (the original cut had twenty-one of them), starting with the parents of poor drowned Little Maria, Hans (Reginald Barlow, a different actor than in the first film) and his wife (Mary Gordon), gets multiplied. The Monster's deformed body looks more hideous as well, displaying ugly scars on his arms and face, lasting reminders of the intense burns he suffered in the windmill blaze that almost killed him. Back home, a different Elizabeth also appears, seventeen-year-old Valerie Hobson. Throughout the movie, Whale cleverly includes various allusions, often ironically, to the earlier film. Here, for example, Elizabeth realizes that the severely injured and feared-dead Henry remains alive when his hand twitches, reminding us that his Creature first signaled his birth by moving the same hand. Recuperating in bed, Henry makes another of his grand-ambition speeches: "What a wonderful vision it was! I dreamed of being the first to give to the world the secret that God is so jealous of—the formula for life. Think of the power to create a man . . . I might even have found the secret of eternal life." In response to this declaration, Elizabeth hysterically discloses that she has been having bizarre visions that "a strange apparition has seemed to appear in the room. It comes, a figure like death, and each time it comes more clearly, nearer." Perhaps Whale meant us to consider these macabre hallucinations as a foreshadowing of the evil man just about to enter their lives and tempt Henry away from their settled, socially acceptable domesticity and lure him back into the murky shadows.

In the midst of this emotional thunderstorm, we hear a loud pounding on the door, again repeating a scene from the first movie. The heavy wooden door slowly swings open to reveal a man shrouded in darkness except for his highlighted, priest-like collar. As the door exposes more of him, the light reveals a gaunt, older figure with rather astonishing eyebrows, his piercing dark eyes seeming like a pathway to an even darker soul. It is the eccentric Dr. Septimus Pretorius, a doctor of philosophy and former physician, who asks Minnie (Una O'Connor), the maid, to conduct him to the young Baron Frankenstein, whose father has apparently died. After he enters the bedroom, Elizabeth and Pretorius stand on opposite sides of the bed with Henry lying between them, an apt visual representation of the competition for his attention and likely his soul as well. We later learn that Pretorius, who stares disdainfully at Elizabeth, has been booted out of the university for "knowing too much," and that he wants Henry to become a partner in his experiments, to work as fellow scientists to "probe the mysteries of life and death and reach a goal undreamed of by science."

Once they enter his cramped laboratory, Pretorius offers a creepy toast, "To a new world of gods and monsters," that shocks Henry before he can even take a sip of the gin. Declared by his new colleague to be his "only weakness," the drinking of gin proves to be but one among his many and far greater moral defects. Pretorius reappears from behind a curtain with a small, coffin-like

James Whale directs Boris Karloff in *Bride of Frankenstein* (1935).

cabinet and now wears an alchemist's skullcap. He smugly displays his exhibits to the stunned Frankenstein, seven tiny figures, homegrown homunculi,
encased within glass jars: a squeaking queen, a randy king modeled on Henry
VIII, a disapproving archbishop, a suave devil to whom Pretorius compares
himself, a dancing (only to Mendelssohn's "Spring Song") ballerina, a mermaid
floating in seaweed, and, viewed from behind in the right front bottle, a baby in
a high chair. This exhibition, which Pretorius grew "from seeds as nature does,"
repels Henry, who calls it "not science but more like black magic"; yet he still
seems initially intrigued when Pretorius offers him the opportunity to collaborate in creating a mate, a woman, that he claims "would be really interesting."
Fade out.

Meantime, the Creature, who has not been seen for an hour or so, has been
getting into trouble. After he arouses the anger of a raucous mob yet again,
they finally hunt him down, bind him, Christ-like, to a pole, and stone him by
hurling rocks. Here, Whale seems to poke fun at religious iconography rather
than simply incorporate it. The image is simply too blatant to read as a straight
equation of "monster equals savior" and, instead, seems more like "monster
equals parody of savior." Indeed, once the Creature frees himself, he commits
several offscreen murders, such as those of little Frieda and Frau Neumann.
Fleeing into a desolate and expressionistic landscape devoid of any foliage, the
Creature chances upon the hut of a blind hermit (O. P. Heggie) in his hut, a
sequence unforgettably parodied by Mel Brooks in *Young Frankenstein*. Yet this

scene when the Creature encounters his only friend remains the most touching sequence in the entire movie, one suffused with religious imagery that Whale never mocks. These desperately lonely people with physical disabilities, at least for a short period of time before the world intrudes, find comfort and solace in the company of each other.

The Creature enters the hut making a plaintive motion with his hands that recalls his famous introduction in the first film and is later repeated when he hopefully greets his intended bride. This gesture represents his desire for friendship, for contact with another being who will not reject and despise him. Religious symbolism permeates the entire sequence: the nondiegetic organ music; the eating of bread and the drinking of wine mimicking the sacrament of the Eucharist (Holy Communion); actual prayers of thanksgiving; and finally a crucifix prominently adorning the walls of the hermit's lodging. The hermit teaches the Creature to speak, a decision that Karloff strongly objected to and that substantially changed his physical appearance in the role: Jack Pierce had to alter Karloff's facial prosthetics to permit him to move his mouth. Driven from the home of the one person who shows him kindness, the Creature hides in a graveyard crypt. There he discovers the irreverent Pretorius chopping up a young girl's corpse to use in his new creation, eating dinner atop a coffin, and blowing smoke in the face of a skull. "I love dead. Hate living," the Creature tells Pretorius, who simply smiles and then responds, "You are wise in your generation."

Nicki Minaj demonstrating the ongoing popularity of the Bride's hairdo.

To save Elizabeth, who has been kidnapped by the Creature, Frankenstein joins Pretorius in his old laboratory and prepares to fashion a mate for his creation. As he does with everything in this sequel, Whale exaggerates the creation scene, constructing a sequence far more elaborate than its predecessor. Fully using his Art Deco set, he conducts a symphony of chaos composed of music (including drums mimicking heartbeats) and lights and thunderstorms and kites and fires and torches and shiny mechanical devices and exploding bulbs and switches and large gears and clanking chains and winches and all manner of sputtering, sparking electrical mechanisms. The swift staccato cutting from instrument to instrument, canted camera angles, off-center compositions, and

The Bride (Elsa Lanchester) rejects her intended mate (Boris Karloff) as Henry Franken-stein (Colin Clive) and Dr. Pretorius (Ernest Thesiger) begin to realize their miscalcula-tion in *Bride of Frankenstein* (1831).

expressionistic lighting form a masterful montage, culminating in the long-awaited birth of a mate. Whale, as several critics note, utilizes what is com-monly called "Rembrandt lighting" throughout this sequence, a technique that fully illuminates only one side of an actor's face while highlighting a triangle on the other cheekbone, and placing his figures against a black background. "She's alive! She's alive!" screams Frankenstein, nearly repeating his now-famous line.

Whale reveals the mate (Elsa Lanchester who played Mary in the opening scene) in a series of quick, jerky cuts, a stitched-together bride with a scar on her neck and an iconic, Nefertiti-inspired hairdo dramatically streaked with lightning bolts; she is dressed in white, and, accompanied by the sounds of wedding bells, stands between her two fathers/creators. The "Bride of Franken-stein," proclaims Pretorius, once more conflating the creator with his creation, perhaps forgetting that another bride of Frankenstein already exists, Elizabeth. Yet, sadly, this beauty cannot stand her beast. Upon seeing the Creature, she hisses, shrieks in terror, and, rather ironically, clings to Frankenstein for moral and physical support, something he steadfastly denied his first creation but now provides his second. The distraught Creature, once more scorned, sends Fran-kenstein and the newly arrived Elizabeth away, telling them to go and live, but he informs Pretorius, "We belong dead." Essentially, then, he commits suicide, pulling down a lever that somehow blows up the lab and sends the entire edifice crashing down upon Pretorius and the two man-made creatures—at least until the next film.

As has been pointed out by numerous scholars, *Bride of Frankenstein* has much to recommend it, including John Mescall's dramatic cinematography, Franz Waxman's operatic musical score, Charles Hall's arty sets, Vera West's sumptuous costumes, and, of course, Jack Pierce's famous makeup for Karloff and Lanchester. Whether one understands it as a straightforward horror movie or a campy and queer (see below) creation that both mocks and embraces the first *Frankenstein* film, it remains a product of Whale's heightened vision and arguably his greatest work.

A Queer Reading of Whale's Frankenstein Films

In a 2003 episode of *Will & Grace*, Will compares his dating life to Dr. Frankenstein's relationship with his monster.

WILL: I'm intimidated, okay? It's like I've—I've created a guy that's too hot for me to date. It's the same reason Dr. Frankenstein didn't date his monster.
GRACE: What? Dr. Frankenstein wasn't a homo.
WILL: Oh, really? He sewed together a bunch of guys to create the perfect man? Wrapped him in linen. Give him a flat head, so you can set a drink on it. Dr. Frank was a 'mo, my friend. [*chuckling*] He was a 'mo.[23]

Along these same lines, Henry Benshoff regards Whale's *Frankenstein* as one of the iconic gay monster movies of the classic era, a prototype establishing many tropes found in later films, including "the queer villain's desire for one or both members of the couple," the monster destroyed by a public mob or its patriarchal representatives, the "normal" couple "reinstated after safely passing through their queer experience," and "the mad scientist, who, with the . . . aid of a male assistant, sets out to create life homosexually—without the benefit of heterosexual intercourse."[24] Turning his attention specifically to Whale's *Bride of Frankenstein*, Benshoff focuses on the image of Dr. Pretorius, describing him as a campy gay character whom Minnie, the maid, calls a "very queer looking old gentleman." Invading the couple's bedroom, he lures Henry away from Elizabeth, coyly unveiling his collection of homunculi as part of his plan to seduce Henry into collaborating with him. Noël Carroll, who agrees with this approach to the film, argues that *Bride of Frankenstein* is a "thinly disguised take of homosexual seduction" between Dr. Pretorius and Henry Frankenstein and that the gay director "discovered a theme of latent male desire in Shelley's classic," while Reynold Humphries calls Pretorius a "misogynistic old queen."[25] *Gods and Monsters*, a fictional biography of Whale's last years, makes a queer reading manifest when Whale (Ian McKellen), Colin Clive (Matt McKenzie), and Ernest

Thesiger (Arthur Dignam) prepare the scene when the Bride comes alive: "What a couple of queens we are, Colin," says Thesiger. "Yes, that's right. A couple of flaming queens. Pretorius is a little bit in love with Dr. Frankenstein, you know," adds Whale.

Son of Frankenstein (1939)

The movies released after the two most celebrated examples of Universal's Frankenstein franchise offer a series of idiosyncratic variations on Shelley's, and more accurately Whale's, basic narratives; but as these sequels drift further and further away from their original sources, they degenerate into self-parodies with small production budgets. Finally, and perhaps mercifully, the iconic Creature originally forged by Karloff and Pierce ends his onscreen life in 1948 as a comic foil to Abbott and Costello, more of a joke than a frightening presence. That said, however, the succeeding films offer viewers a series of distinctive twists and turns that add unique innovations to the composite Frankenstein narrative, an ever-expanding and fluid process that shows no sign of stagnating. The following comments on these post–James Whale films are not meant to be exhaustive, but rather to provide a solid sense of what new elements they insert into the evolution of the Frankenstein family tree.

With the ouster of Carl Laemmle and the takeover of Charles R. Rogers in 1936, Universal shifted away from Gothic horror movies, a decision that lead to a drastic decline in the studio's box office revenues. Ultimately, the new studio honchos realized their error and commissioned Wyllis Cooper to script a sequel, secured the services of Boris Karloff and Bela Lugosi, finally allotted a relatively big budget of $420,000 for the project, and produced the longest English-language film in the series: *Son of Frankenstein* (1939), a huge commercial success that the critic Robin Wood praised as "the most intelligent of the Universal series,"[26] and that scholars often characterize as the last truly classic Universal Frankenstein film. Directed by Rowland V. Lee, this version of the tale situates a family drama within the recognizable conventions of a horror movie, with most of the murders occurring offscreen or in the shadows. Wolf Frankenstein (Basil Rathbone, prior to his famous incarnation as Sherlock Holmes), the son of Henry (Colin Clive died in 1937), leaves his teaching position to claim his father's estate some thirty years after the last movie, bringing along his American wife (Josephine Hutchinson) and young son (Donnie Dunagan). Their train ride begins in a seemingly modern world but ultimately deposits the family in the nowhere land of Universal's timeless back lot where everyone speaks in a different accent and people have failed to change their outfits or occupations since Henry's day. Wolf never met his father but reveres him, aspires to have some small portion of his genius, claims that his creation was a miracle, and blames the fatal results totally on his incompetent assistant.

Upon arriving, Wolf tries to reassure the wary villagers that he wants "the dead past to remain buried," but they still ostracize the family, doubting his sincerity. And future events prove them right to do so. Wolf ultimately succumbs to the Frankenstein family's penchant for scientific hubris and seeks to "penetrate the unknown"—and with predictable results. Driven by a passion to vindicate his father, Wolf struggles to rehabilitate Henry's reputation and stature as a scientist so that his "name will be enshrined among the immortals." Soon he emulates his father's ambitious error by bringing his creation (Boris Karloff) back to life from a coma, ironically induced when he was struck by lightning. In a symbolic act, Wolf uses a torch to change the words on Henry's coffin from "maker of monsters" to "maker of men." The newest Frankenstein must continually confront the legacies of the past, including the escalating jealousy of the murderous Ygor (Bela Lugosi), a deformed and demented grave robber who survived a hanging but emerged with a broken neck. Ygor, who manipulates the Creature to wreak revenge on those who crippled him, claims that Wolf and the Creature are brothers, since they share the same father.

The film starts with a factual error; the opening credits note that its narrative was "suggested by" Shelley's novel of 1816, instead of the actual publication dates of either the first version (1818) or the revised printing (1831). Even with this inauspicious beginning, however, several elements and characters make *Son of Frankenstein* worthwhile viewing; some also serve as the basis for jokes in *Young Frankenstein*. While Lee's relatively static images rarely match Whale's elegant and fluid camera work, his visuals emulate some of the best parts of the earlier two movies, particularly his sets—sparse furnishing amid gigantic living spaces/fireplaces that dominate the mise-en-scène—and his strong use of German Expressionistic techniques that make shadows an integral part of almost every scene. The decision to mute Karloff again, in his last full-scale incarnation of the Creature, returns emotional poignancy to his performance, particularly evident when he compares his distorted image to Wolf's aristocratic demeanor, mourns the death of his only friend, and forms an affectionate (uncle-like) bond with Wolf's son. Ygor's devious malevolence transforms the Creature into a hapless victim willing to commit murder if his only friend demands it. Karloff's limited screen time and the wooly vest he wears make him appear more animalistic and at times less sympathetic than in the earlier movies.

Most crucially, Lee adds the fascinating character of Police Inspector Krogh (Lionel Atwill), a monocled representative of civilized and stable society. Krogh was still a child when the Monster attacked his family and tore out his arm by the roots; it has been replaced by a cumbersome wooden prosthetic, a permanent alteration that separates him from the rest of society and forever ends his dreams of a glorious military career. Krogh, Ygor, and the Creature all possess physical deformities that disconnect them from commonplace life in the village, making them, as well as the Frankenstein family, outsiders. Other clever little touches also abound. For example, Wolf's initial diagnosis of the Creature's condition using sophisticated medical language and contemporary technology (such as an X-ray machine) modernizes the rebirthing segment, concluding, "This Creature is indeed a monster. There is not one part of his physical being that's like that of human beings. . . . He's unearthly." Finally, the village is called "Frankenstein" (no longer Goldstadt) and those who live within it "Frankenstei-nians." These citizens grumble that Henry's blighted experiments decimated the tourist trade, and they later form a raucous mob that attacks the castle. Wolf also complains that in the popular imagination the creator's name has been conflated with his Creature, a mélange of father, son, creation, town, and townspeople who all share a blurred and tainted identity.

The Ghost of Frankenstein (1942)

If *Son of Frankenstein* is a family movie, then *The Ghost of Frankenstein* is a buddy film, perhaps even the weird epitome of this genre formulation. It also marks the last time in the cycle that the Monster appears as the singular Creature in the story. Now that Henry is dead, Wolf has abandoned the ancestral cas-tle to the villagers, and the Frankenstein family has presumably returned to America, the narrative focus shifts to the home of Ludwig Frankenstein (Sir Ced-ric Hardwicke), a prominent doctor in Vasaria who performs brain surgery on the criminally insane, with the help of Drs. Kettering (Barton Yarborough) and Bohmer (Lionel Atwill)—the latter Frankenstein's former teacher but now his resentful subordinate. Ludwig, the second son of Henry and brother of Wolf, has distanced himself and his daughter, Elsa (Evelyn Ankers), from the disrepu-table experiments of his family, but the ghost of his father implores him not to destroy his creation but rather to enhance it by implanting a proper brain. Seek-ing to make amends for all the misery caused by his family, as well as to restore the good name of Frankenstein, Ludwig decides to replace the Creature's (Lon Chaney Jr.) criminal brain with the moral brain of Dr. Kettering, his latest vic-tim. "No, no, no," Ygor pleads. "You cannot take my friend away from me. . . . You can put *my* brain in his body. You can make us one." Frankenstein refuses, but Ygor secretly turns to his jealous rival, Dr. Bohmer, who (after the Creature acci-dentally injures Ygor severely, perhaps fatally) removes Ygor's brain and wheels it, not Kettering's, into the operating theater where Frankenstein is waiting. The operation thus creates not a gentle giant but an extremely powerful being with the devious cunning of a sociopath.

Ygor's attempt to literally become one with his only friend, whose blue-collar costume again consists of his original ill-fitting jacket and large work-man's boots, is both disturbing and at least somewhat understandable. Even more so is the Creature's friendship with a young girl in the village, Cloestine

Hussman (Janet Ann Gallow), which initially seems touchingly reminiscent of his sad experience with Little Maria in the original film. As the film progresses, however, this connection takes a swift turn toward the macabre when he requests that her brain be placed in his body. One can only imagine what out-landish events would transpire if a child's brain controlled that gigantic body. Who could deny her/his demands for ice cream, discipline him/her, or refuse to take him/her to the zoo?

The film offers a vague and fleeting moral note: Bohmer rejects Franken-stein's request to help him dissect the tranquilized Creature, calling it murder. "How can you call the removal of a thing that is not human murder?" responds Frankenstein, who later calls the Creature a "human junk heap." But the rela-tionship between Ygor and the Creature remains at the center of this modifica-tion of the narrative. Ygor wants to merge completely with the Creature and is willing to die, at least physically, to achieve this intense symbiosis and "the promise of a life forever." Although *The Ghost of Frankenstein* was a commer-cial success, the dwindling budgets Universal executives allotted it and the final four Frankenstein movies ultimately demoted the series from A-list to B projects with ever-diminishing box office returns.

The Last Four Universal Studio Pictures

Frankenstein Meets the Wolf Man (1943), *House of Frankenstein* (1944), *House of Dracula* (1945), and *Abbott and Costello Meet Frankenstein* (1948), the last four pictures composing the Universal studio cycle, use "Frankenstein" more as a brand name to lure viewers into the theater rather than adding anything very substantial to the development of the ongoing narrative. For example, during *House of Frankenstein*'s 71-minute running time, the Creature remains inanimate till being defrosted after 62 minutes elapse and never moves till 67 minutes tick off the clock. Instead of focusing on the Creature, it showcases a mad scientist in the mold of the sociopathic Dr. Pretorius rather than the high-strung and often remorseful Henry Frankenstein in the first two movies. In these four films, then, the Creature functions as a bit player rather than a star. The central figure in the financially successful *Frankenstein Meets the Wolf Man* is the tortured Law-rence Talbot/werewolf figure (Lon Chaney Jr.), in *House of Frankenstein* the focus shifts to the revenge narrative of the malevolent Dr. Niemann (Boris Karloff) and later the Wolf Man again, in *House of Dracula* the vampiric Count (John Car-radine) takes center stage, and in the final film the spotlight remains on the two hapless comedians. Although the cycle slides downhill after *Son of Frankenstein*, shuffling the same actors (Atwill, Lugosi, Frye, Carradine, Chaney) from film to film in a kind of horror repertory company, incorporating cheap sets, and offer-ing poor special effects, some interesting elements occasionally bubble to the surface. In *Frankenstein Meets the Wolf Man*, for instance, the gallant hero of the movie, Dr. Mannering (Patric Knowles), gets seduced by the tantalizing lure of continuing Frankenstein's experiment and, instead of destroying the Creature, recharges (quite literally) its superhuman strength, an apt representation of how even good men can be swayed to the murky side of scientific experimentation and corrupted by power.

The image of the anguished Lawrence Talbot, the cursed werewolf, presents a sympathetic monster that rivals, and in these last films surpasses, the appeal of Frankenstein's Creature. Because the viewer experiences the transformation of Talbot into the Wolf Man at the same time as the character through a series of close-ups and superimpositions, we share his pain and empathize with his confusion. Even in his animalistic state, he fights to save Elsa and Dr. Mannering from the Frankenstein monster, presumably finding peace in his own demise. A kind and gentle man much of the time, Talbot relentlessly seeks death as the only means to escape his cruel fate: each time the full moon appears, he metamorphoses into a raging beast whose murderous actions he cannot control. With a contemporary perspective, the deeply depressed Talbot is, in essence, requesting an act of euthanasia to relieve the burden of circumstances he is powerless to alter and finds unbearable to endure. The Wolf Man was added to Universal's monster lineup by the screenwriter Curt Siodmak, a Jewish refugee from Nazi Germany, and some horror film scholars propose that the character is related to Siodmak's experiences there. The *Wolfsangel*, a runic symbol appropriated by the Nazi Party, was used as a divisional insignia by various Nazi storm units (it is currently part of the logo for the neo-Nazi Aryan Nations), and Wolf's Lair was Hitler's initial military headquarters during World War II.

These films also delve into the mob mentality. When driven by fear of what they cannot understand, the townspeople band together to destroy whatever threatens their stability, resulting in violent and destructive actions that never permanently eliminate their problems. The more the viewer identifies with the ostracized monsters, the sympathetic outcasts such as Talbot and the gentle and lovesick hunchback (J. Carrol Naish) in *House of Frankenstein*, the more the angry mob with its pitchforks and torches fulfills the role of the villain in these movies. Modern viewers might well interpret these groups as lynch mobs intent on destroying anyone who looks different or, with an even more contemporary reading, groups vigorously denying rights to those they consider outsiders, such as people with disabilities, or deviant, such as gay members of society.

The first two Universal films forever transformed Shelley's canonical work from required classroom reading into a readily recognizable cultural phenomenon. They indelibly seared images of the creator, the Monster, and his intended bride into the public imagination, where, no matter their modifications over the decades, they have flourished till this day. So immensely popular do these images remain that Universal Studios copyrighted and trademarked them, as it did Kenneth Strickfaden's version of Frankenstein's laboratory. As early as 1932, the studio sued the Mindhyam Theatrical Company in the New York County Supreme Court for "unfair competition" when it rereleased the silent film *Life without Soul* with an ad campaign proclaiming it "the original version of Frankenstein"—and Universal won the suit. Because Shelley's novel has long since slipped into the public domain, anyone can make a movie or write a novel using *Frankenstein*'s basic plot elements and characters, either adhering faithfully to her work or cannibalizing it as a springboard for fanciful variations, but whatever the setting or the medium, replicating Universal's haunting version of the Creature too closely could lead to a lawsuit. Legally, no image not licensed by Universal can incorporate the following characteristics: green skin, flat-top head, scar on the forehead, bolts on the neck, and protruding forehead.[27] Universal has, of course, licensed a multitude of products bearing the likeness of the Creature and his bride, including everything from Halloween costumes to toys to mugs to throw pillows to model kits to iPhone 6 cases to stamps to pluggable fragrance diffusers to mouse pads and much much more (just check out Amazon.com).

The Hammer Film Production Cycle

Flames, ice, floods, quicksand, lightning, lime pits, and torch-wielding villagers never managed to kill off Frankenstein's Creature, but slapstick comedy and a series of low budgets finally expunged him from the screen—at least for a while. The conclusion of Universal's cycle of Frankenstein movies in 1948 removed Shelley's Creature from movie theaters for just under a decade. Yet, once again, he rose from the dead, this time resurrected by Hammer Film Productions. A relatively small and not particularly successful British company content to produce cheap B pictures during the 1940s, Hammer drastically changed its luck—and its future—in 1955 with its release of the contemporary science fiction film *The Quatermass Xperiment* (US title *The Creeping Unknown*). The story of a man infected by an alien parasite and consequently metamorphosing into a hideous and murderous monster became a huge box office hit in both the UK and America. Hammer studio executives attributed the appeal of *The Quatermass Xperiment* to its horror elements and sought to duplicate their financial triumph by giving audiences more blood and guts, quite literally, on the screen. They knew about the early popularity and box office success of the Universal horror cycle, particularly the *Frankenstein* movies, so the creator and his Creature naturally appealed to them. Thus, in 1957 Hammer Film Productions launched the first in the only other sustained series of Frankenstein movies, a cycle that rebooted Shelley's characters, kept the narrative in the public eye, and ultimately resulted in sharing the bloody crown as king of horror studios with Universal.

Because Universal Studios had clearly demonstrated its eagerness to drag *Frankenstein* poachers into court, particularly those who reproduced Jack Pierce's memorable image of the Creature, Hammer executives warned its creative artists to steer far away from any elements of previous Frankenstein movies. Jimmy Sangster, the screenwriter for the first film in the series, embraced such admonitions, claiming that his interest was in the baron, not the Monster, and that he wanted more of Shelley and less of Whale in his version. Terence Fisher, its director, went even further; to avoid dealing with Universal's lawyers, he never viewed either of Whale's movies.[28] Yet, in at least two important ways, Hammer emulated Universal: starting with *The Curse of Frankenstein*, the series produced staggering profits. The Hammer films also turned both Christopher Lee and Peter Cushing into huge international stars, as the Universal films had done for Boris Karloff and Bela Lugosi.

Apparently inspired by the box office achievements of *The Quatermass Xperiment* and *The Curse of Frankenstein*, the bargain-basement studio American International Pictures (AIP) brought a new version of the Creature to the screen in *I Was a Teenage Frankenstein*, part of a drive-in double bill (with *Blood of Dracula*) in 1957 and a follow-up to its financial windfall with *I Was a Teenage Werewolf* earlier the same year. A shoddy production specifically designed to appeal to the burgeoning teen market, the film became a hit and remains a favorite among some horror film fans to this day. Professor Frankenstein (Whit Bissell), a distant descendant of the illustrious baron and a renowned medical researcher, conducts rather sketchy scientific investigations into transplantation. To prove his theory that dead tissue can be reanimated and concomitantly perfect the human race, he and his reluctant assistant, Dr. Karlton (Robert Burton), plan to replicate his ancestor's experiment by stitching together parts from various cadavers, assisted by the professor's secretary/fiancée/receptionist, Margaret (Phyllis Coates).

A flaming car crash fortuitously provides them with the body of a young victim (Gary Conway) to use as suitable fodder for their dangerous research. Because the damaged corpse is missing some extremities, Frankenstein replaces them with parts from other dead teenagers and then brings the composite Creature to life, but he cannot move or speak, possesses no memory of his past, and has a horribly scarred face from the accident. The muscular Creature accidentally kills a college girl, murders Margaret (with Frankenstein's blessing), and slays a teenage boy to replace his ravaged face. As one might expect, the Creature eventually kills Frankenstein, too, and is then accidenally electrocuted, as the black-and-white film bursts into color. While most mainstream critics panned, and continue to pan, *I Was a Teenage Frankenstein*, it has achieved cult status among some online horror aficionados. Typical is El Santo, moderator of *1000 Misspent Hours and Counting*, who writes that the film is "an example of the studio at its best, combining tacky cheap thrills with a surprising amount of wit and intelligence to make a first-rate drive-in experience. Shelley's theme of the cosmic injustice of the Monster's condition is presented here far more cogently than even in her own novel. It's an impressive accomplishment weaving those two strands together, and to the best of my knowledge, no one has ever done it better for so little money."

The Hammer Film Productions branch of the Frankenstein family tree begins with the critically reviled (one reviewer labeled it "for sadists only") but international sleeper hit *The Curse of Frankenstein* (1957): its production budget of £65,000 (under $200,000) returned over $7,000,000 in box office sales internationally. Set a century before its release, in 1857 (Mary Shelley would have died six years earlier), the film opens with a wide shot of a priest (Alex Gallier) slowly riding into the grounds of an isolated prison buried deep in the foreboding mountains, accompanied by the tolling of a solitary church bell. Inside, he encounters a disheveled and emotionally distraught Baron Victor Frankenstein (Peter Cushing) awaiting his execution within the hour for the murder of his maid, Justine (Valerie Gaunt). Contemptuously spurning an offer of spiritual comfort, the baron begs the cleric to hear his story, which he hopes will save him from death, and to tell the world about his strange experiments. He begins his account with the arrogant assertion, "I've always had a brilliant intellect." Then, as the film dissolves into a long flashback, Victor relates how, upon the death of both his parents, he inherited a large fortune and obtained the services of a tutor, Paul Krempe (Robert Urquhart), who later becomes his laboratory partner. Their workplace, while lacking the dazzling pyrotechnics of Universal's version, fills the screen with flashing lights, spinning wheels, bubbling liquids, smoky containers, glowing red blubs, and an assortment of dials and levers. (A later Hammer film, *The Evil of Frankenstein* [1964, will spin quite a different version of these events and the Creature's birth.)

As expected, Frankenstein's experiments soon swerve toward a search for "the source of life itself" that would allow Victor to "build a man with a perfect physique, the hands of an artist, and the mature brain of a genius." Unlike the willing, often grotesque assistants in the Universal series, however, the ethical Paul fears the outcome of this rampant ambition, calling it "a revolt against nature that will only result in evil." Reluctantly, Paul accedes to Frankenstein's manipulative pleas and helps find a suitable body. Because birds have pecked out the eyes and eaten half the head of the hanged highwayman they select, the Baron must find replacement parts, particularly a suitable set of hands; a lovely pair purchased after the death of the famous sculptor Bardello does nicely. During this time, Victor's cousin, Elizabeth (Hazel Court), arrives to live with him and, eventually, to be his bride, a situation that enrages his maid, Justine, with whom he has been having a sexual liaison. To obtain a suitable

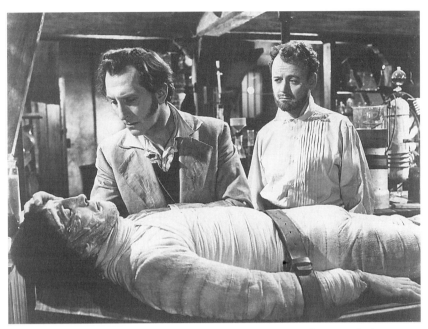

Dr. Frankenstein (Peter Cushing) and his reluctant assistant, Paul Krempe (Robert Urquhart), examine the body of his creation (Christopher Lee) in *The Curse of Frankenstein* (1957).

brain, Frankenstein murders kindly Professor Bernstein (Paul Hardtmuth), but the organ is damaged (as was the brain in Whale's film) in a fight with Paul, who adamantly refuses to collaborate any longer with Victor.

Interestingly, the birth of the Creature (Christopher Lee), which takes place some 50 minutes into the 83-minute movie, occurs with no one present, not even Victor, but results from an accident of nature. After Frankenstein leaves the laboratory believing his experiment has failed, a stray lightning bolt reactivates the machinery and brings the totally bandaged Creature to life. Unlike Shelley's and Karloff's childlike and innocent Creature, however, Lee's mummy-like figure is inherently evil, brutally attempting to strangle Victor, almost killing Elizabeth, murdering a blind man and a little boy (allusions to the Little Maria scene in *Frankenstein* and the hermit scene in *Bride of Frankenstein*), and disposing of Justine. Victor and Paul desperately search for the fleeing Creature in the woods, and Paul shoots him, blinding and apparently killing him. But Victor cannot bring himself to destroy his creation, vowing "to give him life again." This necessitates brain surgery, and, in order to keep his experiments a secret, Victor chains the Creature in the cellar and treats him like a pet (or even a slave), ordering him around with a snap of his fingers. After the Creature eventually escapes his prison, Victor finally shoots him (wounding Elizabeth as well), causing him to fall through the rooftop skylight and into a tank of acid. When the film shifts back to the present and the incarcerated Victor, Paul arrives but refuses to verify Victor's account of events, essentially condemning him to death. The final image is that of a guillotine, the sound of its blade slicing through the air in preparation for the baron's arrival.

One scene in particular resonates with contemporary implications. Victor and Elizabeth dine in a lavish setting that simulates the opulent world of powerful elites and wealthy aristocrats. They politely drink tea, butter their toast, and pass marmalade back and forth, pleasantly talking and indulging in a revered and refined social ritual. A bit later, they host an extravagant formal pre-wedding reception for their neighbors and friends. These gracious, shared conventions occur upstairs amid luxury and mannered courtesy, while downstairs the chained and miserable Creature Frankenstein brought to life and now, presumably without his consent, continues to subject to painful experiments and surgical procedures lives in dark agony. In 1957 England, like the rest of the world, was quite aware of the Nazi atrocities, including the sadistic experimentations of Dr. Josef Mengele on inmates in Auschwitz. Couple this image of Victor and Elizabeth politely enjoying their teatime with the idea of concentration camp commanders having civil conversations with their wives and children over dinner, after spending a hard day indiscriminately torturing women and kids. Such men compartmentalized their lives. Their brutal experiments on and murders of people they considered inferior specimens of humanity, or not human at all, had little effect on the ebb and flow of their daily social lives. Victor replicates their callousness by cordially engaging in elegant communal events without any hint of regret or compassion for the wretched Creature quite literally beneath the highly civilized veneers of these common activities.

Cushing's Frankenstein, unlike his predecessors on the page and in the Universal films, never utters any grandiloquent sentiments about how mankind will benefit because of his experiments or the resulting social good that might justify his research methods. Indeed, the film's one philosophical speech about science in the modern age comes not from Victor but from the eminent Professor Bernstein ("the greatest brain in Europe") during his brief appearance within a typical British domestic scene, as he questions the difference between "knowing a thing is so and knowing how to use it for the good of mankind." When Elizabeth argues that the world would be a far better place without research, the professor agrees and warns Victor against spending too much time isolated "in stuffy rooms in search of obscure truths" and thereby not sufficiently enjoying life. More importantly, he wonders if the world is ready for "the revelations scientists make." Scientists commit a mistake, he continues, by handing over their discoveries to people who will inevitably mishandle them. Frankenstein, obsessed by his experiments, totally rejects this socially oriented and controlled vision of scientific research—and shortly thereafter kills its proponent.

The Curse of Frankenstein resurrected Gothic horror tropes and inspired a general shift away from the common types of science fiction/horror films that dominated screens in the early fifties, such as *The Thing* (1951), *Invaders from Mars* (1953), *Them* (1954), and Hammer's own *The Quatermass Xperiment*. It also provided some sexual titillation, as seen in the baron's lusty affair with the voluptuous and socially ambitious Justine, whose revelation that she is pregnant and demand that he marry her ultimately results in her murder. Their relationship also mocks the oppressive English class system: in the midst of a passionate embrace, he insists she still call him "Herr Baron" rather than "Victor," never letting her forget their disparate social status. Despite its relatively few gory scenes, such as the eyeballs in the jars and the Creature shot in the eye, the film ran afoul of the British Board of Film Censors, who demanded numerous cuts and changes, chastising the project's producers with comments such as "This is a loathsome story and I regret that it should come from a British team."[29] Robert Urquhart, who plays Paul, felt similarly offended when he first saw the finished print, walking out halfway through the film's premiere and vowing never again to appear in a horror movie. By today's bloody standards, the film inspires little squeamish shudders, and most of its deaths take place offscreen.

The Curse of Frankenstein paired Terence Fisher as director with Peter Cushing and Christopher Lee for the first time, actors who would assume the mantle of "horror matinee idols" from Karloff and Lugosi. In his biography of Fisher, Wheeler Winston Dixon notes that "this one film would establish the careers of nearly everyone in its production. Cushing and Lee became overnight stars. Fisher was elevated into the highest ranks of his profession. Jimmy Sangster would never work as an assistant director again. Jack Asher proved himself a master of color photography," and much more.[30] It also indelibly stamped Hammer Film Productions in the minds of the moviegoing public as delivering a certain type of movie. This tradition continues today. Acquired in 2007 by the Dutch producer John De Mol through his firm Cyrte Investments, the studio (in a joint venture with Alliance Films and other production companies) has continued to release films in the horror/monster/thriller genre, including the blockbuster *The Woman in Black* (2012).

Fisher's cinematic style lacks the fluidity and flourish of Whale's visual sensibility at its best, but he skillfully composes long master shots that allow the audience to accept the action as realistic and never jars them out of this illusion with self-consciously arty techniques. Lacking the expressionistic embellishments of Whale's mise-en-scène, Fisher's sets replicate the décor of the mid-1800s, another attempt to maintain some reasonable level of authenticity within which to spin out a fantastical narrative. Yet, despite what most critics characterize as a less visually impressive rendition of Shelley's narrative elements, Dixon argues that the film is groundbreaking in "its use of color, in its iconography, in its framing and syntactical structure, and most prominently in its relaxed choreography."[31] The box office windfall of *Curse* demanded a sequel, one quickly produced with the same star, director, and production team, minus Christopher Lee, who had achieved acclaim as another iconic horror figure: Count Dracula in Fisher's *Dracula* (1958).

Between the releases of *The Curse of Frankenstein* and *The Revenge of Frankenstein*, Screen Gems, a TV subsidiary of Columbia Pictures, made a deal with Universal to package some of the studio's most famous horror movies (including *Frankenstein*) into a syndicated series called *Shock Theatre*. Screen Gems/Columbia also partnered with Hammer (after Hammer's US distribution deal with Warner Bros. ended) for a proposed series of twenty-six original episodes for American television's *Tales of Frankenstein*. Although a pilot was eventually produced—staring Anton Diffring as the baron—the networks ultimately passed on the project, and further episodes were never completed.

Following *The Curse of Frankenstein*, *The Revenge of Frankenstein* (1958) initiates the Hammer cycle's fascination with transplantation in conjunction with re-animation, rather than the creation of a new being. It begins where *The Curse of Frankenstein* ends, in the shadow of the guillotine, but Victor (Peter Cushing) finds a clever way to keep his head attached to his body. Escaping decapitation, he sets up a successful practice in Carlsbruck, reinventing himself as the charismatic Dr. Victor Stein. His scornful refusal to join the local medical society, however, angers his jealous colleagues, particularly Dr. Molke (Arnold Diamond), whose wife has taken a far-too-friendly liking to the new physician. Stein's thriving practice among the wealthy class consists mostly of soothing hypochondriacal women who desire his attention. In a less fashionable section of town, however, Stein sets up a pauper's clinic for destitute citizens, a seemingly benevolent establishment that clandestinely supplies him with a steady stream of organs and limbs for his illicit laboratory experiments. Young Dr. Hans Kleve (Francis Matthews), whose distant relative Christina will appear in *Frankenstein Created Woman*, recognizes Stein as Frankenstein and blackmails him, demanding to become his research assistant. At first denying his identity, the baron archly observes that "uncertainly is one of life's fascinations" and that many branches of the Frankenstein family exist, even in America, an apt prediction for the evolution of this narrative over time.

In all of the preceding Frankenstein movies, the Creature emerges ugly and deformed, particularly Karloff's lumbering giant, and society's cruel treatment, at least in part, turns him into a vindictive murderer. The twist in *Revenge*, however, is that Frankenstein clearly recognizes the earlier mistakes made in his rough draft of a human and now stitches together a handsome and perfectly formed being, one needing only a living brain. The eager donor is the severely crippled Karl (Michael Gwynn), the former prison guard who helped Frankenstein escape the guillotine's blade and willingly trades his brain for a normal body. The baron plans to display Karl's discarded carcass next to his new improved physique, so that skeptical colleagues will finally be forced to acknowledge his genius. Although bringing the Creature with the new brain to life results in a violent birth, the body thrashing in agitated pain, the operation is a medical triumph—for a while. Here, at long last, exists the possibility that Frankenstein's Creature can live a conventional life in society without suffering from prejudice and rejection. The new Karl, at first pleased with his handsome reflection in the mirror, emerges quite unlike the previous Creatures who beheld their own visages with a revulsion that mirrored their creators and society.

But Frankenstein film fans expect to see dreadful things inevitably happen despite good intentions—and they do: Otto, a chimpanzee in Frankenstein's lab and a victim of his earlier transplant experiments, has already eaten his mate—a foreshadowing of cannibalistic things to come. A janitor (George Woodbridge) mistakes Karl for a thief and severely beats him, damaging his brain and forcing his body to revert to its previous condition: partially paralyzed, humped back, hideously twisted features. Eventually, the new Karl strangles a young girl, breaks into a posh music recital, lurches toward Frankenstein, and begs for help. Once Karl exposes Frankenstein as the reviled doctor who mutilated bodies, the indigent-ward patients recognize that he severed their limbs for his own experiments, not their well-being, and almost beat him to death. To save his brain, Kleve performs emergency surgery and transplants Frankenstein's organ into another bandaged figure waiting for life in the laboratory; what emerges (we see in the epilogue) is Dr. Franck, a prominent surgeon with offices on London's prestigious Harley Street. Ironically, Kleve, not the baron, performs the only totally successful surgical procedure in the entire Frankenstein series, either at Universal or at Hammer.

Although the scriptwriter Jimmy Sangster expressed his preference for the baron over the Creature, *Revenge* offers some intriguing alterations in the latter classic figure. The movie features the least scary, slightest deformed, and most normal-sized Creature in the entire Frankenstein family of films, at least until the damaged brain reshapes the body to its previous malformed condition. Indeed, the Creature Frankenstein initially constructs replicates a discernible and intelligent human being with a range of emotions and anxieties. His attraction to the lovely Margaret Conrad (Eunice Gayson), the compassionate daughter of the local minister who volunteers at the clinic, demonstrates that he can feel affection and even love. Their interaction throughout the film represents the first time that a woman treats a Frankenstein-created Creature with kindness, even as his shape changes. (A similar relationship emerges in the modern *Penny Dreadful* TV series.) This quite sympathetic Creature emulates real-life patients who willingly undergo routine cosmetic surgery and even extreme medical procedures via the needle and the knife to enhance their appearance or rectify physical problems. In a related vein, Bruce Hallenbeck notes that the film can "effectively be read as an adventure in eugenics, with the Baron attempting to 'correct' a genetic deficiency in one of his patients."[32]

The film offers other unique elements as well. At its conclusion, the creator totally merges with his Creature—a startling event that occurs in no other Frankenstein movie. By transplanting Victor's brain into a body, like its predecessors assembled from parts sutured together from different people, Kleve becomes another Frankensteinian figure; his surgical skills artificially generate a replica of his mentor (with a mustache and foppish monocle) that can truly be called "Frankenstein," as has often been confused in the mind of the general public. Thus, the maker of monsters has become a product of his own construction: a living amalgamation of past and present, of new and old, of synthetic and natural. *Revenge* also totally avoids incorporating any of the pious moralizing inherent in the "this is against the laws of God and Nature" rhetoric that characterizes many other past and future Frankenstein movies, as well as figuring prominently in Shelley's novel. Frankenstein never doubts the importance of his experiments and never hesitates to continue them. His acts prior to the film's opening have become the stuff of legend, and the local people uniformly believe that his aberrant research reaches beyond moral standards and endangers the community. No shades of gray permeate these black-and-white attitudes. Frankenstein also finds willing and intelligent assistants, rather than the reluctant Paul or the emotionally and physically stunted figures who populate the previous films: both Karl and Hans eagerly participate in Frankenstein's experiments, the latter even threatening blackmail if he is not allowed to partake in the research. Finally, the film seems a thinly veiled critique of, and perhaps even a warning about, the English two-tiered medical system of the late 1950s. Despite passage of the National Health Service Act of 1946, many social critics contended that the poor received far less skillful care than their rich counterparts, who could afford the expensive services of private physicians, often with offices on Harley Street. Here, the poor become unwitting guinea pigs because they cannot afford appropriate medical treatment.

Agreement between Hammer and Universal

A distribution/partnership agreement between Hammer and Universal in 1958 allowed Hammer's makeup artists to fashion a Creature without fear of a lawsuit. The five films made under this agreement included *The Evil of Frankenstein* (1964), *Frankenstein Created Woman* (1967), *Frankenstein Must Be Destroyed*

(1969), *The Horror of Frankenstein* (1970), and *Frankenstein and the Monster from Hell* (1974). The flat-headed being (Ernie "Kiwi" Kingston) in *The Evil of Frankenstein* recalls Karloff's incarnation, and there are also some plot connections to previous Frankenstein narratives, such as finding the Creature trapped and preserved in ice. Many critics label *Evil*, directed by Freddy Francis, as the worst representative of the Hammer Frankenstein series due to its tacky monster makeup, tedious narrative, and one-dimensional, brutish Creature. Frankenstein (Peter Cushing) and his assistant, Hans (Sandor Eles), return to the baron's family castle, but without sufficient funds to continue their experiments; the baron has been banished from the town a decade earlier and his castle's goods distributed among the townspeople. After recounting his past in flashbacks to Hans, a tale that totally ignores the two previous Hammer Frankenstein movies, the baron discovers his Creature buried, but perfectly preserved, in a mountain glacier, still alive but catatonic. They employ the services of Professor Zoltan (Peter Woodthrope), a carnival hypnotist, to bring the Creature back to life, but the greedy Zoltan uses the Creature to wreak revenge by murdering the local officials and to gain wealth by robbing the village church.

Frankenstein Created Woman, the title recalling Brigitte Bardot's international blockbuster *And God Created Woman* (1956), tantalizes potential viewers with a promise of scandalous sex—its publicity poster displayed a naked woman, and its female lead was a Playboy Playmate in 1966—but instead delivers a far more metaphysical quest than any of the other Hammer movies. The baron (Peter Cushing) attempts to discover if the soul dies when the body perishes—a question pondered by some of the world's greatest thinkers, as discussed in our earlier chapters. Ultimately, the baron concludes that death is physical, not spiritual, and that the essence of a person can be transferred from one body to another, although he never specifies his method for an operation that coalesces the soul with the flesh. Assisted by the dim-witted Dr. Hertz (Thorley Walters), he transplants the soul of the unjustly guillotined Hans (Robert Morris), his former assistant, into the body of Christina Kleve (Susan Denberg), a severely scarred and crippled café worker he surgically transforms into a beautiful woman. The soul of Hans eventually controls Christina's body, forcing her to seduce and then kill the sadistic toffs who bullied him in life, and the ensuing guilt drives her to commit suicide.

Frankenstein Created Woman, the last Hammer film shot at Bray Studios, begins with an ironic moment: using himself as an experimental subject, the baron replicates the original condition of his creations by being dead for an hour. Once returning to life, he condescendingly tells his doubtful assistants, "Of course I'm alive. Did I not tell you I would be?" *Frankenstein Created Woman* ignores Shelley's basic premise of creation, as well as later films that focus on reanimation, replacing these procedures with an attempt to relocate souls from

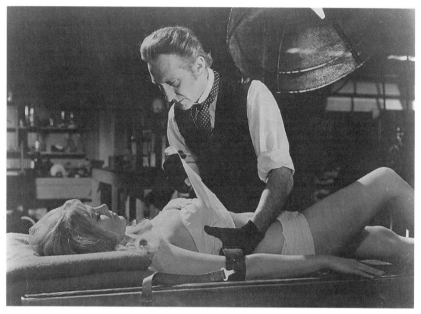

Baron Frankenstein (Peter Cushing) unwraps his newest creation, Christina (Susan Denberg), a woman with a man's soul, in *Frankenstein Created Woman* (1967).

one body to another. Who knew that the science-obsessed baron was equally infatuated with metaphysics and spirituality? Perhaps the director (Terence Fisher again) and screenwriter (John Elder) were appealing to the late-sixties youth market by emphasizing Eastern religions and mysticism, but whatever the reasons, this film's narrative bears no resemblance to the preceding Frankenstein movies from either Universal or Hammer. Here, the recurring horror film premise of the young woman threatened or even abducted by the Monster takes an unfamiliar twist: the Monster resides inside the woman's body, directing her actions like a embittered ventriloquist.

As a result of this premise, a misogynistic fantasy drives the narrative. A vindictive Hans, whose embedded soul remembers past violence against him, takes control of a beautiful woman's body, forcing her to implement a series of retaliatory murders: "Christina's body is but a projection of male fantasy; her identity is even more sharply circumscribed once she has a perfect body and face, given to her by a distant father who is interested in her only for experiments."[33] But troubling questions remain. Does not Christina, too, have a soul, and what happened to it? Or do women not have souls? A beautiful woman who offers the allure of sexual relations, only to assassinate the men she tempts, screams out for a Freudian reading—and not a particularly charitable one. Fisher juxtaposes Christina's seductions and murders with images of her performing mundane chores around the household, displaying what the film purports to be the hidden, twofold aspects of womanhood: dangerous and domestic, loving partner and femme fatale. Such a conception of a male soul inside and dominating a woman's body goes beyond transgenderism or even hermaphrodism. It reaches into realms of Cartesian dualism, which pits body and mind (spirit) in an ongoing battle for supremacy; in this case, it is an irreconcilable split that ends in Christina's suicide when her body becomes unwilling to be manipulated.

In Hammer films like this one, the baron no longer occupies a grand house with obedient servants as in the Universal productions—rather, he has become quite middle-class, living in relatively modest surroundings and dining at the local tavern—but he steadfastly maintains a decidedly aristocratic air. Indeed, Cushing's baron always remains haughty and sarcastic, disdainfully dismissing anyone who forces him to take time away from his demanding work or challenges the morality of his ideas. When called upon to testify at Hans's trial, for example, he scornfully thumbs through the Bible with the condescending air of someone offended by foul-smelling garbage, berating the judge for impinging on his time and taking him away from his experiments. While some critics castigated the film for its basic premise, no less a film expert than the director Martin Scorsese appreciated Fisher's movies, including *Frankenstein Created Woman* in a 1987 National Film Theatre series of his favorite films.[34]

Frankenstein Must Be Destroyed, the fifth installment of the Hammer series, continues the move further and further away from Shelley's and Universal's characters and narratives, flaunting more blood and female flesh than in previous films. The arrogant baron (Peter Cushing) takes up residence in a plush boardinghouse run by Anna Spengler (Veronica Carlson), fiancée of Dr. Karl Holst (Simon Ward), who works in the local insane asylum. He has come to collaborate with Dr. Brandt (George Pravda) about their mutual interest in brain transplantation, but Brandt's mental breakdown has landed him in the madhouse. Frankenstein blackmails Anna and Karl to gain their assistance, frees a catatonic Brandt from the institution, and skillfully transplants his brain into the body of Professor Richter (Freddie Jones) to learn the secret of his colleague's successes. Again, the baron expresses a noble goal: in order "to preserve for all time the great talents and geniuses of the world," he must remove their brains at the instant of death, freeze them, and preserve them for posterity. Needless to say, things quickly disintegrate as Inspector Frisch (Thorley Walters), a snuff-sniffing detective, investigates all the mysterious deaths. Most shockingly, Frankenstein callously rapes the vulnerable Anna, an act out of character for the rather asexual baron that traumatizes her and displays the depraved nature beneath his politely civilized exterior. Indeed, the egotistical baron seems far more condescending and sarcastic to everyone around him than his previous incarnations. In their final confrontation, Richter/Brandt, who fully recognizes

Terence Fisher directing Peter Cushing (Frankenstein) in *Frankenstein Must Be Destroyed* (1969).

the incompatible contradictions inherent in his new physical/mental condition, sets fire to his house and apparently burns Frankenstein and himself alive, claiming he has "become a victim of everything he and Frankenstein have advocated." The Creature has, yet again, destroyed his creator.

The Horror of Frankenstein, usually considered among the weakest of the Hammer productions, simply repeats the basic narrative formula: a randy Victor Frankenstein (Ralph Bates), equally interested in dead and female flesh, again creates an artificial being (David Prowse) that turns into a homicidal maniac for no apparent reason. Directed by Jimmy Sangster, the scriptwriter for many of the earlier Hammer productions, the film meanders between semiserious action and a dark parody of its forefathers, particularly *The Curse of Frankenstein*. Besides the youthful cast, its most unique element is the introduction of patricide into the series: Victor jury-rigs his father's (George Belbin) gun to explode during a hunting trip, killing the patriarch who forbade him to continue his education, thereby inheriting the title and enough funding to enter medical school. Yet, after impregnating the daughter of the dean, he is booted out and forced to return home. His totally unsympathetic Creature kills a number of people, then takes refuge in a vat and is killed when it's flooded with acid. The repetitious plot and almost timid violence of *The Horror of Frankenstein* demonstrate that Hammer had little understanding of the increasingly bloodthirsty audience for horror flicks. With American movies such as *Night of the Living Dead*

(1968) already breaking box office records (making $30,000,000 in profits from a $114,000 budget) and *The Last House on the Left* (1972), *The Exorcist* (1973), and *Texas Chain Saw Massacre* (1974) about to drench movie screens in buckets of gore and blood, Hammer's quaint Gothic films seemed more like fuddy-duddy old relics rather than gruesome films from a thriving shock factory. Ironically, then, Hammer's Frankenstein films became casualties in the increasingly graphic horror film revolution they had set in motion.

Toward the end of *Frankenstein and the Monster from Hell*, the baron (Peter Cushing) remarks, "It's all over now. All over," prophetic words for this final Frankenstein film from Hammer. This was Terence Fisher's last film as a director and Peter Cushing's final portrayal of the egocentric baron. Fans of the series greeted the sixty-one-year-old Cushing's return to his signature role like giddy schoolchildren; although the dashing baron looks grayer and quite gaunt, even cadaverous, he proves surprisingly spry when he leaps off a table onto the back of his Creature to subdue him. Far removed from his previous lavish surroundings, or even an elegant boardinghouse, the baron (using the name Dr. Victor) now lives in a small, sparely furnished apartment within a lunatic asylum, where he tends to the inmates and continues his experiments assisted by the mute Sarah (Madeline Smith), dubbed "the angel" by the inmates. His cramped, barebones laboratory seems hardly suited to his usual grand designs. Enter Simon Helder (Shane Briant), a doctor convicted of sorcery who reveres Frankenstein's work and becomes a willing acolyte, performing the delicate surgical procedures the baron can no longer accomplish due to his severely scarred hands. Winston Wheeler Dixon interprets Frankenstein's diminished condition as a sad reflection of Fisher's deteriorating directorial skills and of his need to rely on others to complete his work due to old age and ill health.[35]

Together, Frankenstein, Helder, and Sarah transplant the brain of Professor Durendel (Charles Lloyd-Pack), a talented violinist and brilliant mathematician whom the baron induced to commit suicide, into the muscular body of a Neolithic-like man (David Prowse, later to find fame as the body of Darth Vader), who was killed when jumping from his cell but resurrected, much to his dismay, by Frankenstein. With no immunosuppressant drugs available, the body begins to reject the brain, which means it will slowly atrophy and finally rot (perhaps an allusion to Christiaan Barnard's early transplant cases). The narrative then plows into new waters for Frankenstein movies, incest: Frankenstein wants the Creature to mate with (read rape) Sarah and reveals that she turned mute after her father (John Stratton), the noxious director of the asylum, tried to rape her. Such a cruel plan proves too much for Helder, who has grown to love Sarah, and he tells Frankenstein that researchers cannot "divorce science from humanity." Finally, the Creature kills the director and, having been wounded in their battle, staggers into the inmate ward, where the frenzied residents tear him apart.

Frankenstein survives, muttering about his mistakes and how he will do things differently "next time"—but the film's tepid box office performance assured there was no "next time" for Hammer's Frankenstein.

Horror films are inherently transgressive because they foreground issues polite society consistently avoids confronting. *Frankenstein and the Monster from Hell* touches on a few of these. For example, the film demonstrates that involuntary incarcerations for "insanity" have become a tool of the state to deal with people it finds uncomfortable to contend with, such as the man who thinks he's God in the film, or is unable to persuade to more "normal" thinking, such as Dr. Helder. Declaring them crazy provides a legal justification to lock them away, out of sight, so they cannot bother, disturb, or challenge members of polite society. With Germany's death camps and the Soviet Union's gulags as potent examples from recent history, such governmental tactics were quite evident in 1974. The film also depicts the poor treatment granted society's castoffs in these institutions, as illustrated by the incompetent and greedy supervisor who steals state funding for his own purposes and sexually abuses female prisoners, and sadistic guards like Ernst (Philip Voss) and Hans (Chris Cunningham) who treat inmates callously. While *Frankenstein Must Be Destroyed* dealt with rape, this film deals with incest, both equally uncomfortable subjects. The film also returns the ugly Creature to the series, here a missing-link-like figure covered with hair and displaying misshapen features, although his pathetic plea "Help me" and his affection for Sarah elicit sympathy. Finally, a level of verisimilitude characterizes the filming of delicate (and quite messy) surgical procedures, filling the screen with blood and black humor: a brain is carelessly kicked across the floor, and as the Monster is torn limb from limb, his body parts and organs get tossed around like unwanted beach balls.

Sibling Rivalry: The Universal versus the Hammer Frankensteins

Both the Universal and the Hammer films circle around the same general ideas gleaned from Mary Shelley but with a different emphasis, including scientific hubris, the morality of medical research and experimentation, and the enduring battle between doing good for society and being seduced by hubris to do evil. While the Universal directors shot in black-and-white, making extensive use of the tropes and shadows characteristic of German Expressionism, their later counterparts saturated Hammer's productions in vibrant color, mostly a lurid red of course. Several commentators detect the influence of the flamboyant coloration and vivid artistry of comic book illustrators in the Hammer palette as well. The settings, too, are quite different, in terms of both place and time. Universal's directors filled their worlds with the cavernous residences of aristocrats, while Hammer's characters work within sometimes lavish but clearly more middle-class environments; ultimately, as mentioned, the baron resides in rather meager surroundings. The Universal Frankenstein films exist in an uncertain time frame, whereas most Hammer versions take place during the Victorian era. As a result, Hammer's movies contain a level of familiar reality absent in the Universal versions, "an illusion of reality that camouflages its mythic dimensions."[36]

Whale and his cohorts usually depict violence offscreen, in the shadows, or in quick sequences, while Fisher and his followers show their characters' nasty deeds and macabre murders in more graphic detail. That said, however, some early reviewers' disgust (one famously suggested an SO rating that stood for "Sadists Only[37]) at the earlier films in the Hammer series seems quite overblown; Fisher more often shows characters reacting to violence than the violence itself. As the scriptwriter James Sangster intended, the Hammer movies focus on the baron, not his Creature, unlike the best films in the Universal series; thus, the baron's evil intentions dominate the narratives, while the Creature's motivations remain opaque. In other words, the creator offers viewers a multifaceted character, while the Creature remains essentially opaque, one-dimensional, and animalistic. Because Cushing was some thirteen years older than Colin Clive, his Frankenstein represents a more mature version than either Whale's or Mary Shelley's: a decisive and self-assured researcher who confidently commands others to do his bidding, rather than a young medical revolutionary rebelling against his stodgy teachers. Most crucially, as James Twitchell points out, "the saga is no longer about creating life but about transplanting it."[38] Such an important alteration in focus seems quite apropos in an age that will witness Christiaan Barnard's successful transplant of a liver and later a heart (1967), astounding feats that forever transformed the topography of medicine.

The Hammer films consciously challenged the standards for acceptability established by the British Board of Film Censors, and thus the social mores of their day, consistently earning and then flaunting the X-certificate ratings (originally "passed for exhibition to persons over the age of sixteen," now eighteen) awarded their productions. Although all good horror films inevitably break rigid societal taboos, the Hammer productions provided far more sexually explicit scenarios than did the Universal series, clearly demonstrated in their ample display of female flesh and the extravagant low-cut gowns that adorned their buxom heroines. Yet, like most other films of this period, Hammer's Frankenstein movies preach that deviant sexuality must be destroyed for society to return to normality. Finally, the Hammer films, despite their pulsating splashes of color, are more downbeat, more melancholy, than their forefathers, tending toward nihilistic at times. Whereas the first Whale film, for example, concludes with the reestablishment of the traditional social order, the last scene of the first Fisher film ends with the unapologetic Frankenstein about to be guillotined. Similarly, Christina in *Frankenstein Created Woman* commits suicide when she can no longer control her actions, and Frankenstein apparently perishes in a burning house in *Frankenstein Must Be Destroyed.*

The Hammer cycle shifts the focus of the Frankenstein films from reanimating dead tissue to transplanting organs and body parts. When Whale's Creature awakes, he has no idea about whose body parts and organs compose him or any memory of a past history. In fact, he never even inquires about the identities of his donors. Therefore, the philosophical issues swirl around concepts of artificial versus natural life and the inevitable quandaries that arise when trying to discern who is human and what is not. The Hammer films, however, never question whether the Creature is human. In these movies, once the amalgamated beings—brains and spirits, sometimes damaged, housed in new bodies, often deformed—return to life, they immediately search out answers about who they are, not what they are. The question never arises of who is human and what is not. Some retain no memories, such as Christina (*Frankenstein Created Woman*). Others, like Brandt (*Frankenstein Must Be Destroyed*), one of the most sympathetic victims of Frankenstein's experiments, retain vivid memories of their past lives only to face rejection by those they most love. When, for example, Brandt returns home to see his wife, Ella (Maxine Audley), one last time, she refuses to accept a man claiming to be her husband but not looking like him. Similarly, Professor Durendel (*Frankenstein and the Monster from Hell*) clearly remembers his love of music and artistic talent, but angrily crushes his violin when his new, gigantic hands can no longer finger the bridge.

Such fundamental identity questions strike a decidedly modern note, as our formerly rigid definitions of gender, ethnicity, and sexuality are currently undergoing intense scrutiny and serious challenges. What was once black and white is now fifty or more shades of gray as "are" categories give way to "neither, either, both, or multiple" groupings. The difficulties facing a person like Bruce Jenner living inside a body that feels like someone else's, a foreigner inhabiting a shell that is not who he/she really is, speaks directly to current issues within the transgender community and plays a prominent role in the Hammer movies. More specific to these productions, patients receiving organ transplants, in particular, often wonder about the personalities and qualities of the persons who donated their organs. Contemporary movies also play with this Frankenstein theme across genres. *Return to Me* (2000) features a man (David Duchovny) who falls in love with a woman (Minnie Driver) he later discovers has received the heart of his dead wife, and in *Heaven Can Wait* (1978) the soul and mind of a football quarterback (Warren Beatty) inhabit the body of a murdered millionaire. On a more sinister level, *Body Parts* (1991) introduces a criminal psychologist (Jeff Fahey) who agrees to an experimental transplant procedure to replace his severed arm by grafting on the limb of an executed serial killer, an appendage that soon begins to act more like its former host than its current body. Finally, in the comic *All of Me* (1984), a dying rich woman (Lily Tomlin) has her soul mistakenly transplanted into the body of her lawyer (Steve Martin). Among other movies that play with the concept of switching one person's consciousness into the body of another person are *Freaky Friday* (1976), *Dream a Little Dream* (1989), *Prelude to a Kiss* (1992), and *The Change-Up* (2011). Thus, real experiences and reel tales share some similar questions and fears about transplantation and the role such surgical procedures play in both our individual lives and the broader culture we all inhabit.

Although the Hammer series endures as one of the largest and most important branches of the Frankenstein family tree, the studio's profound effect on the British cinema industry and the overall evolution of the horror film remains an equally significant part of its legacy. In an obvious challenge to the polite drawing-rooms of stiff upper lips and Oxbridge accents that characterize British classical cinema, Hammer presented a visually garish alternative designed to titillate rather than educate. Its uncanny mingling of low art, high art, and camp reached into the balcony and behind the walls of ivy, a series that somehow appealed both to hormonal teenagers and serious scholars. Brian Wilson notes how Hammer's "subversive ideology" both reflects and "subverts a conservative value system." "Hammer," he argues, challenged the dominant moral codes and proper standards of good taste imposed by the establishment."[39] The Hammer productions revived the Gothic horror film, replacing giant, often mutant monsters with atmospheric environments dominated by a sense of foreboding and inhabited by human predators. In doing so, Hammer became a brand name for horror, as recognizable as MGM was for musicals and Warner Bros. for crime dramas.

5

=================================

Mary Shelley's Stepchildren

Transitions, Translations, and Transformations

No culture is philosophically monolithic, or promotes a single conception of the human. A culture is an internecine contest between alternative conceptions of the human.

　　　　　—Leon Wieseltier, "Among the Disrupted"

In looking over the broad spectrum of films containing the name "Frankenstein" in the title, a seemingly simple question arises: What is a Frankenstein film? If the answer demands strict adherence to Shelley's novel, then no quintessential model exists. No film faithfully translates all the events and characters in her novel to the screen, a predictable outcome with movies based on literary works. Instead, directors and screenwriters treat her novel like a delicious buffet overflowing with a tempting assortment of treats; they choose what items they find most appealing and leave untouched those they consider indigestible. Every film alleging Shelley's novel as its progenitor contains both embellishments and alterations. Even those productions professing to be "the True Story" take substantial liberties that belie their earnest declarations of authenticity. More confusion arises when films with "Frankenstein" in their titles—such as *Frankenstein's Army* (2013), situated toward the end of World War II, *The Frankenstein Syndrome* (aka *The Prometheus Plot*, 2010), set in the present, or *I, Frankenstein* (2014), located in the future—have minimal if any connections with Mary Shelley's original narrative and characters. To utilize a sliding scale of how much a particular film precisely replicates the events and characters in her novel to determine if it qualifies as a "Frankenstein film," therefore, leads to exasperating hairsplitting rather than clarification. In the final analysis, Shelley's book often serves merely as a starting point, often an inspiration or simply an allusion for name recognition, that feeds the various branches of the Frankenstein family tree.

　　A more constructive approach to answering the baseline question "What is a Frankenstein movie?" would employ Mary Shelley's essential narrative structure as a significant factor in any practical solution. Her bare-bones, three-part configuration acts as a pragmatic guideline to identify what movies constitute the assorted branches of the family tree: act 1—Frankenstein generates a Creature; act 2—Frankenstein cannot control the Creature, who runs amok murdering people; act 3—Frankenstein's Creature destroys the creator, sometimes by his own hand and other times by the consequences of his actions. Even this primary organizational pattern, however, fails to encompass some important Frankenstein spin-offs because Victor does not appear in every film, the Creature sometimes perishes while his maker survives, and numerous other variations emerge over the decades. Such narrative fluctuations aside, however, a stark definition of the thematic spine that supports all the Frankenstein films would be that they examine the outcomes, costs, and responsibilities of creating artificial beings or reanimating dead bodies. Yet even such a seemingly straightforward assertion raises a series of complex issues, the most fundamental being how to define "artificial" as it relates to traditionally accepted designations of the "natural," an ongoing debate discussed later in this chapter.

These elemental definitions of dramatic structure and thematic backbone raise additional problems, for example, conceptual elasticity. How far can they be stretched before snapping back to strike our faces—or breaking? Caroline Joan S. Picart, for example, directly connects reanimated to newly manufactured beings, thereby constructing a continuum from the nineteenth century into the twenty-first. Focusing on the evolutionary depictions of masculinity and femininity in what she calls the Frankenstein "cinemyth," she highlights parthenogenetic births and representations of "the feminine-as-monstrous" in the hybrid comic-horror genre, exploring the *Alien* and *Terminator* series and then probing humorous offshoots such as *The Rocky Horror Picture Show*.[1] Picart's amalgamation of mechanical and reanimated creations ignores the structural and thematic guidelines established above—where is the Frankenstein figure who constructs the monster out of dead tissue in the *Alien* series? Instead, we concentrate on movies that fall within the following three broad categories:

1. Transitions, featuring narratives about organisms that were never alive being given life, in purported adaptations of the novel and in comedies humorously incorporating Shelley's basic narrative
2. Translations, incorporating tales about hybrid creations and once-dead organisms brought back to life resulting in biological mutations, in films that do not use Shelley's characters or settings
3. Transformations, exploring artificially created beings in cyborg and robot movies, a logical evolution of Shelley's novel

Thus, rather than drowning in a sea of arguments about what constitutes a "true" Frankenstein movie, a delicate task best left to philosophers, theologians, and late-night discussions among English graduate students, we use the basic three-part structural definition and thematic spine (Frankenstein films examine the outcomes, costs, and responsibilities of creating artificial beings or reanimating dead bodies) to explore a range of films with straight and crooked links back to Shelley's novel. Understanding that individual films inevitably straddle multiple genres and may transgress organizational boundaries, this definition allows for the division of movies into three broad categories outlined above. Thus, the following lineup of representative movies is useful for discussions and placements within the Frankenstein family tree.

Transitions 1: Adaptations such as *Flesh for Frankenstein* (1973), *The Bride* (1985), and *Mary Shelley's Frankenstein* (1994).

Transitions 2: Comedies such as *Young Frankenstein* (1974), *The Rocky Horror Picture Show* (1975), *Igor* (2008), and *Frankenweenie* (2012).

Translations 1: Biological mutation movies such as *The Fly* (1958/1986), *Jurassic Park* (1993), *Species* (1995), *Godsend* (2004), and *Splice* (2009)

Translations 2: Reanimation films such as *Re-Animator* (1985), *Bride of Re-Animator* (1989), *Pet Sematary* (1989), and *The Lazarus Effect* (2015)

Transformations 1: Cyborg films such as *RoboCop* (1987)

Transformations 2: Robot movies such as *Blade Runner* (1982) and *A.I. Artificial Intelligence* (2001)

The representative films in each of these clusters prominently feature the intricate chemistry between creators and creations, animators and reanimations, scientists and their experiments, and normality and deviation—themes at the beating heart of the Frankenstein narrative.

The inclusion of the "transformations" category, incorporating movie cyborgs and robots, occasioned some lively disagreements between the coauthors. Were these new "monsters" legitimate heirs of Frankenstein's Creature or some alternate configuration that belonged in a different book? Although plots featuring cyborgs and robots do not necessarily incorporate the tripartite dramatic structure of most Frankenstein films outlined above, we agreed that the subject matter surrounding them affords new pathways to scrutinize issues that Shelley raises in the novel and that play a prominent role in the more traditional Frankenstein movies. Fundamentally, our difference of opinion revolved around considerations of how questions of artificial versus natural life in cyborg and robot dramas relate to Shelley's narrative. The novel clearly explores whether a sentient being constructed by using organic materials but circumventing the standard procreative process should be granted personhood status and thereby acknowledged as a member of the human race, with the moral considerations that designation implies. The cyborg films extend this inquiry to a being comprised of biological parts merged with nonnatural materials and subsequently granted life through technology. The robot films, however, turn the question upside down. They probe whether a totally artificial creation that imitates life—perhaps too perfectly—but is assembled using synthetic parts can be granted the same personhood status as an ordinary citizen. Put another way, and more specific to our project, are David (the robot child in *A.I.*), Murphy (the cyborg policeman in *RoboCop*), Frankenstein's Creature, and Victor himself all part of the same species, all afforded the same moral rights, and consequently should all be held to the same behavioral and ethical standards?

Such entangled issues led us to reflect about the manner by which a society defines the qualities necessarily to achieve personhood. In America's not so ancient history, for example, both minorities (sexual, ethnic, racial, religious) and women were legally denied rights customarily granted to citizens, and current abortion disputes often center around who determines the moment when a fetus should be granted the same legal status and protections as a child and whether those are more important than the protections granted the living woman bearing it. Cyborg and robot narratives compelled us to wonder: Should the standard definition of being human be based solely on what types of materials comprise a living body or rather on the means by which that body receives life? Alternatively, should considerations other than physical or intellectual, such as the capacity to display a range of emotions or to form personal attachments, be part of this designation? If so, what shared qualities and characteristics connect David, Murphy, the Creature, and Victor? After some deliberation, therefore, we decided to keep cyborgs and robots in this book, believing that the cultural anxieties and individual concerns they raise are germane to Shelley's work and the movies inspired by it. All these cyborg and robot films investigate what constitutes life, how emotions intersect with rationality, the price of gaining knowledge, and the responses to unmet expectations of being loved and accepted by individuals and society as a whole.

Transitions 1: Adaptations

In the late sixties, the breakdown of the aging Hollywood studio system that had dominated mainstream filmmaking around the world for decades left room for more independent productions, as the once-autonomous studios became mere divisions of large, multinational corporations. Concomitantly, the film industry's abandonment of the restrictive Motion Picture Production Code and its replacement in 1968 with the far more flexible Motion Picture Association of America ratings system liberated filmmakers to explore more mature subject matter and to intensify their graphic depictions of sex and violence. These director-driven movies reflected the profound cultural shift occurring throughout the country, as brutal images permeated citizens' daily lives: from the morning newspaper to the evening TV news, a barrage of increasingly violent pictures from the pro-tracted, bitter and divisive Vietnam War conditioned audiences to accept new levels of bloodshed, both on and off the screen. Within this chaotic era of artis-tic innovation, wretched excess, individual brilliance, and egotistical fiascos, horror movie directors quickly took full advantage of their emancipation from the Motion Picture Production Code to titillate viewers with sexual scenarios, inundate the screen with blood, and parade a plethora of slimy body organs for their audiences. This grisly escalation in explicit sex, violence, and carnage alienated older audiences, expanding a consumer demographic composed pri-marily of teenage boys that convinced moviemakers to include younger screen characters with whom this target audience could identify.

An outlandish illustration of the trend to exploit the new rating system is *Flesh for Frankenstein* (aka *Andy Warhol's Flesh for Frankenstein* and *Andy Warhol's Frankenstein*, 1973) written and directed by Paul Morrissey. Within its frames, a viewer watches acts of incest, voyeurism, male and female full frontal nudity, blood spurting from severed body parts, decapitation, rape, oral sex, explicit medical procedures, impaled bodies, exposed organs, hints of child molesta-tion, and enough dead bodies to rival a Tarantino movie. The height, or depth if you prefer, occurs when the frenzied Serbian Baron Frankenstein (Udo Kier) has sex with his newly created female zombie (Dalila Di Lazzaro), burrowing his hands deeply into her body and proudly proclaiming to his assistant, Otto (Arno Juerging), that "to know death, you have to fuck life in the gall bladder!" The baron, a fanatical eugenicist, desires to fashion "a new race responding only to his bidding," while his hypocritical sister/wife/ mother of his children (Monique van Vooren) indulges in a Lady Chatterlyesque affair with a horny local herds-men (Joe Dallesandro). Although the campy film has the saturated color of a Hammer production and the aristocratic setting of a Universal picture, neither Fisher nor Whale would recognize it, as Morrissey thrusts his movie's images over the threshold of seventies censorship. Even today, *Flesh for Frankenstein* still shocks viewers with its stomach-churning display of bloody organs and dismem-berments, not to mention taboo sexuality.

Expanding on a premise already developed in *Frankenstein Created Woman* and set during roughly the same time period, *The Bride* (1985) also takes advan-tage of the ongoing relaxation of censorship restrictions. Dr. Charles Franken-stein (Sting) creates a beautiful female mate, the aptly named Eva (Jennifer Beals), for his distorted Creature (Clancy Brown), whom he derisively labels "an abortion." But when Eva refuses to be his bride, the distraught Creature demol-ishes the laboratory and escapes into the surrounding countryside. Franken-stein, believing his Creature has perished along with his equipment, rescues Eva, but he decides not to reveal the reason and truth of her birth. Over time, the creator grows increasingly jealous and more possessive of his creation, par-

Benedict Cumberbatch (Frankenstein) and Jonny Lee Miller (the Creature) in the National Theatre's stage production of *Frankenstein* (2011).

ticularly after she develops a passionate fascination with the handsome Captain Schoden (Cary Elwes), who ultimately proves unworthy of her affections. Meantime, the isolated Creature finally forms a friendship with another outcast, the dwarf Rinaldo (David Rappaport), who christens him Viktor. At the end of the movie, a lust-driven Frankenstein becomes so fixated on sexually possessing Eva that he attempts to rape her, but Viktor arrives, literally on horseback, to rescue her, and in the ensuing fight between creator and creature, Frankenstein plummets from his laboratory's damaged roof to his death on the stones of the courtyard below. In the last scene, beauty and beast sail to Venice together, perhaps the most joyful ending the Creature experiences in all the Frankenstein movies.

Some productions, most TV miniseries, lay claim to the title of "authentic" productions by claiming to be merely visualizations of Shelley's novel, such as *Frankenstein: The True Story* (TV, 1973), *Kyofu densetsu: Kaiki! Furankenshutain* (TV-Animation, 1981), *Frankenstein* (TV, 1984), *Frankenstein* (TV, 1992), *Frankenstein* (TV, 2004), *Frankenstein* (TV, 2007). Victor Frankenstein (Harry Treadaway) emerges as an ongoing character in the HBO series *Penny Dreadful*, while *Victor Frankenstein*, told from the perspective of Igor (Daniel Radcliffe), traces the early life of the young scientist (James McAvoy), despite the fact that Frankenstein has no assistant in the novel. The National Theatre's stage production of *Frankenstein* (London, 2011), directed by Danny Boyle and starring Benedict Cumberbatch and Jonny Lee Miller (who traded the roles of Victor and his creation in alternate performances), was broadcast via satellite to over three hundred cinemas and around the world in 2011 and again in 2013. Finally, the director Guillermo del Toro, whose favorite book is *Frankenstein*, plans to film an adaptation of the novel (and a remake of *Bride of Frankenstein* as well) set during Shelley's era.

Mary Shelley's Frankenstein (1994), directed by Kenneth Branagh, remains the most widely known modern adaptation. This lavish production, with Branagh in the role of Victor Frankenstein and Robert De Niro as the Creature, features gigantic sets in exotic locations and begins with words taken directly from Mary Shelley's preface to the 1831 version of the novel: "I busied myself to think of a story which would speak to the mysterious fears of our nature and awaken thrilling horror, one to make the reader dread to look around, to curdle the blood and quicken the beatings of the heart." The film incorporates some of Shelley's characters and their stories rarely seen in adaptations—including Walton (Aidan Quinn), Justine (Tervyn McDowell), and the De Lacey family—along with images such as the tree blasted by lightning, as well as scenes from Victor's childhood in Geneva and his time in medical studies in Ingolstadt. Thus, Branagh imitates the novel's nesting structure, allowing the narrative focus to shift from Walton to Victor to the Creature, with detours to Elizabeth and Justine. More than any dedication to society's welfare, Victor's motivation is galvanized by the psychological devastation emanating from his mother's death after giving birth to his younger brother—not his future bride. He fully commits himself to eliminate this scourge forever, but the overpopulation of the planet if he is successful never occurs to him: his personal loss trumps any broader, communal considerations.

Branagh, like so many directors before him, understands the inherent visual possibilities in the Creature's emergence. He edits his extravagant birth scene with a series of quick cuts establishing a breakneck pace that, combined with an operatic score, reaches a visual level equal to the hysterical heights of Shelley's language. It begins with Victor's rejection of Elizabeth (Helena Bonham Carter) and Henry (Tom Hulce), followed by a bare-chested Frankenstein performing the acts necessary to bring his Creature to life. He hoists the carcass up on a slab, sends it flying across his laboratory, drops it into a tin birthing tank filled with collected amniotic fluid, and rolls the tank over flames to bring it to a boil, as if preparing an elaborate meal. He then punctures the marked energy points of the body with large needles, setting various dials humming, gears spinning, and lights flashing. From the ceiling, he lowers a pulsating balloon-like contraption, perhaps a representation of a womb, filled with electric eels that he dumps into the tank to harness even more electricity for his purposes. "Live! Live! Liiiivvve," he screams, jumping atop the tank and peering through the window. With unmitigated joy, he sees the Creature momentarily flick open his eyes, but then

Victor Frankenstein (Kenneth Branagh) brings his Creature (Robert De Niro) to life in *Mary Shelley's Frankenstein* (1994).

return to an inert and lifeless mass, a seemingly failed experiment. Walking away with the bitter taste of defeat nearly choking him, Frankenstein hears a dramatic noise that causes him to look back at his work: a hand knocks against the window of the tank, the reverberating sound causing Frankenstein to utter the now-famous phrase, "It's alive."

What follows is a slippery, homoerotic ballet between two men covered in gooey fluid, one trying to help the other stand and both slipping and sliding across the slimy floor. Finally, Victor ties up his creation with some chains, hoists him up to the ceiling, accidentally banging his head along the way, and leaves him hanging aloft, a misshapen being apparently dead. Branagh's camera starts with a high shot just below the feet of the sagging Creature and slowly zooms down to a close-up of the stunned and disgusted Frankenstein. "What have I done?" he asks, a question that should have been posed at the start, not the conclusion, of his experiment. He reaches down for his leather-bound notebook and writes that the new being has "massive birth defects . . . is malfunctional and pitiful and dead," adding that the journal containing his notes must be destroyed—forever. But, as we all know, the Creature is far from dead and will revenge himself upon Victor and his family. After the Creature rips out Elizabeth's heart and sets her hair ablaze, Victor attempts to stitch her badly scarred head onto the hanged Justine's body, but the newly amalgamated being commits suicide rather than live as a hideous outcast. Enraged, Frankenstein pursues his Creature into the frozen realms of the Arctic Circle to kill him, but dies in the attempt, and the Creature burns himself alive on the funeral pyre of his creator.

Branagh's Creature, like his literary predecessor, learns to read, talk, think, and "know the ways of man" voyeuristically by watching the cottagers in the woods, particularly the blind grandfather (Richard Briers). Indeed, a philosophical discussion reminiscent of those found in the novel occurs when Frankenstein and his Creature confront each other within a cave of ice. Here, the Creature raises some of Shelley's most important questions. Not only does he ask if Frankenstein thinks his creation has a soul, but he inquires whose bodies were conjoined to create him, wondering, for example, who provided him with the ability to play the flute. "Who am I?" he demands of his maker, his body literalizing the most basic question of individual human identity. Most importantly, the Creature has memories, claiming that his various skills are "remembered, not learned." Finally, the Creature raises the crucial role of ethical responsibility in scientific research. "Did you ever consider the consequences of your actions?" he asks a bewildered Victor. All these questions lead to his bold request for "a friend—a companion—a wife"; he vows that "the sympathy of one living being" will allow him to "make peace" and to travel north to where "no human eye would ever see them again." Victor will eventually attempt to fulfill this request, more for himself than for his Creature, but with disastrous results.

Branagh's film represents a struggle to cram as much of Mary Shelley's novel into a film as possible in 123 minutes. As such, it remains one of the most serious attempts to translate her literary creation to the screen, although the director could not resist adding his own elements to the already overstuffed plot. Yet, as seen in the chapter's next segment, the heightened emotions and hyperbolic characters present in the novel provide ample materials for comedy as well as tragedy. Broadly speaking, scholars have noted that comedies and tragedies both contain conflicts, but resolve them in different ways: comedies usually end with reconciliations and a reestablishment of social communities, whereas tragedies conclude with the death or destruction of the protagonist. Thus, comedies reaffirm an individual's role in communal life and tragedies the inability of characters to conform (or reunite) with those around them. Such a pattern is evident when comparing the dramatic adaptations of the novel with their comic counterparts.

Transitions 2: Comedies

Horror movies often incorporate various degrees and types of comic elements as a technique that momentarily modifies or lightens the viewer's response to the more gruesome events that dominate the film. Inserting humor into productions devoted to scaring or grossing out an audience allows them to function in the kind of "self conscious textual mode" that Philip Brophy christens "horrality."[2] It provides viewers with temporary relief from the onslaught of shock and gore, an "emotional release that can be wielded as effectively as a crucifix against a vampire."[3] As Stephen King observes: "They're very close, humor and horror. . . . They're the only two genres I know that cause an audience to make an audible reaction. . . . As far as I know the only difference is it starts being horror and stops being humor when it stops being somebody else and starts being you."[4] These moments of comedy in blood-soaked movies allow viewers to catch their breath before being bombarded with more carnage. Specifically regarding Frankenstein narratives, Picart's book *Remaking the Frankenstein Myth on Film: Between Laughter and Horror* deftly explores how "the Frankensteinian cinemyth" ranges in a continuum across horror and laughter and elicits a complex range of reactions "from fear, terror, and awe to laughter, ridicule, ironic sympathy, and distance."[5] In this section, however, we do not examine horror movies with humorous splinters wedged between their more scary segments; instead, we concentrate on variations of narratives that clearly announce themselves as comic interpretations of Shelley's basic story. Within the Frankenstein family tree, comedies like *Young Frankenstein* (1974), *The Rocky Horror Picture Show* (1975), *Igor* (2008), and *Frankenweenie* (2012) incorporate elements from Shelley, Whale, and Fisher that initially shocked or frightened earlier audiences as the basis for evoking laughter from viewers in subsequent decades. Such productions assume at least a passing familiarity with the arsenal of tropes and characters previously provided by Shelley's novel, as well as the Universal and Hammer cycles: the better one knows the originals, the funnier the parodies. Although primarily meant to evoke laughter, these comedies provide significant alternative interpretations of Shelley's story, emphasizing fundamental aspects of the Frankenstein narrative and offering new insights wrapped within congenial packages.

Film buffs and scholars alike usually accord Mel Brooks's *Young Frankenstein* (adapted into a Broadway musical in 2007) the top spot in any listing of horror film parodies and place it among the best movie parodies of all time. The American Movie Channel's online review christened it "the gold standard of cinematic spoofs" and concluded that "even three decades after its initial release, there's enough rapier wit and repeatable dialogue to redesign its cult of cleverness."[6] The movie ranks as number thirteen on the American Film Institute's list of the hundred funniest American films of all time. The unexpected box office success of *Young Frankenstein* (over $86,000,000 adjusted gross on a budget of $2,800,000) was primarily responsible for the spate of horror film parodies that followed, such as *Attack of the Killer Tomatoes* (1978), *Love at First Bite* (1979), *An American Werewolf in London* (1981), *The Monster Squad* (1987), *Killer Klowns from Outer Space* (1988), and later perhaps even *Shaun of the Dead* (2004).

Academic disagreements regarding how to define and classify comic replications of prior works include intricate distinctions among satires, spoofs, burlesques, lampoons, pastiches, caricatures, and more, but an exaggerated imitation of a previous film for comic effect, as exemplified in *Young Frankenstein*, fulfills any basic definition of a parody. Such humorous works function as a representative feature of our fragmented, self-reflexive postmodern life, as Linda Hutcheon claims:

> I think with postmodernism and the breaking of the fixed borders between popular culture and "high art" came the realization that parody was a popular mode of recovering the past (in this case, a past work) but at the same time making a different statement using it. Parody relies on our knowing the parodied text, right? So, using popular cultural examples as parodied works that are shared by many people, across cultures, even, is one way of making a work accessible, while at the same time challenging the audience to rethink that work and its ideological baggage.[7]

The manner in which *Young Frankenstein* jokes about various genre subjects continues a long-established technique in the cinema that stretches from the silent days to contemporary times. Such productions take the sting out of horror movies by robbing them of their power to traumatize, scare, or offend us.

Freud noted, for example, how "children create games around the very things they most fear as a way of subduing those fears and gaining control."[8] To laugh at something that once was frightening loosens its psychological grip on us; it allows our rational mind to triumph, at least temporarily, over the instinctual trepidations that lay beneath the level of conscious articulation. It also makes us feel rather gullible for originally being afraid of imaginary actions enacted on a screen and watched within the confines of a safe environment. Horror movies that once acted as a barometer to measure a particular era's fears can devolve into figures of fun. Spoofs such as the popular *Scary Movie* (1991–2013) franchise lampoon the horror film's easily recognized conventions, but they also pay homage to and express a continuing fascination with the essential components of this genre as well.

Young Frankenstein's director and (with Gene Wilder) cowriter, Mel Brooks, verifies Freud's observation as he recounts his frightened reaction upon first seeing Whale's *Frankenstein* as a young boy growing up in Brooklyn: "It terrified me and stayed with me. I think I made a comedy out of it, in a strange way, to exorcise it from my soul so I wouldn't worry about Frankenstein climbing up the fire escape and coming into my bedroom." (Brooks, of course, dreads the Creature sneaking into his bedroom, not a relatively more civilized Dr. Frankenstein.) Shooting the movie in black-and-white, as well as resurrecting the original laboratory, which its designer, Kenneth Strickfaden, had saved almost intact, Brooks explicitly "tried to stay with the look and feel and texture" of Whale's original movie and incorporated many of the by-now classic characters drawn from the previous iterations produced by Universal and Hammer and slumbering in film history's graveyard: Frankenstein's grandson Frederick (Gene Wilder), the huge monster (Peter Boyle), the lovely fiancée Elizabeth (Madeline Kahn), the wooden-armed police office Inspector Kemp (Kenneth Mars), the hunchbacked laboratory assistant Igor (Marty Feldman), the pretty ingénue Inga (Teri Garr), and the faithful housekeeper Frau Blücher (Cloris Leachman). To maintain the spirit of earlier versions, Brooks integrates early film transitional devices such as vertical and horizontal wipes, as well as in and out irises.[9]

Yet for all its old-fashioned mise-en-scène, *Young Frankenstein*'s characters have a decidedly modern consciousness of their roles within the Frankenstein legend; they mug for the camera, overact, and offer sly smirks of understanding that establish their knowing wit within a whimsical playground of nostalgic parody. Brooks twists his arsenal of Frankenstein motifs and conventions to invert the typical preoccupation with scientific hubris and shift elements from Whale and Fisher into an exploration of society's callous treatment of outsiders. In this film, the reasons society ostracizes the Monster become much more important than what the Monster does to alienate society. Brooks's comments regarding *Young Frankenstein* reveal his slant on materials borrowed from

Shelley and Whale. The film, he says, "deals with the ignorant vs. the intelligent, the mob vs. the intelligent people. The story of Dr. Frankenstein addresses itself to the fear quotient. The monster is symbolic of his mind, and the mob hates his mind. They hate his imagination."[10] Brooks's Creature desperately struggles to fit into society, even donning a white tie and tails to accompany his maker in a duet before the Bucharest Academy of Science, where he performs like a trained seal before ultimately regressing to his instinctual fear of fire. Reading the *Wall Street Journal* at the movie's conclusion, the domesticated monster eventually gains the social acceptance he so ardently craves, at the cost losing some of his animal sexuality and freedom.

In addition to altering the Creature drastically, *Young Frankenstein* also reverses the traditional view of Frankenstein as a dangerous, egotistical researcher, making him a far more supportive and finally a benevolent figure who risks his life to save his Creature. Throughout the early part of the film, Frederick struggles to escape his tainted ancestry. Pronouncing his name "Fron-ken-steen" rather than acknowledging his relation to the infamous Frankenstein lineage, he heatedly denies any affinity, either emotionally ("he was a kook") or intellectually ("his work was doo-doo") with his notorious grandfather, whom he physically resembles. Brooks presents this Frankenstein as dramatically different from his forebears, a compassionate and brilliant scientist thwarted by a prejudiced and superstitious mob bent on destroying what it cannot understand. More like Shelley's characters than Whale's, both Frankenstein and his creation become outsiders who have more in common with each other than with those who harass and fear them. In the early Universal films Frankenstein, the privileged aristocrat, ultimately reaffirms the prevailing social order by reestablishing a tender bond with Elizabeth; Brooks's Frankenstein identifies more with his creation than with the symbolic representatives of the traditional social order, ultimately rejecting the glacial Elizabeth for the sexually liberated Inga. By the film's ending, Frederick has reconciled himself to his familial heritage and proudly proclaims the direct linkage between himself and his progenitor: "My name is *Frank*-en-stine!"

Dominated stylistically by German Expressionistic techniques, the scene that most clearly displays Brook's perspective, as well as his innate understanding of Shelley's novel and the Frankenstein narrative, occurs when the doctor enters the cellar where the distraught Creature has been chained. Shelley's novel, as noted in earlier chapters, is a virtual meditation on bad parenting and the lack of scientific responsibility, as Victor pays a terrible price for his insufficient fatherly empathy and emotional understanding of his creation. In contrast to his counterpart on the page, Brooks's Frankenstein instinctively realizes that "love is the only thing that can save this poor Creature" and resolves to risk his life "to convince him that he is loved" despite the danger posed by such a strong

Frankenstein (Gene Wilder) as a father figure to his emotionally needy creation in Mel
Brooks's *Young Frankenstein* (1974).

potential adversary. Frederick abandons the detached scientific mode demonstrated by earlier incarnations, particularly in the Hammer series, and provides
his Creature with the acceptance and kinship necessary to soothe his battered
psyche. First, he confronts the Creature's physical appearance. "Hello, handsome!" he begins, a greeting that confuses the Creature. "You're a good-looking
fellow, do you know that?" he continues, to the Creature's amazement. "People
laugh at you. People hate you. But why do they hate you?" he asks and then
quickly answers: "Because they are jealous. Look at that boyish face. Look at that
sweet smile," he tells him. Next, he emphasizes the Creature's positive qualities:

"Do you want to talk about physical strength? Do you want to talk about sheer muscle? Do you want to talk about the Olympian ideal?" he proclaims, adding grandly, "You are a god." Finally, Frankenstein accentuates the Creature's self-worth and inherent morality: "You are not evil. You are good."

Such tender sentiments move the powerful Creature to moan aloud and burst into tears, to which Frankenstein literally responds with parental pride and affection: "This is a nice boy. This is a good boy. [*He caresses the Monster and rocks him tenderly back and forth.*] This is a mother's angel. And I want the world to know, once and for all and without any shame, that we love him." The Creature sobs as Frankenstein cradles him in his arms and kisses him gently on the head. Finally, he turns to their future together, how he will become a doting father, but simultaneously share his triumph with his offspring: "I'm going to teach you how to walk, how to speak, how to move, how to think. Together, you and I are going to make the greatest single contribution to science since the creation of fire!" The allusion to fire specifically recalls the Creature's initial fear and erratic relationship to this element from Shelley's novel onward. Accepting his fearful progeny frees Frankenstein to acknowledge his checkered heritage: it is immediately following this tearful scene that he pronounces his name in the traditional manner, acknowledging that he has repeated the actions of his grandfather—with some crucial differences.

Toward the end of the movie, Frankenstein and his Creature exchange more than just loving declarations: each sacrifices part of himself for the good, indeed for the actual survival, of the other. Frankenstein donates some of his brain to rescue his creation, and the postoperative, now-articulate being responds with affection: "For as long as I can remember, people have hated me. They looked at my face and my body and they ran away in horror. In my loneliness, I decided if I could not inspire love, which is my deepest hope, I would instead cause fear. I live because this poor, half-crazed genius has given me life. He alone held an image of me as something beautiful. And then, when it would have been easy enough to stay out of danger, he used his own body as a guinea pig to give me a calmer brain." Brooks comments: "This creator loves his creature so much that he risks his sanity and his life to help his brainchild survive."[11] In essence, Brooks transforms the heartless, cold, and calculating researcher we have seen in numerous versions into a devoted parent who delights in the accomplishments of his offspring's talent and intelligence. In exchange, he gains not only emotionally but even becomes an improved lover because the creature has donated part of his well-endowed sexual anatomy to his creator. Rather than remaining bitter antagonists, therefore, the maker and creation now share parts of each other, establishing an emotional, physical, and intellectual union that benefits both of them.

While *Young Frankenstein* pokes gentle fun at the collection of tropes and conventions that have become clichés—most derived from the Universal series—and developed into the standard narrative and iconographic foundations of the Frankenstein films, *The Rocky Horror Picture Show* augments many of these same elements with an onslaught of raucous humor and pounding music that assaulted mainstream America's hypocritical Puritanism. Based on Richard O'Brien's stage musical (which premiered in London on June 19, 1973) and destined to live on as a participatory cult classic, and directed by Jim Sharman, the film foregrounds the polymorphous sexuality emerging in the late sixties and continuing into the seventies, challenging conventional cultural mores. Its main character, Dr. Frank-N-Furter (Tim Curry), a bisexual transvestite from the planet Transsexual in the Transylvania galaxy, fashions a male toy boy, Rocky Horror (Peter Hinwood), for his own erotic pleasure. In the midst of his bizarre celebration to accompany the unveiling of his creation, including a rousing group performance of the "Time Warp" (again), two middle-class innocents, Brad Majors (Barry Bostwick) and Janet Weiss (Susan Sarandon), take shelter from the raging storm in his spooky castle, also home to his creepy collection of assistants: Riff Raff (Richard O'Brien), Magenta (Patricia Quinn), and Columbia (Nell Campbell). The young couple talk as if they just stepped out of a fifties Doris Day movie and dress like extras in an episode of *The Brady Bunch*, but both ultimately succumb to the doctor's sexual advances; Janet even abandons her frigid reserve ("Touch-a, Touch-a, Touch-a, Touch Me"), puts a semi-nude Rocky's hands on her breasts, and seduces "the Creature of the night" by telling him how much she "wants to be dirty," much to the amusement of the voyeuristic Magenta and Columbia.

The charismatic Frank-N-Furter, wearing a pink triangle on his green lab coat, brings his newest Creature to life not as an ugly misfit but rather as a muscular blond hunk. In an ironic reversal of the traditional Frankenstein narrative, the Creature takes one frightened look at his creator and flees, claiming that "the sword of Damocles" hangs over his head. Frank's song upon first glimpsing Rocky immediately aligns him with a God-like power, its lyrics proclaiming that "in just seven days / Oh, baby / I can make you a man." Unlike Shelley's and Whale's Frankenstein, this incarnation never aspires to achieve any grand scientific breakthrough or ascribes his motives to bettering the fragile condition of mankind. He is driven by passion, like his predecessors, but only for his own selfish gratification, and, while in the throes of his fervor, he forsakes his earthly mission for sexual indulgence: "Give yourself over to absolute pleasure / Swim in the warm waters of sins of the flesh / Erotic nightmares beyond any measure / And sensual daydreams to treasure forever / Can't you just see it? / Don't dream it—be it." Sadly for Frank-N-Furter, Rocky initially prefers Janet as a partner, an

"Just a sweet transvestite from Transexual, Transylvania": the gender-bending Dr. Frank-N-Furter (Tim Curry) in *The Rocky Horror Picture Show* (1975).

odd reinforcement of heterosexuality in an otherwise transgressive movie. Following Frank's death, a distraught Rocky hoists him on his back and climbs the RKO Radio Picture logo tower, in imitation of the famous *King Kong* scene on the Empire State Building, finally plummeting into the swimming pool—thus joining the lascivious doctor/creator in death.

The *Rocky Horror Picture Show*'s budget was only $1,200,000, but its lifetime gross ballooned to $112,892,319. During its heyday from the midseventies into the eighties, theaters across the country hosted midnight shows to the delight of costumed fans who came equipped with squirt guns, noisemakers, flashlights, and cards, knew the lyrics and the dialogue by heart, happily danced the "Time Warp" along with the film's characters, attended multiple showings, threw various objects (rice, newspapers, confetti, toilet paper, toast, etc.) at the screen, and shouted sarcastic commentaries at the action. ("The man's got no neck." "Think about it, asshole." "Don't ask Janet, she'll lie." "Take a Quaalude, bitch.") With its jumble of glam rock and drag costumes, horror film tropes, old movie references, and taboo sexual practices, not to mention a cannibalism scene, *The Rocky Horror Picture Show* amuses more than frightens. Other musical versions of the story, such as *Frankenstein—The Rock Opera* (2003), *Frankenstein—A New Musical* (2007), and the BBC's *Frankenstein's Wedding . . . Live in Leeds* (2011), stick closer to Shelley's narrative, but none approach *Rocky Horror*'s subversive battering of mainstream society's sexual duplicity. At its sybaritic climax, the formerly prim Brad and Janet meld into a balletic, hedonistic underwater orgy where male, female, and newly created bodies blissfully touch, kiss, and intermingle without shame, guilt, or gender distinctions. Although less shocking in today's world of Jerry Springer confessionalism and hard-core Internet porn than in 1975, the movie's critique of both excess and repression using the novel's fundamental narrative outline demonstrates both its adaptability and its elasticity.

Tim Burton's black-and-white, animated *Frankenweenie*, a 3D, stop-action, extended version of a short film he made in 1984, has an affectionate tone more akin to the nostalgic *Young Frankenstein* than to the rowdy *Rocky Horror Picture Show*. Burton fuses a basic boy-and-his-dog story with fundamental segments of the Frankenstein plot but reshapes the narrative with distinctive variations. Lonely young Victor Frankenstein (Charlie Tahan), an aspiring filmmaker and nascent scientist, only has one real companion: Sparky (Frank Welker), his friendly bull terrier, who is run over by a car as he chases after a baseball. After Victor's science teacher, Mr. Rzykruski (Martin Landau), ignites his curiosity by demonstrating how electricity can affect dead frogs, the clever boy resolves to use the same procedure to bring Sparky back to life. "Science is not good or bad," warns Mr. Rzykruski, "but it can be used in both ways," as the film—like all the other Frankenstein movies—aptly demonstrates. Following in the footsteps of his adult progenitors, this grade-school Frankenstein digs up Sparky (perhaps an allusion to the robotic dog Sparko, who joined Westinghouse's mechanical man at the 1939 New York's World Fair) from his grave, hooks him up to improvised laboratory instruments made mostly from household items, and harnesses lighting to resurrect him—with spectacular results and a characteristic Karloffian bolt plugged into his neck.

Victor decides to hide his newly reanimated pet from his parents (Martin Short and Catherine O'Hara) and, more essentially, safely conceal him from his nasty classmates: Edgar "E" Gore (Atticus Shaffer), Bob (Robert Capron), Toshiaki (James Hiroyuki Liao), and Nassor (Martin Short). Eventually, however, these scheming boys discover Victor's secret experiment and blackmail him into reviving their dead pets as well, but, unlike the faithful Sparky, these mutant reanimations develop into ferocious monsters bent on destroying the entire town of New Holland. While trying to save the somber Elsa Van Helsing (Winona Ryder), Victor gets trapped inside a fiery windmill, echoing the dramatic scene in Whale's *Frankenstein*. Sparky bravely drags him to safety, but the windmill collapses on the dog, killing him a second time. After witnessing his bravery, however, the grateful townspeople pool the electricity from their car batteries, reanimating Sparky again and uniting him not only with Victor but with Persephone (Dee Bradley Baker), Elsa's pet poodle: a spark from his neck bolt shocks her hair into the same beehive-with-side-lightning-bolts style worn by the Bride in Whale's second Frankenstein movie.

Visually, *Frankenweenie* pays homage to Whale's German Expressionistic style, particularly the distorted shapes of Burton's characters (like the bug-eyed Weird Girl and the hunchbacked Edgar Gore) and the tilted angles prevalent in Victor's attic and the pet cemetery. Yet the film's obvious deviations from prior Frankenstein narratives configure a totally different version of the scientist, his experiments, and his creations. Viewers thoroughly empathize with the young dreamer as he evolves from a shy introvert to a depressed survivor of his dog's death to a triumphant researcher to the town's hero. Rather than reject his re-creation, his "monster," Victor rejoices in having his lovable playmate back in his life, despite the fact that he sometimes runs low on power and must be recharged. Burton updates those torch-wielding townspeople from earlier movies into the narrow-minded citizens of a bland suburbia, governed by an intolerant adult villain haunting the piece, Mayor Burgemeister (Martin Short). The director's offbeat sense of humor and thorough understanding of horror movies saturate *Frankenweenie*. The Van Helsings, who live next door to the Frankensteins, allude to the hero of the Dracula movies, and Victor's parents actually watch a production of *Dracula* on TV. Toshiaki's mutant turtle, Shelley, refers, of course, to Mary Wollstonecraft Shelley, and it rampages through the town like a crazed Godzilla. The other transformed pets also parody famous horror film monsters, including the Mummy, the Invisible Man, the Fly, the Wolf Man, and the Creature from the Black Lagoon.

Burton radically shifts the familiar narrative so that the Creature need not seek revenge on—or destroy—his creator, for Victor loves and totally accepts his reanimated hound. Sparky, unlike previous Creatures, never embarks on a murderous rampage; the other revived pets eventually do so, but without any of the social rejection that motivated Shelley's Creature to attack innocent victims. *Frankenweenie*, then, is fundamentally about love, particularly the powerful bond between Victor and Sparky, rather than being a tale of hatred, murder, and revenge. The grief-stricken boy engages in scientific experimentation to bring back his friend, not because of hubris, a desire to make a giant contribution to research, or the compulsion to do something positive for humanity. "I just wanted my dog back," he tells his frightened parents. But, much like his adult predecessors, Victor never considers the consequences of his actions, and tragedies do result. Most importantly, Burton shifts the ending's tone. By having the once-frightened townspeople accept the pieced-together Sparky, the film strikes a far more optimistic and positive note than most of the other Frankenstein narratives.

Igor, another animated production, cannibalizes the formula in a very different way, telling the tale of a brave and smart hunchback (John Cusack) condemned to life as a slave because of his physical deformity. Ruled by the evil King Malbert (Jay Leno) and populated by equally nefarious scientists who routinely abuse their assistants, all called Igors and all having humps, the once sunny and prosperous kingdom of Malaria now languishes under the tyranny of greedy men who control the weather. Left alone after his master, Dr. Glickenstein (John Cleese), dies testing his experimental rocket, this clever Igor constructs a giant woman, Eva (Molly Shannon), with a misshapen head and asymmetrical appendages. Because she enjoys singing, Igor convinces Eva to audition for the musical *Annie* (later, she does sing "Tomorrow," as in when the sun will come out), when in reality he wants to display her to win first place at the prestigious Evil Science Fair. Ultimately, Igor's previous creations—the sarcastic rabbit Scamper (Steve Buscemi) and the Brain (Sean Hayes) that exists within a life-support jar attached to a mechanical body—join his quest, save his life, befriend Eva, help restore their land's sunshine and thriving economy, and finally allow Igor to become its benevolent king.

Although some elements of *Igor* mimic parts of the Frankenstein narrative, its director, Anthony Leondis, alters the focus of earlier works by including significant differences, particularly that Igor falls in love with his creation, risks his life to rescue her, and becomes one half of a couple at the film's conclusion, similar to Elizabeth and the Creature in *Young Frankenstein*. The film also spotlights the bigotry faced by people with physical disabilities. All the Igors suffer segregation and discrimination because of their abnormal bodies; they are never allowed to rise above their assigned socioeconomic status, remaining a permanent underclass within this world. (Curiously, other figures in the movie, such as Dr. Glickenstein, possess equally irregular bodies but face no similar social prejudice.) Igor's motivation for creating Eva, like Victor's, is personal glory; he wants to be recognized as more than a hunchbacked and subservient assistant. Leondis also parodies the blind man in the hut sequences in *Bride of Frankenstein* when Eva dances with a group of blind orphans, the soundtrack ironically proclaiming "I Can See Clearly Now." Most crucially, the film incorporates the unruly nature displayed by characters in most Frankenstein films by showing Igor rebelling against his society's bigoted norms and its unjust denial of human rights to people with disabilities.

Taken as a whole, these representative comedies, as expected, soften the rougher edges of the Frankenstein narrative by emphasizing love, compassion, and acceptance. The makers of the two animated films anticipated that children would comprise a major part of their audience, and, although they offer enough in-jokes to keep adults attentive, they never offer violent shocks that might traumatize their younger viewers. In *Young Frankenstein* and *Rocky Horror*, bawdy humor and rock music replace the bloodshed and butchery that become ever more prominent as the Frankenstein narrative evolves over the decades. All of the comedies reconfigure the stature and function of the scientist, depriving him of any grandiose justifications and supplanting these rationalizations with private needs for love, companionship, and sexual gratification. Similarly, the monsters have changed as well. None of the newly created or reanimated creatures threaten social mayhem or familial destruction, and their creators never fear that they or their loved ones will be murdered in their sleep. If anything, the symbiosis between creator and creation is even stronger in these movies than in the more serious Frankenstein productions, ranging from parental devotion to love to lust. Each of the comedies presupposes a familiarity with the Universal films, more than with Shelley's novel, and incorporates familiar characters and stylistic flourishes inspired by these earlier movies. Comedies, however, should not be undervalued and dismissed as superficial fantasies. They can offer acute observations about society and, at the very least, illustrate some of the continuing alterations within the evolution of Shelley's narrative. As such, they comprise a noteworthy branch of the Frankenstein family free.

Translations 1: Biological Mutations

Every film in the Frankenstein family incorporates some type of organic anomaly. That acknowledged, two familiar elements bind together the following ten representative films divided into two subcategories: biological mutations and reanimations. The first component is a scientist who becomes obsessed with an audacious research project that falls outside the traditional boundaries of scientific investigation, and the second is that events occur within reasonable extensions of recognizable settings and everyday realities. None of these movies contain direct references to Shelley's characters, but they all fit comfortably within this cluster of films that features bodily alterations, distinctive creations, and destructive reanimations. These Frankenstein descendants do not live in earlier centuries, dwell in exotic foreign locations, or conduct experiments in secluded laboratories atop mountains or deep within gloomy castles; instead, they reside in contemporary times and work in realistic environments that audiences can readily identify as part of their world. They could easily be our neighbors, and that fact makes them even scarier. Like many other horror and science fiction movies, these Frankensteinian productions begin with a seemingly logical set of circumstances that could plausibly take place and then push events into the speculative realms of "what if" or "what might happen."

Frankenstein films including biological mutations graphically illustrate how the unstable marriage of science and technology can result in creations that overwhelm and finally devour their creators, as the outcomes of their experimentation predictably become unmanageable monsters. In these movies, the most brilliant stars among the galaxy of research scientists, those audacious voyagers who chart the mysterious unknown, possess a prodigious amount of potent knowledge and consequently develop into dangerous renegades because they exempt themselves and their projects from any conventional code of morality, as did Victor. While their revolutionary procedures could potentially enhance human life, their blind intoxication with pioneering experiments inevitably results in callous and selfish actions that jeopardize the security and welfare of the entire community. These movies, therefore, function as manifestations of an anti-intellectual bent of mind that distrusts scientific experimentation, particularly secular endeavors that challenge religious authorities' zeal to determine the proper scope of research and subject it to their sometimes quite narrow moral standards. The cultural anthropologist Christopher Toumey, among others, contends that this kind of narrative "reveals a visceral fear of science" and that fictional mad scientists have increasingly been depicted as depraved and amoral.[12] Films in these two subcategories recommend that, at the very least, some level of institutional authority is required to keep such endeavors within ethical boundaries and responsible to professional oversight—as does Mary Shelley in her novel.

Jurassic Park (1993), based on Michael Crichton's novel (1990) optioned by the director Steven Spielberg before the author even finished writing it, follows the tripartite structure of Shelley's narrative, replays some of the warnings commonly associated with *Frankenstein*, and substitutes newly minted dinosaurs for

Victor's Creature. John Hammond (Richard Attenborough), a wealthy entrepreneur, falls within a long tradition of literary and cinematic Frankenstein figures who tamper with the natural world only to reap dire consequences. Hammond disrupts the endless cycle of creation and destruction, of survival and extinction, best left to natural selection, species evolution, or pure chance. His reasons, like Victor's, are complex and, at times, even contradictory. Driven by obsession, pride, and greed, Hammond hatches disaster by endeavoring to reconfigure the brutality of the wild into an entertaining amusement park ride, which is almost ready to open when the movie begins—an arrogant and ultimately unsuccessful attempt to domesticate violent natural instincts and turn ferocious animals from past eras into tourist attractions for the modern family. He has spared no expense, he constantly assures everyone, and after an employee is killed by a velociraptor he purchases the expert services of a paleontologist, Dr. Grant (Sam Neill), and a paleobotanist, Dr. Sattler (Laura Dern), to assuage the fears of his nervous investors. Despite his avuncular appearance and concern for his grandchildren, Lex (Ariana Richards) and Tim (Joseph Mazzello)—his park's "target audience"—the industrialist willingly allows them to venture into the jungle, even after the employee's grisly death. Though the potential for danger is clearly evident, Hammond risks turning his grandchildren into palate cleansers for financial reasons and commercial expediency. Thus, Hammond—and the corporate mentality he embodies—becomes an irresponsible and ultimately dangerous figure, despite his considerably appealing personal qualities.

At crucial times, Hammond offers reasons other than monetary gain for his obsession with creating this vast and ingenious attraction. His first explanation comes during a lunchtime debate and undergirds defenses of scientific investigation stretching from Galileo to Darwin to the Human Genome Project. Countering Dr. Malcolm's (Jeff Goldblum) insistent charges of scientific egotism, lack of responsibility, and crass commercialism—of being so preoccupied with seeing if something *could* be done that no one bothered to ask if it *should* be done—an exasperated Hammond justifies his actions by citing the need for human progress: "How can we stand in the light of discovery and not act?" he demands. Not surprisingly, the cynical chaos theorist Malcolm rejects this reasoning, calling discovery a "violent, penetrative act . . . the rape of the natural world." Later, after the dinosaurs escape, Hammond reveals a more personal reason to Sattler. The first attraction he built was a flea circus in Petticoat Lane, a deception based on persuading customers to see something that did not exist. In his prehistoric theme park, however, he "wanted to show them something that wasn't an illusion, something that was real, something they could see and touch." He aspired, in explicitly Frankensteinian terms, to bring something back to life that once was extinct, to take the past and turn it into the present as Victor wanted to turn death into life. Yet whereas Victor stands as an isolated and aberrational figure within his societal surroundings, a solitary scientist trapped in a neurotic and lethal cycle, John Hammond represents even more of a social danger: a multinational corporate perspective funded by untold wealth that values increased profits over communal safety and moral responsibilities.

In a particularly crucial scene, Hammond and Sattler meet in the park's cafeteria as chaos engulfs the outside world. Spielberg starts this sequence by panning over the numerous dino-items for sale in the visitors center and ending with a shot of Hammond eating melting ice cream, a perishable treat representing his crumbling theme park. With such a visual linking, Spielberg explicitly ties Hammond to the park's strident commercialism so that, while he intimately shares his past with Sattler, we never lose sight of his materialistic objective. As previously noted, Hammond started his career as a huckster, a fraud, and a creator of illusions. Yet as he sits in the ruins of his consumable playground, this voracious industrialist fails to comprehend what has transpired—and more importantly why. He never takes personal responsibility for the catastrophes caused by his creation of Jurassic Park and its rupture of natural progression. When Hammond prattles on with almost maniacal desperation about how things will be flawless next time, how overdependence on automation was his major mistake, and how "creation is an act of sheer will," Sattler brusquely interrupts him and insists he grasp what he should now understand but sadly fails to comprehend: "You never have control; that's the illusion." Ultimately, Sattler joins him in eating the liquefying ice cream. To her comment that the ice cream is good, Hammond can only add his once-jaunty tag line, now a barren capitalistic slogan, "Spared no expense."

Hammond's dual nature is symbolized by his cane. On the one hand, it highlights his frailty, his need to lean on something sturdy to travel from one place to another. Metaphorically, it represents his scientific endeavors; in Malcolm's words, "You stood on the shoulders of geniuses to accomplish something as fast as you could, and before you even knew what you had, you patented it, and packaged it, and slapped it on a plastic lunch box, and now you're selling it." Most crucially its head, a prehistoric mosquito sealed in tree sap and encased in glass, visually encapsulates his hubristic endeavor: attempting to trap nature and the awesome power of genetics in a seemingly innocuous commercial project designed exclusively for the pleasure and use of mankind. (In 2015 scientists found three well-preserved, amber-encased insects some 230 million years old, from the Triassic Period.) But objects meant to support can break, and those designed for their beauty can be used as weapons—sometimes even against those who create and trademark them. Hammond remains guilty of severely underestimating the power he unleashes and, like his nineteenth-century forebear, of not considering the consequences of his actions, both to his immediate family and to the intricate social system that forms the world around

Ian Malcolm (Jeff Goldblum), John Hammond (Richard Attenborough), Ellie Sattler (Laura Dern), and Alan Grant (Sam Neill) watch the birth of baby dinosaurs—Frankensaurs—in *Jurassic Park* (1993).

him. Although Victor's scientific obsession brings death to innocent victims, John Hammond's presumptuousness, backed by huge corporate resources, can reach devastating proportions far beyond a relatively small circle of family and friends. *Jurassic Park* never posits scientific and technological developments as intrinsically evil but fears the motivations of those who bankroll it. In doing so, it demonstrates how corporate avarice can pose a menace far beyond the capabilities of a single human being, even if that lone researcher is Victor Frankenstein.

Jurassic Park, like so many of the other Frankenstein films, ultimately presents an ambiguous attitude that both celebrates and castigates technological progress. Although the park's human inhabitants become prey hunted by the products of science and technology (the dinosaurs), they can only be saved by Lex's knowledge of computer programming and a helicopter that whisks them off the island. Hammond and his researchers develop an idealized reconfiguration of the natural world and its inhabitants, a tranquil dream of scientific rationalism and technological domination that becomes a nightmare when the dinosaurs display unruly instinctual behavior. Jurassic Park is Sea World writ large and, as such, represents a human projection of how things ought to be, not how they are: performing orcas in tiny pools, rather than pods hunting free in the ocean. Its creators never take into account nature's erratic inconsistency, exemplified by the freak storm that attacks the island. In Hammond's circumscribed view of "the wild," animals can kill each other only in prescribed and systematic ways monitored by technocrats. As a result, Jurassic Park represents a human attempt to impose mechanical predictability upon natural uncertainty via technological inventiveness. The irony resting at the heart of *Jurassic Park* and every other work inspired by *Frankenstein* is that scientific advancements and technological developments, which purport to be rational and orderly endeavors, repeatedly bring forth results as unpredictable and chaotic as the wildest natural environment.

In *Godsend* Dr. Richard Wells (Robert De Niro), a seemingly benevolent genetic researcher much like John Hammond, offers a bereaved couple, Paul (Greg Kinnear) and Jessie (Rebecca Romijn-Stamos) Duncan, an opportunity to clone their dead eight-year-old son through an illegal regeneration process secretly accomplished at the Godsend Fertility Clinic (visit their website at http://www.godsendinstitute.org). All appears relatively normal until the new boy, Adam (Cameron Bright), reaches his eighth birthday, when his personality drastically changes due to a series of terrifying flashbacks, nightmares, and strange visions. Ultimately, Paul discovers Wells's disturbing secret: he has mingled DNA from his own dead son, a profoundly troubled youth named Zachary who murdered his mother and set his school on fire, with Adam's in an attempt to clone and presumably improve his own child rather than the Duncans' boy. Paul and Jessie, along with Adam, move far away from the clinic, hoping that distancing themselves from Dr. Wells will save their son, but the film's final frames reveal that Zachary, not Adam, has survived. In *Godsend*, the mutation is not physical, for the resulting child is outwardly ordinary, but a dramatic psychological alteration, an internal manifestation of evil wrought by a scientist whose private obsession endangers society and continues at the movie's conclusion.

Godsend remains one of the few braches of the Frankenstein family tree that features a female character giving birth in the traditional manner, as opposed to a scientist piecing an artificial being together in a laboratory or reanimating a corpse. Traditionally, the being that results from radical scientific experimentation emerges as a disfigured "monster" feared and shunned by ordinary people, an alienated Creature who lives on the fringes of mainstream society deprived of human affection and denied love. *Godsend*, however, situates Adam/Zackary right in the center of an affectionate family unit as a beloved only child, shifting the horror from close to home to right inside it. The dramatic strategy of making an innocent and attractive child the perpetrator of evil makes it harder both for the other characters to recognize these dangerous traits and for the viewer to accept that someone with such a lovely exterior harbors murderous intentions. Once that understanding occurs, however, the harsh disjunction between exterior beauty and interior evil makes the deeds even more disturbing because they transpire in a world similar to our own and among people who resemble us: "It is the human, the facade of the normal, that tends to become the place of terror within postmodern Gothic."[13] Although not a particularly outstanding example of visual artistry, *Godsend* cleverly embeds two particularly resonant visual images in domestic spaces: a horizontal figure eight on a birthday cake that mimics the sign for infinity and a spiral staircase in the Duncan house that resembles the double helix.

Assisted reproductive technologies (ART)—such as artificial insemination, surrogates, gamete intrafallopian transfer, donor eggs, in vitro fertilization, frozen embryo transfer, and fertility treatments—have become common medical practices; as a result, the emergence of what some label as "synthetic children" no longer qualifies as science fiction. But *Godsend*, like the various Frankenstein narratives, cautions against allowing scientists to intrude into the natural process of reproduction, warning that transgressions of moral boundaries can result in personal tragedies. From the birth in 1978 of Louise Brown, the world's first "test tube baby," a spirited public debate has raged around the moral implications of assisted reproduction and the rights of infertile couples to seek out such procedures, with the label "Frankensteinian" often attached to describe the newest advances in the field. As the sociologist Michael Mulkay argues, "Frankenstein's dream of systematic, science-based control over the creation of human beings can be seen as having become a reality in the modern fertility clinic"; he goes on, prefacing his discussion of the 1984–1990 public debate in Britain about research on human embryos, to assert that "narrative structures available in the mad scientist genre will be used regularly in the course of public debate concerning new, science-based technologies," shoving fictional representations like *Frankenstein* into policy disputes.[14]

Like *Godsend*, *Splice* focuses on the creation of new forms of life, but it extends the process far further in a narrative arc reminiscent of how the female monsters in the more current *Species* series (1995, 1998, 2004) result from mixing human with nonhuman (in this case alien) DNA. It opens with a deceptively familiar scene. The director, Vincent Natali, plunges the viewer into what seems like a conventional hospital birth. "OK. OK. I can see him," says an unseen man, while the soundtrack relays the steady, recognizable, comforting beeping of a normal EKG. "That's it. Here he comes," continues the calm voice. The screen image clears, displaying a man and woman gowned in scrubs, their surgical mask exposing only their eyes. "All right. I got him. I got him," the man continues. The vitals are checked, and they are stable; the man severs the umbilical cord. Panic ensues a moment later when the patient's BP starts dropping fast and respirations become slow, shallow, and irregular. "He's in V-tach!" The EKG registers a flat line, and the woman quickly administers a dopamine injection. "Clear!" Cardioversion brings the abnormal heart rhythm back to normal. "Heart rate stable," says a relieved female voice, adding, "He's perfect." The doctors, now behaving like parents, enter the incubation room, discuss names, and take pictures of the new arrival. "He's so cute," says the woman. But the organism finally uncovered looks far from cute; in fact, it resembles nothing identifiable, nothing anyone has ever seen before this moment. The doctors/parents now reveal that it is, indeed, a new species, a hybrid formed from the combined DNA of various animal groups.

Splice merges elements from both *Frankenstein* and *Jurassic Park*, tossing gender bending and sexual taboos into the amalgamation as well. Updating *Frankenstein*, two brilliant biochemists—contemporary versions of the mad scientist—generate a new being that runs rampant. As in *Jurassic Park*, a greedy multinational company, Newstead (the name of Byron's childhood home) Pharmaceuticals—a far more malevolent corporate entity than John Hammond's InGen—puts its profit margin ahead of society's well-being. The film's irresponsible researchers, Clive (Adrien Brody—invoking *Frankenstein*'s Colin Clive) and Elsa (Sarah Polley—recalling *Bride of Frankenstein*'s Elsa Lanchester), even utter Frankenstein's famous words when first setting eyes on Dren (Delphine Chaneac), their creation: "It's alive." Clive and Elsa hope to revolutionize medicine by virtue of their experiments, addressing genetically influenced diseases, but they ardently desire scientific glory as well. Instead, they create a lethal monster with the face of a lovely and hairless woman, powerful springy legs that resemble an animal's, a whip-like tail complete with a deadly stinger, and wings.

Clive and Elsa, like Victor Frankenstein, attempt to keep their illegal experiment secret by isolating Dren and ultimately locking her away from prying eyes—and conventional ethical codes imposed by institutional oversight. Over time, the pair become more parents than scientists, alternatively caring for and attempting to destroy their creation when they become unable to control her. Near the end of the film, Clive discovers that Elsa used her own DNA in their experiment, so Dren is her daughter; nevertheless, he responds to Dren's seduction and becomes her lover—despite the incestuous implications of sex with, essentially, his stepdaughter. Dren changes gender, however—an unintended consequence of the experiment—and kills Clive, then rapes and impregnates Elsa, who resolves to have their offspring with the clandestine financial backing of Newstead, which hopes to reap huge profits from research conducted on it. Again, these biological connections and gender reformulations challenge social taboos: Dren, as a female, is partly Elsa's daughter, but as a male, still containing Elsa's DNA, he/she impregnates his/her "mother," so the child will result from the union of daughter/son and mother. As Kimberly Jackson notes, the sexual scene between them seems wrong on so many levels, "incestuous, bestial, and pedophilic all at once," a violation of "the most primal of taboos."[15]

Frankenstein and *Jurassic Park* conclude by restoring the traditional social order and providing audiences with a sense of security, but *Splice* ends with the frightening promise of an evolutionary nightmare: the human race—or more accurately the posthuman race—radically and irrevocably altered. As a hybrid brought to life outside the womb and containing both human and animal parts, Dren, like most of the Frankenstein Creatures, raises complex definitional and personhood issues. The fact that she/he appears alternately sympathetic, lovable, dangerous, and deadly compounds these problems, not to mention uncomfortable gender confusion when the physical metamorphosis transpires. Clive and Elsa seem unsure how to respond to Dren. Initially, Elsa treats her like a child, teaching her to speak and cuddling with her, while Clive increasingly feels they have made a terrible mistake by letting her live, at one point even attempting to drown their creation. Later, however, he finds her sexually attractive with deadly consequences. *Splice*, like *Godsend*, takes Mary Shelley's concepts further than she could ever have imagined in the nineteenth century, depicting a brave new world of designer organisms and hybrid procreation that would make 100 percent human beings obsolete and over time perhaps even extinct.

A final representative film of the biological mutations branch of the Frankenstein family tree is the most recent iteration of *The Fly* (1986), David Cronenberg's remake of the 1958 film that starred Vincent Price and was directed by Kurt Neumann. Its crucial shift in the evolution of the Frankenstein narrative fuses the creator and the creation, the scientist and the product of his experiments. Seth Brundle (Jeff Goldblum), like his predecessor Victor Frankenstein, emerges as an inspired, quirky genius bent on an obsessive quest that finally destroys him. He invents teleporter pods ("telepods") that can move matter across space, but the items must be totally fragmented into pieces at the starting point and reconstructed at their final destination. As the movie opens, he can only transfer inorganic items from one place to another and struggles to achieve his ultimate objective: a method to transport human beings over larger spaces. Brundle reveals his invention to Veronica Quaife (Geena Davis), a feisty reporter who immediately recognizes its immense potential and becomes involved with his mission to upgrade the telepods for human use. Eventually, they become lovers, and she gets pregnant, a fact she initially hides from Seth.

Brundle's first attempt to transport a living creature, a baboon, ends in tragedy, as the animal reappears in the reception pod inside out. His second attempt, with another baboon, proves more successful, but Brundle, mistakenly believing that Veronica has returned to her previous lover (John Getz), decides to transport himself. Unfortunately, and unknown to the inventor, a housefly gets trapped with him in the first pod, and the two become molecularly spliced together into a single creature, later called the Brundlefly. Although Seth's transportation seems initially successful, he slowly begins to exhibit unmistakable characteristics of a fly, a horrifying process videotaped by Veronica that transforms him from human being into insect. Every day parts of his body fall off—he stores them in the Brundle Museum of Natural History—as he becomes increasingly fly-like: spewing out digestive enzymes, climbing the walls, and realizing that primitive instincts are overcoming his human intelligence. He comes to believe that his only salvation lies in using the pods to fuse himself with Veronica, along with her fetus, but his attempt at this union goes dreadfully awry, leaving him an even more hideous hybrid of human, fly, and now machinery as well. Finally, Seth begs Veronica to kill him, and she reluctantly does so with a shotgun. But what about the baby: a human being, a fly, a mutant, or another species entirely?

Unlike the other films in this section, *The Fly* confronts the frightening proposition of losing control over one's own body and being converted, against one's will and despite one's strongest efforts, into an unrecognizable mutation of one's original self. Here the monster is not a designed new species, a revived ancient animal, or a cloned child. Rather, the ravaged body of the creator results from his own technological endeavors, not an attempt to bring dead matter to life. The protracted colonization of Seth Brundle's body functions as a potent metaphor for losing control of our bodily functions due to disfiguring diseases, accidents, or disasters—events that occur beyond the physical and rational control of the person to whom they happen. Upon its initial release, many critics interpreted *The Fly* as an expression of the growing social alarm about the AIDS epidemic spreading across the country, but today it registers more broadly as the dread of any set of symptoms attacking, taking over, and transforming the body despite our best attempts at prevention and treatment. Like Dren in *Splice*, the Brundlefly is an interspecies hybrid, and both emerge as a one-of-a-kind type with no comparable life forms. But Dren's existence results from a planned birth, while the Brundlefly appears as the unintended outcome of an inadvertent catastrophe, an accidental result rather an anticipated product of intense research, experimentation, and development.

All Frankenstein films explore the interface between human beings and technology. Given the inspiration of Shelley's novel, most also issue dire warnings about products generated by scientific research and technological innovations that beget social changes ranging from slight to transformative. The films in the biological mutations subdivision share a fascination with bodily manipulations, both internal and external, and what society labels as the malformations that result from human intervention into natural processes—most often birth. Indeed, most horror/monster movies contain a disfigured being at their center that defies traditional definitions of human. Sometimes, as in *Godsend*, the manifestation of pathology hides beneath a seemingly normal exterior, whereas in other films, like *The Fly*, *Jurassic Park*, and *Splice*, it exists in plain sight. But predatory impulses usually lurk within these engendered beings. The juxtaposition of what is known and what is unknown, what is rational and what is irrational, what is seen and what is unseen, forces viewers of these films to share the restrictive point of view of the potential victims of the engineered creature. Often, as in Shelley's novel, this living thing conceived and forged in a laboratory is larger and more powerful than the common folk it threatens, thus increasing our sense of vulnerability; we become children in need of a protecting parent, a brave hero, to escape and survive. Such manufactured creations, according to Elaine Graham, blur the fragile boundaries between humans and almost-humans, challenging "the demarcations by which cultures have separated nature from artifice, human from non-human, normal from pathological."[16]

Translations 2: Reanimations

The *Re-Animator* trilogy of splatter films pays homage to previous Frankenstein movies, with *Bride of Re-Animator* directly alluding to Universal's *Bride of Frankenstein* (creating a woman) and *Beyond Re-Animator* to Hammer's *Frankenstein Created Woman* (transplanting souls). The first film in the series, which became a cult favorite and won a Critics Prize at the Cannes Film Festival, is loosely based on the six-part serialized (September 1921–June 1922) novella called *Herbert West—Reanimator* written by H. P. Lovecraft. Directed by Stuart Gordon, this darkly comic narrative begins in the Zurich Institute of Medicine laboratory, where the police break into the laboratory of Dr. Hans Gruber (Al Berry) and discover has metamorphosed into a bug-eyed monster who drops dead in front of them. When questioned, Herbert West (Jeffrey Combs), Gruber's medical student assistant, replies that he did not kill the professor but rather "gave him life." Cut to Miskatonic University in New England, where the newly arrived West rents a room from another medical student, Dan Cain (Bruce Abbott), who is secretly romancing Megan Halsey (Barbara Crampton), the daughter of the medical school's Dean Halsey (Robert Sampson). She has also become the object of lust for Dr. Carl Hill (David Gale), a brain surgeon with an uncanny resemblance to Karloff's monster. West quickly turns the basement into a makeshift laboratory to continue his reanimation experiments, injecting his glowing green "reagent" into the dead household cat, Rufus, and enlisting Dan as a co-investigator. The revived Rufus's violent attacks and scrambled remains fail to discourage West, and, even after being dismissed from the school, he continues resurrecting dead beings. He and Dan slink into the morgue to test the reagent on cadavers, but the reanimated zombies (Lovecraft's story was one of the first in which zombies appeared) turn on their "saviors" and murder Dr. Halsey, who inadvertently interrupts the illicit experiment. West injects Halsey with reagent, and he turns into a catatonic zombie; during all this chaos, Hill seizes control of the medical school, lobotomizes Halsey, and then attempts to blackmail West

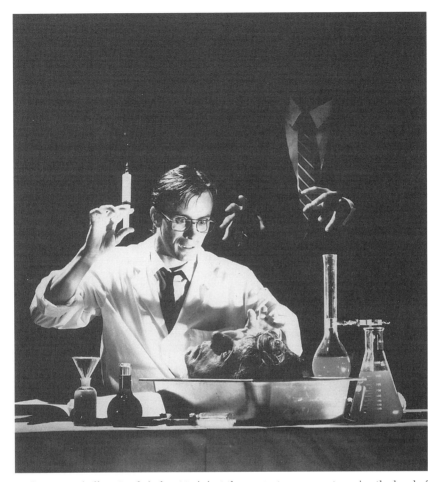

Herbert West (Jeffrey Combs) about to inject the reagent necessary to revive the head of Dr. Carl Hill (David Gale) in *Re-Animator* (1985).

in order to steal his research. In response, West decapitates him with a shovel and injects both the severed head and the headless body with the serum. Hill's mind now compels his torso to do its will, including the detached head's weird sexual assault of Megan and a reanimation of several corpses in the morgue. In the ensuing battle between living and reanimated beings, Halsey destroys Hill's head but is killed by the zombies, as is Megan. In a desperate attempt to save her, Dan injects her corpse with the reagent, and, as the movie ends, the sound of Megan's anguished scream punctures the final dark frames.

Rick Worland, who believes that *Re-Animator* encapsulates "a century of horror tradition," speculates that the film's successful mix of medical horrors, sexual titillation and absurdist comedy results from its manner of "synthesizing stylistic and thematic strains of classic and contemporary horror while hewing to the principle of social transgression inherent in the most audacious horror and comedy." This, he concludes, makes it "one of the truest cinematic expressions of the Grand Guignol aesthetic."[17] West, like Victor Frankenstein, seeks to defy death, to eliminate it from the human experience; unlike his nineteenth century predecessor's, this modern scientist's procedures spawn a trail of corpses, many destroyed by him after they return to life as murderous zombies. At the start of the movie, viewers perceive West, with his condescending sarcasm and arrogant superiority, as the typical mad scientist villain, the man with the monstrous ego who refuses to let anything stand in the way of his reckless obsession. But, as the narrative progresses, West's sins pale in comparison to those perpetrated by the dour Dr. Hill, including his cruel lobotomy of Dr. Halsey and sadistic rape of Megan, his bloody decapitated head licking down her naked body and ending between her legs. This latter scene, the consistently most remarked upon in the film, demonstrates how the adroit melding of humor and horror, the merging of grotesque fantasies with slapstick physicality—not to mention an overt visual pun—can provide a riveting brew of repulsion, laughter, and mortification possible in few other genres.

Bride of Re-Animator, directed by Brian Yuzna, never specifically references Whale's Bride of Frankenstein, but it reworks the tale by blending a modern sensibility with the unsettling mixture of humor and gore characteristic of this series. For eight months following the hospital massacre in Re-Animator, Herbert West (Jeffrey Combs) and Dan Cain (Bruce Abbott) work as medics in a Peruvian civil war zone, barely escaping with their lives and compelling a return to bucolic Miskatonic University in Arkham, Massachusetts. This time, however, West inflates his initially grandiose goal even further; instead of merely reanimating carcasses, he strives to generate life from dead tissue, an ill-considered quest that aligns his ego, ambition, and aspiration directly with Victor Frankenstein's. Dan, a ruggedly handsome Igor figure, reluctantly agrees to assist Herbert, who pledges to implant Meg's heart in this creature and, in this way, keep Dan's lover (somewhat) alive. Of course, frenzied anarchy ensues (why do these smart men never learn that using this reagent guarantees disaster?) from Herbert's audacious attempt to do "what others dare not dream about." As a result, we see Dr. Hill's severed head attached to bat wings, a policeman turned into a raging zombie, an attack by slobbering reanimated beings, living corpses with mismatched body parts, a blood-spattered catfight between Dan's two loves, lots of gory medical procedures, hacked-off limbs, dead pets, and other assorted mayhem.

Although campy, Bride of Re-Animator confronts some interesting bioethical issues. At one point Dan refuses Herbert's request for help, proclaiming, "I am a doctor," to which West caustically responds, "Well, be a scientist." Such a basic distinction emphasizes the uncomfortable dichotomy between a physician's primary duty to do the best for his/her patient and a researcher's fundamental responsibility toward her/his experimental agenda—particularly when the practitioner and researcher are the same person. The creation of the Bride (Kathleen Kinmont) results from the fusion of incongruent body parts pilfered from the morgue and cemetery, including the feet of a ballet dancer, the legs of a hooker, the heart of Meg, the womb of a virgin, the arms of a waitress, the hands of both a lawyer (male) and a murderess (female), and the head of Dan's beloved patient Gloria. Or, as Herbert calls them, "cast-off remnants of a meaningless existence . . . just dead tissue, but in our hands the clay of life." In response to the reporter Francesca Daneilli's (Fabiana Udenio) accusation that he has committed blasphemy, Herbert utters sentiments beyond even Victor's arrogance: "I created what no man's mind or any woman's womb could ever hope to achieve," he boldly asserts. "Blasphemy? Before what God? A God repulsed by the miserable humanity He created in His own image? I will not be shackled by the failures of your God. The only blasphemy is to wallow in insignificance. I have taken the refuse of your God's failures and I have triumphed."

Note should also be made of the sexual elements in *Bride of Re-Animator.* Throughout the series Herbert, like Victor, remains almost stridently asexual, although he clearly appreciates Dan's shirtless torso. At one point, he even warns his coinvestigator not to "let the little head rule the big head" in dealing with Francesca. Indeed, Herbert views Dan's Italian love interest as an impediment that distracts his roommate from their primary mission: to find the key to creating life. At one point, Herbert voyeuristically watches Dan and Francesca naked and having sex, perhaps the most traditionally romantic moment in the movie, but quickly turns away from them with disgust (or perhaps jealousy) pasted on his face. Herbert consistently claims sole responsibility for the Bride's creation and remains upset when she rejects him for Dan and his six-pack abs. He callously tells Dan not to worry as she rips out her heart and splits it in half, spitefully remarking that she is "just an assemblage of dead tissue" and clearly denying both her personhood and her sexuality as he murders her. Finally, one needs to ask, why a female? Of course, this decision allows Yuzna to parade a topless woman around the set, but it also ties Dan to Herbert in a medical partnership. Dan's overwhelming desire to keep his former lover and favorite patient at least partially alive compels him to work with Herbert despite his strong moral reservations. Making a man would not have appealed to Dan at all, but the incorporation of various parts from women he loves binds him to Herbert. In essence, then, Dan becomes more than just West's assistant; he becomes his Creature as well.

If Tim Burton's *Frankenweenie* is a child's happy-ending dream of reanimating his beloved pet, then Stephen King's *Pet Sematary* (directed by Mary Lambert) is an adult's nightmare of the same fervent pursuit. Both movies hark back to Shelley's novel by infusing the Frankensteinian themes directly into the family unit: in *Pet Sematary*, that family is Dr. Louis Creed (Dale Midkiff), his wife, Rachel (Denise Crosby), and their children, Gage (Miko Hughes) and Ellie (Blaze Berdahl). Upon moving from urban Chicago to seemingly bucolic Ludlow, Maine, they become friends with an elderly neighbor, Jud Crandall (Fred Gwynne—the Karloff figure in the hit TV show *The Munsters*), who acquaints them with the pet "sematary" (purposely misspelled) outside the boundaries of their red-roofed house and manicured backyard. Despite the warnings of a dying patient (Brad Greenquist), who later reappears in a cautionary nightmare desperately warning that "the barrier was not made to be broken," Louis and Jud lay the family's dead cat, Winston Churchill (nicknamed Church), to rest in a Micmac Indian burial site, only to have the animal return later that evening as a ferocious version of its former self (shades of *Re-Animator*) that slashes Louis's face with its claws. After a truck kills Gage, Louis tries to convince Jud to bring his son's body to the Indian burial grounds, but Jud relates how another father tried the same tactic after his son, Timmy Bateman (Peter Stader), died and the reanimated corpse terrorized the town. Louis, however, ignores Jud. When Gage returns, he steals one of Louis's scalpels and murders Jud and then his mother. Louis kills Gage with a shot of morphine, but makes the same mistake for a third time: he buries Rachel in the Indian cemetery, and upon her homecoming, she stabs him in the back with a butcher knife as the screen goes black.

Louis Creed takes his place among the modern Frankenstein surrogates who reanimate dead loved ones only to have the resurrected beings become psychotic murderers. Their goal is not power, glory, or the betterment of human life; they are not inherently bad men, but rather psychologically distraught figures who cannot accept the overwhelming personal tragedy of a loved one's death and will do anything to bring him or her back to life. Ironically, Louis's attempt to reanimate both Church and Gage springs from his desire to protect his family from pain, to give them back a pet and a child they loved. To be attacked and finally killed by two of the people he most loved in the world, his son and wife, represents the cruelest of punishments for a man trying to do the best he can for his family. King's Louis Creed finds evil lurking in the wilderness just outside the touch of civilization and appears powerless to resists its lure, a weakness that leads to his doom. In these films even those most aligned with the rational science of healing, like Frankenstein and Creed, cannot withstand a Faustian temptation to fulfill their most ardent desires, and they succumb to the darkness by choosing their desires over their intellect.

Two contemporary films that employ similar reanimation themes deserve at least brief mention to demonstrate that this premise is still alive and taking advantage of the zombie craze. *The Frankenstein Syndrome* (2011, originally titled *The Prometheus Project*), a grindhouse production directed by Sean Tretta with credit given to Mary Shelley as one of the writers, follows a research group that discovers how to regenerate dead tissue and, like their forebears, quickly begins reanimating corpses. The story is told from the perspective of Elizabeth Barnes (Tiffany Shepis) through a series of flashbacks and a shaky handheld camera shots, so the viewer immediately shares the victim's point of view, a visual strategy that forces us to feel her fear and tension. Once Dr. Walton (Ed Lauter), whose name recalls Shelley's seafaring explorer, and his team start injecting corpses, the resulting beings, now supernaturally strong, spiral out of control. The hunky David (Scott Anthony Leet) becomes a Jesus-like figure with the power to read minds and heal but also to kill. The movie plugs into the vociferous debate swirling around stem cell research but incorporates a host of religious connotations, including biblical names, Christian imagery, and suggestive actions such as the killing (crucifixion) of David, who returns with what appears to be a crown stapled on his head. He even turns water into fruit punch, although not wine. As in Shelley's novel, the Creature, David, becomes a real threat to his creators once he acquires knowledge taught by Elizabeth. In the most recent reanimation film, *The Lazarus Effect* (2015), as in *The Frankenstein Syndrome*, a group of pioneering scientists discovers a serum (called Lazarus) that can bring dead animals—and ultimately people—back to life, but in a more vicious state. After they have been banned from the university, Zoe McConnell (Olivia Wilde) leads the team on a stealth mission to break into their laboratory and duplicate their successful reanimation procedure; she is inadvertently electrocuted in the process, and the group allows her fiancé, Frank (Mark Duplass), to inject her with the reanimating liquid. Ultimately, Zoe turns into a killing machine, murdering the other members of the team, including Frank. Then, getting the band back together, she injects all of them with the serum. Of course, this entire bloody scenario could have been easily avoided if only these characters had simply watched previous reanimation movies.

As of this writing, the most current and innovative reformulation of Shelley's novel appears not in movie theaters but on television screens. *Penny Dreadful* (2014), the popular series currently running on Showtime in America and Sky in England, offers both a reiteration and an expansion of the basic Frankenstein narrative nestled within a mélange of Eastern and Western myths and occult superstitions blended with generous helpings of sex, violence, gore, profanity, and death. Historically, in the Victorian era penny dreadfuls were cheap, fiction books (including reprints of famous Gothic novels) published weekly and featuring supernatural events and criminal exploits presented in lurid detail, the most famous being the story of Sweeney Todd, later adapted by Stephen Sondheim into a musical. Because they were inexpensive and broadly available, these volumes formed a vital part of the era's mass media, bringing horror stories and tales of the supernatural into the daily lives of England's population.

Dr. Frankenstein (Harry Treadaway) contemplates shooting his murderous creation (Rory Kinnear) in the Showtime series *Penny Dreadful.*

The TV series follows the adventures of an eccentric team put together to help Sir Malcolm Murray (Timothy Dalton) rescue his daughter, Mina Harker (Olivia Llewellyn), from a powerful vampire (Robert Nairne) and fight the dark power of evil forces, including Vanessa Ives (Eva Green), Sembene (Danny Sapani), and Ethan Chandler (Josh Hartnett). Sir Malcolm recruits Victor Frankenstein (Harry Treadaway) into this band, knowing that he possesses exceptional surgical skills but not that he has been experimenting with creating life from pieces of dead matter. Like an contemporary Avengers movie that embraces several superheroes, *Penny Dreadful* unites powerful icons in supernatural/horror fiction: the created being and its creator from Shelley's *Frankenstein*, the vampires of *Dracula*, and the immortal youth from Oscar Wilde's *The Picture of Dorian Gray*, along with classic figures such as an American gunslinger (who turns into a werewolf), an African warrior, an English aristocrat, and a woman fighting demonic possession, not to mention mother and daughter witches in league with the devil—a bouillabaisse of Gothic and movie archetypes.

After lightning accidentally animates his creature in the first episode of season 1 ("Night Work"), Victor responds far differently than most previous Frankenstein figures; he becomes, in essence, a father to his offspring, teaching him to read, speak, and eat, taking him for a walk, and even allowing him to select a name for himself, Proteus (Alex Price). Viewers familiar with Shelley's Frankenstein and so many of its cinematic iterations watch in amazement as Victor, at long last, assumes parental responsibility for his tender-hearted creation, a construction rather than a reanimation. This Victor quotes passages from *Lyrical Ballads*, carries copies of Wordsworth's poetry, and tells Vanessa,

"Man does not live only in the empirical world. We must seek the ephemeral, or why live?" In a sly nod to the Universal production in episode 2 ("Séance"), Victor and Proteus speak of hunting whales, a clever allusion to the director of the two most famous Frankenstein movies. At times, Proteus stares up at the sunlight, mesmerized and mimicking Boris Karloff in the 1931 film. Victor may have finally learned from his past mistakes, but for the tormented characters inhabiting the Frankenstein universe, peaceful harmony never proves to provide a permanent resting place.

A jarring moment occurs at the end of episode 2 and continues to reverberate into episode 3 ("Resurrection"). A pair of bloody hands thrusts its way through the innocent Proteus's chest wall, ripping him in half, and a sneering voice proclaims: "Your firstborn has returned, Father." We later discover that the damaged figure who bursts, quite literally, though Proteus's dead body is Victor's prior creation (Rory Kennear). Like so many of his literary and cinematic ancestors, Victor first rejected and then abandoned his creation following an agonizing birth that resulted in an "abomination," a helpless creature left alone to learn about life through an attic window. But this articulate being has an acute and sophisticated sense of who he is: "I am modernity personified," he tells Victor, asserting that he is one with the men of iron, the steam engines and turbines that drive society. From our twenty-first-century vantage point, Victor's Creature embodies the contemporary evolution of artificial intelligence, the inventions of modern man that will eventually make him obsolete: humans are "things of the past. The future belongs to the strong, to the immortal races, to me and my kind," he boasts in episode 4 ("Demimonde"). Once the Creature is out in the world, his scarred visage frightens and enrages people, but he eventually finds mercy in the kindness of Vincent Brand (Alun Armstrong), an actor who provides him with stagehand work and a place to live in the Grand Guignol theater, where "hideous can be beautiful" and "strangeness is not shunned but celebrated." And, as we now fully expect, he commands Victor to make him an immortal mate, a woman, or he will destroy all that his maker loves.

Although Victor quotes the Romantic Wordsworth, his creature references the far more stern Puritan John Milton's *Paradise Lost* in episode 8 ("Grand Guignol") when he recites the lines that speak to him, "Did I request thee, Maker, from my clay / To mould me Man?" The same quote appears in Shelley's novel, as Adam laments his unbidden creation by an unforgiving God who banishes him from the Garden of Eden after one transgression. In these lines, Milton's Adam and Shelley's Creature both appeal to their makers' sense of justice, assigning them partial responsibility for their sins because they never asked to be born; as the line continues in *Paradise Lost*: "Did I solicit thee / From Darkness to promote me?" Ironically, the Creature mistakes the compassion of an actress who pities him, Maude Gunneson (Hannah Tointon), for a deeper affection and, after assaulting her, loses his temporary sanctuary. Like Adam, he is banished from his Eden for attempting to taste the forbidden fruit of female affection and sexual love. Later in the series, however, he will encounter (at least temporarily) a sympathetic woman in Miss Ives, an equally damaged being haunted by her past who recognizes his sensitive humanity.

After leaving the theater, the Creature returns to Frankenstein's laboratory, his only place of seeming refuge, not realizing his creator intends to shoot him. With his pasty white face, stringy hair, and multiple scars, he resembles a sad refugee from Kabuki theater or, perhaps, Gene Simmons still in his Kiss makeup after a long night of debauchery. "This shattered visage merely reflects the abomination that is my heart," he tells Victor, adding, "Why did you not make me of steel and stone? Why did you allow me to feel? I would rather be the corpse I was than the man I am." Knowing that Frankenstein is creeping up behind him with a loaded pistol, he says that to kill him "would be a blessing," but such obvious emotional pain arouses pity in his creator, and Victor cannot pull the trigger on the child he has brought to life. Instead, he agrees to make his creature a mate.

In the first episode ("Fresh Hell") of *Penny Dreadful*'s second season, the Creature renames himself John Clare, after the minor Romantic poet, and tells Victor, "We are bound on a wheel of pain, thee and me. . . . What is Doctor Frankenstein without his creature?" A Frankenphile hearing these words cannot help but recall the importance of the rotating windmill in the first Universal pictures, and how the Creature and his creator face each other around the moving gearshift that drives its blades. Here, however, both figures join together to reanimate Brona Croft, the consumptive Irish prostitute, into Lily (Billie Piper), named, as Victor tells her in the second episode, after the flower of resurrection and rebirth. She rises naked from the water like a modern Aphrodite given birth by lightning and science, and like the Greek goddess, she will inspire passion and love. "I want to fill her heart with poetry," says the Creature, but it is Victor who gives her the love and compassion that he has denied his own creations. He tenderly washes her hair and gives her memories of her past, falsehoods to shield her from the truth of her origins, as he falls deeply in love with his newest creation much to the disappointment and lethal anger of his first one. Later, we discover that Lily has been cruelly manipulating Victor during their time together. She has always known that Victor created her and, in the arms of her new lover, mocks his fumbling sexual advances, even taunting him about taking his virginity.

The final episode of season 2 ("And They Were Enemies") offers the first glimpse of a sinister, narcissistic union. First, Victor's creations, his "children," unite to torment and drive him almost to the point of suicide in a nightmarish apparition stirred up by the witches. Even more frightening, however, Lily and

Dorian Gray (Reeve Carney) use Nazi-like imagery to announce their intention to sire a race of immortal beings that will forever dominate humanity—"a master race. A race of immortals meant to command" and make mankind kneel before them. "When our day has come," Lily tells Victor, "you will know terror." She then curses him to "live with the knowledge of what you have spawned—and suffer." Victor shoots both of them at point-blank range, but the couple continues to waltz gracefully around Dorian's elaborate, candle-lit ballroom, elegantly dressed all in white, leaving swirls of blood on the marble floor but showing no signs of pain. Realizing his seminal role in this apocalyptic abyss drives Frankenstein to near-insanity. Exceedingly pale and emaciated, he retreats to his shabby garret with misery and pain etched on his face. Addicted to morphine from an early bout with asthma, he has few veins left for the needle so injects himself between his fingers. Tears escape from his hollow, bloodshot eyes as he sinks back on his cot, a victim of his own obsessions and, perhaps, a destroyer of mankind.

As is the case with all the books and movies and comics and games and every other iteration of the Frankenstein narrative, *Penny Dreadful* forces viewers to confront a world that resembles our known experience but exists outside the boundaries of our daily existence. Common elements seem familiar to us, but they conceal another world overflowing with danger, horror, and death. Evil beings stalk these tormented characters with a relentless malevolence that fills their days with fear and their nights with terror. Each is ravaged by a jagged past crammed with mistakes and sorrows, bitter disappointments and devastating loses. All seek some type of atonement for their sins, perhaps redemption, but at least peace—however provisional. Only the brave and the lucky survive in this world filled more with demonic beings than heavenly hosts, and the pitched battle with supernatural forces irreversibly damages those who strive to combat the creatures of the night. The possible becomes the accessible: the nightmare becomes flesh that compels us to face the moral and practical consequences of our choices. At its heart, the Frankenstein narrative brings forth the frightening reality that inside the deepest layers of ourselves we all possess a monster always ready to destroy us and those we love.

Transformations 1: Cyborgs

These last sections of this chapter explore two Frankenstein film clusters that contain few if any, direct allusions to Shelley's novel or Whale's film but that incorporate their narrative, thematic, and/or iconographic elements, often situating their characters and plots in futuristic settings with resemblances to the present. These movies fit the fundamental definition arrived at earlier by examining the outcomes, costs, and responsibilities of artificial creation and, in doing so, revealing "specific, changing configurations of human-technological interaction: patterns, tendencies, and deviations that mark moments in a richly variable history that is at once a history of cinema, of media, of technology, and of the affective channels of our own embodiment."[18] Another way to characterize the intricate tensions between concepts of the real and of the artificial that dominate these various works is to consider Donna Haraway's pithy observation in her "Cyborg's Manifesto": "Monsters have always defined the limits of community in Western imaginations."[19]

When Luke Skywalker finally removes Darth Vader's black helmet, acceding to his father's wish ("Just for once, let me look on you with my own eyes"), we see not only mechanical insertions jammed cruelly into his flesh but also the scarred visage and tired eyes of an old man who remembers his romantic past and finally wants to make peace with his son: he is, in fact, a cyborg. Simply defined, a cyborg is a mechanical and biological hybrid. Two aeronautics experts, Manfred Clynes and Nathan Kline, coined the term "cyborg" (short for "cybernetic organism") in their paper "Cyborgs and Space"(1960), arguing it would be easier to change a human being's bodily functions than provide earthly environments in space, a biological evolution that would enlarge the human spirit as well. While this process never truly materialized, it captured the imagination of both writers—such as Marge Piercy, Martin Caidin, Samuel Delany, Anne McCaffrey, William Gibson, and many others—and the public at large, who embraced a series of pop culture images ranging from the Six Million Dollar Man to Darth Vader.

Being a combination of the biological and the biomechanical, cyborgs represent the logical evolutionary phase in the Frankenstein narrative, since they embody the jagged fault lines along the increasingly blurry boundaries between human and nonhuman figures. Robert W. Anderson argues that the "modern Gothic monster pre-figures the post-modern science-fiction cyborg, the significant difference being that the monster is reviled and the cyborg is celebrated."[20] Indeed, cyborgs dwell in an often-precarious middle ground between the "us" and the "them" precisely because they are both: part organic and part synthetic. They are simultaneously the "other" and the "self," the one and the many, who both define and transgress traditional boundaries of gender, sexuality, race, and, of course, humanity.

In her influential essay "A Cyborg Manifesto," Donna Haraway conceptualizes a "cybernetic organism," both as a literal fact and as a mythic configuration. For her, it becomes both a "creature of social reality as well as a creature of fiction" that maps "our social and bodily reality" and functions "as an imaginative resource suggesting some very fruitful couplings." Haraway understands the power of cyborgs, whether real or imagined, to collapse three critical boundaries: the first between the human and the animal, the second between the organism and the machine, and the third between the physical and the non-physical. By the very nature of being capable of being imagined, the myth of the cyborg functions as a very dynamic force, one fully capable of transgressing boundaries, containing potent fusions, and possessing dangerous possibilities. "It is not clear who makes and who is made in the relation between human and machine," she asserts near the end of the essay, "it is not clear what is mind and what body in machines that resolve into coding practices."[21] At the heart of her essay lies Haraway's intoxicating characterization of cyborgs as a force for desta-bilization and, as such, symbols of liberation that allow individuals to break free from the limitations of dualistic thinking about a wide variety of subjects. Such conceptions, of course, might describe Frankenstein's Creature as well as modern cyborgs.

Many of Haraway's abstract concepts can be illustrated in the Dutch direc-tor Paul Verhoeven's police drama *RoboCop*, a film that emerges in equal mea-sure as a satire on corporate America and a cyborg action movie. In futuristic Detroit, a crumbling, crime-infested warren dominated by savage criminals, Clarence Boddicker (Kurtwood Smith), a vicious, drug-dealing kingpin, delights in killing police officers—over thirty at last count. Government officials, desper-ate to curtail illegal activities, contract with the multinational conglomerate Omni Consumer Products (OCP) to purge the streets of criminals. Over at the Metro West Precinct, Alex Murphy (Peter Weller) reports for duty and gets part-nered with the tough Anne Lewis (Nancy Allen) for his first patrol into the dan-gerous heart of this gritty, dystopic world. Simultaneously, at a meeting at OCP headquarters, the CEO (Dan O'Herlihy) reveals his grandiose plans to decimate "Old Detroit" and erect "Delta City," a shiny metal-and-glass metropolis with the motto "The Future Has a Silver Lining" in its place. He commissions his next-in-command, Dick Jones (Ronny Cox), to oversee the development of a heav-ily armored droid law enforcer, ED-209, but the initial demonstration of the robot's lethal prowess goes spectacularly astray, as it kills one of the company's executives (Kevin [credited as Ken] Page) before being unplugged. Seizing the moment, one of Jones's competitors within OCP, Bob Morton (Miguel Ferrer), divulges his alternative project, RoboCop.

While Lewis and Murphy are on patrol, Boddicker and his renegade gang capture Murphy, shoot off his hand, pulverize his face, and riddle his body with bullets. The disorienting sequence that follows this barbaric attack depicts events from Murphy's confused, semiconscious perspective as scientists con-vert him into a cyborg police officer programmed with three prime directives: serve the public trust, protect the innocent, and uphold the law. Later we dis-cover a fourth: never take action against a company official. Once on the street, RoboCop proves a highly efficient crime fighter, a true knight in shining bullet-proof armor with super strength, whose deadly accurate aim saves the mayor from being murdered by a disgruntled former council member. Although his deeds make RoboCop a sleek celebrity, all is not well. He suffers disturbing flashbacks of his former life as Alex Murphy, particularly fond scenes of his family, and terrifying memories of his execution at the hands of Boddicker and his gang of sadistic thugs. RoboCop eventually locates Boddicker and forces him to reveal that Jones secretly controls much of the city's crime and has equipped Boddicker's gang with military-level weapons to hunt him down. In a cyborg-versus-robot showdown worthy of a Ford Western, RoboCop and ED-209 (created via stop-action animation) square off, and RoboCop reduces ED-209 to a heap of busted hardware. But RoboCop cannot kill Jones, since he is a company officer, until the CEO summarily fires him: RoboCop then shoots Jones enough times to send him flying out the conference room window to his death. When the CEO asks his name, he replies, "Murphy"—an acknowledgment of the man still inside the machine.

Because Murphy has been officially pronounced dead, his reincarnation is really a reanimation, but the title *RoboCop* is a misnomer; it should be *Cyborg-Cop*, since Murphy is still part human as well as part machine. Citing this hybrid state, Slavoj Žižek comments that RoboCop's hero represents "a phenomenon that fully deserves to be called the 'fundamental fantasy of contemporary mass culture,' . . . [the] fantasy of the return of the living dead: the fantasy of a person who does not want to stay dead but returns again and again to pose a threat to the living."[22] Such a description harks back to the silent Frankenstein movies, mentioned in previous chapters, in which murdered people returned from the dead to seek revenge against their killers. The dramatic arc of Verhoeven's film, however, hinges on Murphy rediscovering his humanity by remembering his buried past. Once he is resurrected, encased within the gleaming exoskeleton, and dispatched to fight crime, this action film also becomes a search for the soul inside the machine so that morality can override programming. To do so, *RoboCop* intermingles elements from the Frankenstein narrative with Western gunslinging motifs and overt Christian symbology. Verhoeven, in the documentary *Flesh + Steel: The Making of RoboCop*, characterizes Murphy as "an American Jesus that uses his gun, " a guy who had been crucified, resurrected, and even walks on water."[23]

Most of the early Frankenstein films paint Victor, or his surrogate, as a lone researcher isolated from the cultural forces and social conventions of society, a solitary figure struggling to complete his research, despite its hazards. As the narrative evolves over time, however, the creators of the creatures tend to function within larger and more affluent institutional settings, such as high-tech medical centers and flourishing research facilities (*Jurassic Park* and *The Fly*). *RoboCop*'s creator, for example, is not one person, but rather a team of corporate yuppies, anonymous scientists, and nameless technicians who lack individuality

A corporate Frankenstein creature: the part human/part machine cyborg (Peter Weller) in *RoboCop* (1987).

and remain mostly minor characters as the drama unfolds. Thus, more contemporary Frankensteinian monsters do not emerge from gloomy caves or secluded mountaintop laboratories but instead lumber out of brightly lit operating rooms (*Splice*) and richly funded research centers (*Godsend*) that boast the most costly modern equipment available. Other than the loathsome Boddicker, for example, the villain in *RoboCop* is not a single person, not just Dick Jones, but rather the capitalistic greed, corporate corruption, and lack of concern for the public that fuel OCP and its experimental protocols. The enemy occupies boardrooms and wears custom-tailored suits: John Hammond has become Gordon Gekko.

Seeing *RoboCop* in light of Haraway's "Cyborg's Manifesto" allows viewers to viscerally grasp the power of cyborgs and how such figures necessarily collapse static boundaries, particularly those established between mechanized creations and biological organisms. Murphy's emerging memories trap him between his past and his present, his former relationships and his new companions, his previous body and his new physical formulation. Their emergence raises disturbing questions central to Haraway's comments about the sometimes-discordant roles played by the mind and the body in cyborgs. How can Murphy reconcile what he was with what he has become? How can his past function within his present? As Haraway notes, cyborgs like Murphy necessarily transgress strict boundaries by their very nature, existing in a precarious reality that makes them both fascinating and dangerous to the well-established precepts of the status quo. Like the robots described below, they force a societal consideration of complicated ethical and legal issues and demand a personal response to a rapidly changing way of life that will undoubtedly influence our future.

Looking at the original *RoboCop* today (a reboot was done in 2014), the film's stealth satire seems quite prescient, despite the fact that its director cites older films, such as *The Day the Earth Stood Still* and *Metropolis*, as his visual models. Verhoeven even talks about his RoboCop as a male version of the seductive machine/human (*Maschinenmensch*) in Lang's influential movie.[24] Derisive attitudes toward the financial excess and conservatism of the late 1980s inspire the film's most satiric elements, such as a news report of human tragedies followed by a slick commercial for a new family game, Nukem—whose motto is "Get them before they get you." In the swanky OCP corporate headquarters towering above the mean city streets, a robot kills a man and the only concern of those gathered around the executive table is how to make their product more efficient, a truly heartless response. Some parts of the film are realities today. The collapse of the American automobile industry in 2007, for example, made Detroit and other rust belt cities resemble the bleak vision offered in *RoboCop*. Drones now kill people, police forces and terrorists both have military-grade weapons, and parents buy ever more violent games for their children. (A toy line actually based on the film called "*RoboCop*: Ultra Police," had crime-fighting figures that fired caps at the bad guys.) So what seemed like outlandish science fiction and biting social satire in 1987 seems far closer to reality in 2015.

Transformations 2: Robots

Robots abound in the cinema. Some are playful companions that charm and delight viewers, while others pose more lethal threats to humanity. For every cute and friendly R2-D2 or Wall-E, a Megatron or a Terminator stands ready to kill anyone who crosses its path. Just as movies, quite literally, merge technology with artistry and fantasy, so too cinematic robots amalgamate advanced mechanization with inventive designs and human desires. Not tethered to or restricted by the actual levels of technological advances that exist in the real world, robots that inhabit the reel world inevitably reflect the anxieties, social conditions, and passions of the age that conceptualizes them. As Despina Kakoudaki observes in *Anatomy of a Robot*: "When it is possible to imagine any type of being or type of body, then the beings and bodies imagined express a range of cultural expectations, projections, and desires. Artificial people are useful cultural fictions" and play a dynamic role "in a political and existential negotiation of what it means to be human."[25] Robots, then, embody a collection of very human values and aspirations; they are designed to meet specific needs, amplify areas of human weakness, perform certain functions, or satisfy cravings. Like films themselves, robots are both part of the time period in which they were created and can transcend that specific moment in history to wander into the future.

At first glance robots—a term coined by Karel Čapek in his classic 1920 science fiction play *R.U.R.* (Rossum's Universal Robots) and derived from the Czechoslovakian word (*robota*) for "work"—seem like the branch on the Frankenstein family tree most distant from Shelley's novel. Yet in very specific ways these narratives bring us full circle back to her work again. Robots, like Frankenstein's Creature, are not reanimations of dead corpses but rather new creations, manufactured adult beings without any memories of childhood experiences because they never had a past. Although robots are not composed of organic materials like Frankenstein's Creature, electricity plays a vital role in both creations: it is the spark of life for the Creature and the source of power that drives the tools that create robots. Both the Creature and robots are assembled entities rather than products of the womb, with no physical or psychological connection to the biological birth process. They always remain archetypal outsiders whose conspicuous "otherness" forces a reconsideration of mainstream society's relationships with marginalized groups. Robots and Frankenstein's Creature, therefore, remain unique inventions inhabiting a perpetually liminal state that contests strict boundaries between machines and humans and challenges seemingly stable definitions of personhood. Finally, as in *Frankenstein*, the robot often emerges as a lethal menace to its creators.

As the Frankenstein movies illustrate, not everyone feels sanguine about a future where the consequences of unbridled technological evolution can range from individual discomfort to social devastation. In *Rise of the Robot*, for example, Martin Ford argues that American culture is currently experiencing a seismic alteration in the relationship between workers and machines: the field of artificial intelligence, exemplified by IBM's Watson, will significantly alter our economic landscape, constructing a less labor-intensive and more technology-dependent system that will eliminate humans from a variety of increasingly upper-level jobs, including lawyers, radiologists, journalists, pharmacists, and other professions. Some experts predict that by 2025 fully one-third of all American jobs will be replaced by software, robots, and smart machines.[26] Even Bill Gates has expressed serious concerns about the future of super intelligence: "First, the machines will do a lot of jobs for us and not be super intelligent. That should be positive, if we manage it well. A few decades after that, though, the intelligence is strong enough to be a concern."[27] In a similar manner, Stephen Hawking told a BBC interviewer that "the development of full artificial intelligence could spell the end of the human race; it could take off on its own, and re-design itself at an ever increasing rate," he continued, "humans who are limited by slow biological evolution couldn't compete and would be superseded."[28] Put another way by Kakoudaki, robot stories consistently ask "whether we control our technologies or whether they control us"—a very Frankensteinian question.[29]

The more scientists design robots to resemble human beings, the greater the opportunities for difficult questions to be raised about distinguishing "us" from "them," starting with the uncertainty and propriety of robot ownership. Do those who forge the robots own them? Are robots basically property fabricated merely to do the bidding of human beings and thus easily discarded when their usefulness ends? Should we have second thoughts about consigning an outworn robot to a closet and purchasing a more efficient model? Do robots have any moral or legal rights? All of these considerations become far more complicated when the robot can speak intelligently, looks like a human being, and may even possess feelings. Such issues appear in two of the most famous and complex films featuring robots, *Blade Runner* and *A.I. Artificial Intelligence.* Both foreground simulacra of the highest possible order: artificial but attractive beings that can easily pass for humans and, as a result, make it increasingly difficult to treat them as machines. Such concerns may at first seem farfetched off the screen, but they are increasingly appearing in the real world. Magazines report stories of robots designed to help autistic children learn to communicate and to comfort dementia patients. More than a hundred different models of so-called social robots currently exist, including a Japanese robot already being sold for around $1,600 that "senses human emotions based on vocal inflections and facial expressions"; it gets lonely if you ignore it, and laughs if you tell it a joke.[30] The most popular robot, Sony's dog Aibo, has sold some fourteen thousand units among a market that generates over $5 billion yearly: "Researchers have documented people kissing their Mechanized companions, confiding in them, giving them gifts—and being heartbroken when the robot breaks, or the study ends and it's time to say good-bye."[31] Perhaps, then, the anxiety in the modern-day Frankenstein movies containing robots expresses a substantial feeling among viewers; as the saying goes: just because you're paranoid doesn't mean that people aren't after you!

Almost every commentator who writes about the genre agrees that *Blade Runner*, directed by Ridley Scott, remains one of "the most visually dense, thematically challenging, and influential" science fiction films ever made.[32] (In an "it's a small world" moment relevant to our discussion, Ed Neumeier stumbled onto Scott's set while working as a young script reader, and it inspired him to write *RoboCop*.)[33] Many also agree that *Blade Runner* remains one of the preeminent cinematic renditions of Mary Shelley's essential themes updated to reflect contemporary technological advances. Indeed, no science fiction film, with the possible exceptions of *2001: A Space Odyssey* and *Star Wars*, has stimulated more academic writing and general trade books. Although *Blade Runner* was first theatrically released in 1982, the following section refers to the "Director's Cut" released in 1992 that excises the world-weary Marlowesque voice-over, includes Deckard's unicorn dream, and removes the happy ending insisted upon by the studio. Warner Bros. released a "Final Cut" edition in 2007 on the twenty-fifth anniversary of the movie, another of seven total versions, which reportedly provided Sir Ridley Scott (knighted in 2003) with complete artistic control. (IMDB lists Scott listed as one of the producers and writers of an untitled *Blade Runner Project* featuring Ryan Gosling and Harrison Ford currently in preproduction.)

Loosely based on Philip K. Dick's dystopian novella *Do Androids Dream of Electric Sheep?* (1968), *Blade Runner* meshes a film noir private-eye visual style with a science fiction premise that perfectly fits the previous definition of Frankenstein movies: they examine the outcomes, costs, and responsibilities of creating artificial beings or reanimating dead bodies. Scott depicts the Los Angeles of 2019 as a dark, dank, and perpetually rainy cityscape, a crime ridden jumble of multiethnic life with decidedly Asian flavors; anyone who can afford it escapes to Offworld sites far from this urban decay and decadence, leaving behind those too poor to evacuate and those rich enough to insulate themselves from the teeming masses. Amid this inner-city squalor towers the imposing headquarters of the Tyrell Corporation, the producer of genetically engineered androids, called Replicants, who form a slave force that toils at tasks too odious for humans, provides manual labor wherever necessary, and supplies sexual services for those living in the Offworld. Strict laws forbid them from returning to Earth. If Replicants do manage to reach their home planet, Blade Runners, a skilled group of mercenaries/policemen, track down and kill (called "retire") these renegade robot terrorists.

The best of these futuristic American Snipers is Rick Deckard (Harrison Ford), a former Blade Runner forced back into service by his old boss, Bryant (M. Emmet Walsh), and Bryant's origami-making assistant, Gaff (Edward James Olmos), to hunt down four escaped and extremely dangerous Nexus 6 model

Replicants who have battled their way back to Earth: Roy Batty (Rutger Hauer) possess strength and advanced intelligence; Zhora (Joanna Cassidy) has super-human endurance and combat skills; Leon Kowalski (Brion James) uses brute force; Pris (Daryl Hannah) provides readily available sex. Although some commentators allege these four are cyborgs, they are strictly mechanical beings, not half human/half machines like *RoboCop*'s Murphy. Bryant fears that, despite the preventive programming that limits their life span to four years, these Replicants have acquired emotions, which makes it harder to distinguish them from human beings. Upon going to the Tyrell Corporation's headquarters, Deckard meets Rachel (Sean Young), a beautiful assistant to Eldon Tyrell (Joe Turkel), the CEO of the company, whose motto is "More Human than Human." Tyrell reveals that although Rachel, who resembles a 1940s femme fatale, believes herself to be human, she actually is the most advanced Replicant ever manufactured, one implanted with memories gleaned from Tyrell's family members.

Deckard eventually "retires" two of the Replicants, Leon (actually killed by Rachel to save Deckard) and Zhora (killed amid shattered glass and transparent plastic), but Roy and Pris locate J. F. Sebastian (William Sanderson), a talented genetic designer suffering from Methuselah syndrome, which rapidly ages him. Roy forces the frightened Sebastian to provide entrance into Tyrell's lavish pent-house atop a pyramid-like skyscraper ascending high above the decaying city. The Replicant begs Tyrell for an extended life span and, after learning that he cannot be reprogrammed to live longer, kills his maker. In the meantime, Deck-ard finds the acrobatic Pris hiding in Sebastian's apartment, where she almost tears off his head before he manages to shoot her. Roy returns to find his lover dead and engages the wounded Deckard in a furious battle that clearly dem-onstrates the Replicant's superior physical strength and mental dominance. A moment before Deckard would have plunged to his death, Roy saves him and then, after releasing a dove into the heavens, dies himself. A battered Deckard returns to his apartment, wakes up Rachel, with whom he has fallen in love, and leaves with her to find somewhere safe for them to survive.

Blade Runner, as is the case with *A.I.*, raises complicated questions about the ever more blurred boundaries between human and artificial life. In most earlier Frankenstein films, these borders were clearer, as deformed monsters spawned in laboratories bore little physical resemblance to traditional, and far more attractive, representatives of the human race. These Replicants, however, are not only stronger and often smarter than their biological counterparts but look more physically appealing as well. Thus, sight itself, the use of visual acu-ity to distinguish the human from the nonhuman, becomes a central motif, an intersecting web of images present throughout the film. One of the first images a viewer encounters is a disembodied eyeball, and Scott piles physical depic-tions and dialogue about vision, sight, and eyes upon each other as *Blade Runner*

Roy Batty (Rutger Hauer) and Pris (Daryl Hannah), the "more human than human" Replicants hunted in *Blade Runner* (1982).

progresses: from the Voight-Kampff (VK) empathy test, to the genetic designer Chew (the owner of Eye World who devises the Replicant eyes), to a mechanical Owl, to Pris' blacked eyes, to Roy holding up toy eyes to amuse J.F., to Roy's speeches first to Chew ("if only you could see what I've seen with your eyes") and most importantly to Deckard right before he dies, "I've seen things you people wouldn't believe. Attack ships on fire off the shoulder of Orion. I watched seabeams glitter in the dark near the Tannhauser Gate. All those moments will be lost in time, like tears in the rain. Time to die." As this poetic moment indicates, Blade Runner's Replicants often appear far more sensitive, humane, and affectionate than their biological counterparts. Deckard's love for Rachel reinvigorates his commitment to living rather than merely surviving, an emotional revival that sweeps away his cynicism and replaces it with compassion—an ironic reaffirmation of the corporation's "More Human than Human" slogan that Tyrell never envisioned.

The scene in *Blade Runner* most inspired by *Frankenstein* occurs when Roy finally confronts Tyrell, reminiscent of all those scenes in prior Frankenstein films when the Creature challenges his creator. Although Tyrell is a high-tech guru, his bedroom, lit by glittering candles, could easily pass for one decorated in the nineteenth century, with its owner swathed in a bulky white robe and wearing thick trifocals. "It's not an easy thing to meet your maker," Roy tells Tyrell, asking if "the maker can repair what he makes" and then demanding, "I want more life, fucker!" (The DVD interestingly subtitles "father" as a substitute. The inclusion of "fucker" often puzzles critics, but it seems that Roy, sweaty and intense, verbally resorts to the basics of procreation even though his birth has nothing to do with the traditional way of conceiving children: by granting him only four years, Tyrell has "fucked" him over.) Any alteration in his interior wiring system, contends Tyrell, would be fatal, meaning that Roy's coding cannot be revised. "The light that burns twice as bright burns half as long, and you have burned so very very brightly," he tells Roy, using light/fire/ knowledge imagery common in the Frankenstein movies to calm his "prodigal son." Thinking he is now safe, Tyrell sits next to him on the bed, stroking back Roy's hair like a proud parent and putting his arm around the dejected Replicant's shoulders. Admitting he has done "questionable things," Roy peers at his maker and asks, "Nothing the god of bio-mechanics wouldn't let you in heaven for?" Roy reaches up to caress Tyrell's cheek, moves his other arm up to hold his face between his hands, smiles, pulls him close, and kisses him on the lips. As the operatic music swells, Roy's thumbs edge upward till they plunge into Tyrell's eyes and, as he hears the screams of his creator, dig so deeply into the sockets that blood spurts from them. The lifeless Tyrell falls backward—killed by the product he manufactured.

Like *Blade Runner*, *A.I. Artificial Intelligence* (2001, based on Brian Aldiss's short story "Super-Toys Last All Summer Long") also presents viewers with an appealing and totally artificial being, this time an adorable robot child who desperately wants to become a real boy to gain his mother's love. The flaw in this conception is that while David (Haley Joel Osment), "caught in a freeze-frame, always loving, never ill, never changing" will never age, his human parents will eventually do so and ultimately die, leaving him an orphan while still a child, a fact totally ignored by his creators. Monica (Frances O'Connor) and Henry (Sam Robards) Swinton, like the couple in *Godsend*, are devastated by the loss of their son, Martin (Jake Thomas), who remains cryogenically frozen until a miracle cure can be found for his potentially fatal disease. To ease the emotional pain of his wife, Henry brings home the latest invention by Professor Hobby (William Hurt), the CEO of Cybertronics, where he works: David, a perfect mechanical replication (Mecha) of an endearing human (Orga) child—the simulacrum as part of the family circle, not outside it. Over time, Monica grows to accept David as a replacement for Martin, finally activating the imprinting code that will make him love her permanently. All goes well until a revived Martin comes back to live with them, initiating a sibling rivalry that involves torturing and almost killing the naïve David. Eventually, the Swintons decide to return David to Cybertronics, where he will be destroyed, but instead Monica abandons the distraught child in the woods, a not particularly Edenic garden or Shakespearean green world.

A.I. combines the mythological tales of Pinocchio, Frankenstein, and Peter Pan as the forsaken David embarks on a series of adventures to win the love of his mother by becoming a real boy. Along the way, he meets a male-prostitute Mecha, Gigolo Joe (Jude Law), who takes care of him for a while, barely escaping a Flesh Fair designed by angry Orgas to kill Mechas. This central section of the film provides a transition from the human to the android world. In particular, Gigolo Joe, a robot designed to pleasure women, evolves from mechanical device to moral agent who acts as a care provider. While he is not programmed for such responsibilities, he demonstrates that creations may become ethically superior to those who created them. He also reveals the cruel truth to his young friend about his mother: "She loves what you do for her. . . . But she does not love you, David. She cannot love you. You are neither flesh nor blood. . . . And you are alone now only because they tired of you, or replaced you with a younger model or were displeased with something you said or broke. . . . We are suffering for the mistakes they made." David needs protection and guidance. His Orga parents abandon him, but his Mecha father shelters him. Joe demonstrates far more human qualities than any person in the film by befriending David, educating him, and aiding him on his quest. Eventually, David meets up with Professor Hobby, learns he is not unique, plunges into the water, and comes to rest in front of the Blue Fairy figure from a Pinocchio children's park in Coney Island, where he sleeps for two thousand years. Finally awakened by surviving Mechas, David shares his memories of life with human beings with them; in return, they grant him the thing he most wants: to spend time alone with his mother, Monica, after which he will go to sleep, at last, forever.

A.I.'s director, Steven Spielberg, forces viewers to share the perspective of the "other" by compelling us to experience David's adventures from his childlike point of view. Such a dramatic strategy aligns us with the hunted rather than the hunter, with the alienated outsider rather than the mainstream figures that would ordinarily be our surrogates on the screen. As in the early Universal Frankenstein films, David is given life but denied parental love, kindness, and compassion, but unlike Karloff's Creature he never turns to violence. As such, the artificial creation garners our sympathy rather than the flesh-and-blood representatives of traditional society who seek to destroy him. Although technologically superior, the human beings in the film act morally inferior to the lifelike robots they create for work and emotional comfort: despite his angelic appearance, David faces both personal and societal cruelty as a deserted child, a hounded fugitive, and a frozen supplicant. Indeed, the kindest figures in the

The Mechas David (Haley Joel Osment) and his surrogate father, Gigolo Joe (Jude Law), confront the Orga world in *A.I. Artificial Intelligence* (2001).

film, the mechanical gigolo who befriends him and the androids (called "the Specialists" in Spielberg's shooting script) who appear long after the humans have perished, are the only ones who grant him any consistent peace and fulfillment. The final narrator intones, "There was no Henry. There was no Martin. There was no grief. There was only David," although Freud would undoubtedly have much to say about desires that involve sleeping with Mom, deleting your sibling, and eliminating Dad.

In the film's opening scene, Professor Hobby proposes to create a robot child who "can love . . . love like the love of a child for its parents. A robot child who will genuinely love . . . with a love that will never end." Yet, asks a black female colleague, "It isn't simply a question of creating a robot who can love. But isn't the real conundrum—can you get a human to love them back? . . . If a robot could genuinely love a person, what responsibility does that person hold toward that Mecha in return? It's a moral question, isn't it?" Hobby never really answers here and, in an ironic reversal reminiscent of Mary Shelley, the technological creations in *A.I.* possess a sense of morality beyond the imagination of their makers and a conception of ethical responsibility that far outstrips the cold experiments of Professor Hobby, the jealousy of brother Martin, the distant curiosity of Henry, and the tearful betrayal of Monica. Robots transcend their programming to act as surrogate parents, an action that makes their violent destruction at the Flesh Fair, which Spielberg depicts using Holocaust imagery, accompanied by the cheers of frenzied humans, even more horrific. These mechanical creatures care about David as a sentient being, not—as do their human counterparts—as a replacement for a lost son, a product opening up a

new market, or an experiment in robotic engineering. In response to his colleague's question, Hobby cites "God and Adam" as the apt analogy for such a
momentous venture with metaphysical overtones, but the film demonstrates
the inverse of this creator/creation connection.

In *A.I.* the very human desire for an emotional bond, which often rests at
the heart of the Frankenstein films, can be fulfilled only via technology. The
Specialists use their sophisticated power to scan David's mind for his memories
and, joining into a circle, pass those images from machine to machine. Rapidly
moving scenes from his past jump from the face of one mechanical being to the
next, forming a virtual movie of his life stretched around the ring and shared
by all members of the interpretive community: memory preserved by technology; memory filtered through technology; memory as technology. Ironically, this
robot boy who desperately wants to become a flesh-and-blood child remains
the only creation who actually saw and touched the human progenitors. He possesses unique, experiential knowledge of the species that first invented robots
and then sought their destruction: "They made us too smart, too quick, and too
many," Joe tells David, adding prophetically, "When the end comes, all that will
be left is us. That is why they hate us." Human beings become the ghosts in the
machines, new works of art in the age of mechanical reproduction, with David
the only apparatus capable of accessing remembrances of Orgas past. Thus, the
film directly renders "popular uncertainty regarding core questions about origins and futures, and mediated representations themselves." It "affords a reflex-
ive perspective on the anxieties about digital culture, though with an emphasis
on the component process of subjectivity itself."[34]

Both *Blade Runner* and *A.I.*, along with many other films such as the *Star
Trek* series (especially in the characters of Spock and Data), posit that the main
difference between human and artificial beings is that the former demonstrate
emotions, mostly compassion, while the latter respond to all situations with
rational and impassive composure. They tacitly assume that moral decisions
spring mostly from our affective ability to identify with someone in danger or
suffering, rather than our reasoning capabilities to respond to such situations
logically. The choice ultimately made to deal with any given situation might
result from analytical assessment, but the initial impulse to act morally springs
from a sympathetic recognition of another person's need. Such an assumption
appears ironic if pushed a bit further. To assign the foundation of our humanity, the fundamental basis of what makes us distinct from machines, to emotions, rather than logic, is to situate it within a realm traditionally assigned to
women and, in fact, for which they have often been maligned and castigated. In
essence, then, the traditional traits that rightly or wrongly characterize men—
namely physical strength and rational thought—can be duplicated and even
surpassed by machines, but those of women—compassion and identification

with others—cannot be replicated by any sort of apparatus, tool, or robot. It is the tear, not the rational response, that defines us as human and separates us from the machines.

These two films (as well as newer movies such as *Ex Machina* [2015] with its lethal femme fatale Ava [Alicia Vikander]) compel viewers to consider what happens as machines become more like human beings, only smarter, faster, more attractive, stronger—and perhaps even more moral. Robin Marantz Henig writes about teams of philosophers, psychologists, linguists, lawyers, theologians, and human rights experts trying to teach robots to choose between right and wrong in the same ways as human beings, assuming that "ethics can be calculated by an algorithm."[35] But in some of the contemporary Frankenstein movies this lesson has already been learned. Throughout these movies, artificial beings care more about each other than do human beings about their fellow human beings. Is it a perversion, or perhaps a crime, for Deckard to love Rachel? She is, after all, a machine, so their interaction represents something akin to interspecies relationships, a mixing of species that might be considered blasphemous or at the very least illegal (although a sizable number of commentators, including Ridley Scott, feel that considerable evidence proves that Deckard is a Replicant as well).[36] Does David's mother bear any more moral responsibility for abandoning him than she would for replacing a defective washing machine? Sherry Turkle, director of MIT's Initiative on Technology and Self, warns that human-robot relations are inherently deceptive because "they encourage people to feel things for machines that can't feel anything."[37] So who is fooling whom?

6

======================================

Fifty Ways to Leave Your Monster

Who ever thought they would not hear the dead?
Who ever thought that they could quarantine
Those who are not, who once had been?
　　　　　　　　　　　–Stephen Edgar, "Nocturnal"

Frankenstein is inescapable. A quick tour around the cultural landscape bears witness to the omnipresence of Shelley's novel and the influence of Whale's films, as well as to the surprisingly divergent fates of their main characters. While the Monster has morphed from wretched outcast to intrepid hero—even becoming child-friendly toys and cereal-box designs—Victor Frankenstein has become fossilized as the embodiment of the mad scientist, a figure trapped in amber like the ancient mosquitoes in *Jurassic Park.* Karloff's ubiquitous image saturates our culture, while Colin Clive's face remains familiar only to film enthusiasts. Comic books such as "Doc Frankenstein," "Frankenstein, Agent of S.H.A.D.E.," and "Frankenstein Alive, Alive!" and children's books such as *Frankenstein Makes a Sandwich*, *Robot Zombie Frankenstein*, and *Frankenstein Takes the Cake* demonstrate how the Creature has morphed into a benefactor of mankind and, at the same time, become an appropriate subject for younger readers. Literary tales inspired by *Frankenstein* range from pornographic titles such as the Erotic Monsters series and *The Darker Passions: Frankenstein* to fictional reimaginings as in Joanne Rendell's *Out of the Shadows* (2010), about a modern writer's link to Mary Shelley, and Peter Ackroyd's *The Casebook of Victor Frankenstein* (2008), recounting the fictional meeting of Percy Shelley and Victor Frankenstein at Oxford. Mary Shelley's creature inspired 180 "Rock, Punk, & Low-Brow Artists" in the poster-art book *Electric Frankenstein*, edited by Sal Canzonieri. An elaborate exhibition at the National Library of Medicine in 2002, "Frankenstein: Penetrating the Secrets of Nature," examined Mary Shelley's life, the history of science, and contemporary ethical questions using *Frankenstein* as both a myth and a metaphor; its curator, Susan E. Lederer, posted the exhibit online, thereby widely circulating the materials. Action figures, Halloween masks, TV

Images from the National Library of Medicine's exhibition "Frankenstein: Penetrating the Secrets of Nature" (2002).

The Burger King next to the House of Frankenstein tourist attraction in Niagara Falls, Ontario.

shows, a Burger King, political cartoons, numerous websites, and even a US postage stamp have all featured elements drawn from Mary Shelley's tale and James Whale's movies—and that is just a partial list.

An in-depth review of the cultural effects of this Gothic story seems superfluous after over hundreds of pages devoted to discussing them, since it likely would read as a laundry list of every book, idea, experiment, and discussion conducted since 1818 even remotely related to science, science fiction, medical experimentation, bioethics, and exploration. It remains easier to discuss what is not the product of *Frankenstein*: perhaps Marshmallow Peeps, though the extreme experiments conducted on them by sleep-deprived graduate students invite closer scholarly investigation.[1] Suffice to say that one novel dreamed up on a rainy lakeside to entertain a group of bored (and probably low on drugs) Romantics has, for the last two centuries, grown roots that permeate the Western cultural imagination. This morning, you could have eaten a marshmallow Frankenstein's creature for breakfast and, while reading your newspaper, encountered an analogy between Monsanto's genetic manipulation of crops and Victor Frankenstein's creation. On the way to work, you might well have seen a billboard advertising the latest Frankenstein film while your local radio station compared the generation of organs from stem cells to Victor's transformation of

Boris Karloff as the Creature on a US postage stamp.

Frankenstein's Creature as a commodity —Franken Berry cereal.

dead flesh into a living monster. At the Dairy Queen, you could purchase an ice cream bar—in an attractive shade of green—made to look like the Creature while watching his cartoonish offshoot on *The Munsters*. Frankenstein and his

The Munsters of Mockingbird Lane, with Fred Gwynne embodying the Boris Karloff imagery as Herman Munster (1964–1966).

creature appear as icons of scientific hubris, (weirdly) consumable tasty treats, and artistic representations of the monstrous—sometimes comic, sometimes tragic, but always the same story with the same characters struggling through serial murders, madness, despair, and pitchfork-wielding mobs, then finally confronting each other.

To be fair, most of the novel's context has been lost over the decades in this cultural obsession with creation and monstrosity. Rarely outside of academic work—and rarely even there, now—do you stumble across anything about the obvious class biases evident in the discussions of the villagers, the Irish prison wardress, and Victor's opportunities for education in opposition to the limits Clerval's bourgeois father imposed on his intellectual aspirations. Likewise, discussions of race and gender in the novel have been largely crafted around modern scholarly theory and thus have little to do with the late eighteenth-century culture that produced the material, with exceptions made for arguments about the author's biography and its impact on the novel. And finally, while claims about the manic desire for medical and scientific progress depend upon the label "Frankensteinian" to make them appropriately horrific, they rarely reference the medical and scientific practice that provided the framework for the novel itself. In becoming timeless, *Frankenstein* has lost its moment in time, and with that, some important tools for understanding it.

The late eighteenth and early nineteenth centuries do not play a huge role in modern culture. We love the Tudors (as evidenced in our plethora of TV programs and movies about them) and then happily skip forward several centuries for Victoria, Oscar Wilde, and the fin de siècle. But that earlier turn of the century is a complicated and interesting one whose many shifting priorities and preoccupations are beautifully present in *Frankenstein.* It is a veritable crossroads of intersecting ideas about the place of religion and the divine in daily life, the relationship between the soul and the body, the balance between obtaining knowledge and the sacrifices necessarily made for it, the kind of knowledge production that would become "legitimate" as opposed to that which would be termed imprudent and unacceptable, and the intellectual authorities whose ideas would provide the essential groundwork for future scientific and theological work.

This novel is not liminal, which suggests being between worlds but also outside of their influences. It is, instead, facing machine guns of cultural and intellectual expectations and anxieties from every side. Ironically, we don't recognize them as the products of two centuries ago, but those expectations and anxieties continue to wreak havoc on our modern psyche. We turn back to Mary Shelley's   Frankenstein's Creature as a toy.

fictional character and his grotesque creation to tell us more about how to be human, and we are frustrated when we find more questions than answers. Of course, the novel emphasizes the importance of limiting scientific inquiry to approved topics and methodologies, but it also goes silent on some very important points—not the least of which is what constitutes humanity, and can it be manufactured? The flip side of that question is also important: Are all people inherently capable of humane behavior, or must the extraordinarily human characteristics of ambition and desire derail the angels of our better natures and thus endanger our ability to be human? These are not simple questions, and they keep us coming back. Our constant need for *Frankenstein* tells us not how far we have come in the last two hundred years, but how little distance we have covered in reconciling ourselves to the complicated competing demands of defining "good" scientific work in balance with ethical treatment of subjects, a nuanced understanding of the relationship between life, death, and the soul, and the place of God in the world. Like the Creature himself, these questions remain omnipresent despite our best efforts to banish them.

Who is the hero and who the monster in Mary Shelley's *Frankenstein*? Surely, one of its most potent attractions remains Shelley's decision not to assign any traditionally heroic or truly evil role to either the creator or his creation. In this sense, then, the novel adopts a decidedly modern point of view, refusing to paint its portraits in black or in white and offering readers relativity in the place of stability. Although it allows readers—at least at times—to admire Frankenstein for his daring ideas and absolute commitment to his goal, we cannot totally identify with a man who ignores the possibly dire consequences of his actions, refuses to accept his parental responsibilities, and continually makes disastrous decisions that eventually destroy his family and friends. There also isn't a lot of nonhuman monstrosity to be found in *Frankenstein*, although many science fiction authors and film directors have run far with the possibility of a scientist torturing dead flesh into life. That said, the literary trick of eventually making Victor the lesser human of the piece is clever and allows the novel to explore some profound questions of human nature vs. artificial life.

Well, then, what about the product of Frankenstein's experiments? The Creature certainly garners our sympathies when society brands him an outcast and his maker cruelly rejects him because of his physical features, something over which he has no control. Indeed, Frankenstein bears the blame for these painful rebuffs more than does the initially innocent Creature. Later in the evolution of the Frankenstein narrative, however, even beautiful artificial beings—either reanimated or newly constructed—experience the same prejudice, social exclusion, and grief as their ugly progenitor; deviations from the human-defined norm, not physical appearance, motivate violent actions against beings thrust into the world without their consent or any concern for their welfare.

Frankenstein's Creature (Boris Karloff) displays childlike innocence and becomes a sympathetic figure in *Frankenstein* (1931).

Even sympathizing with the emotional anguish of the Creature, however, does not excuse his murder of children and other innocent victims. Readers are left, therefore, with a novel that adamantly discards traditional generic conventions and abstains from allowing character identification. Shelley provides a dynamic and ultimately influential tale of two lost and lonely beings who, instead of comforting and perhaps even loving each other, cause their mutual destruction.

So if not the ladies, the antihero, or the Creature, then what keeps us coming back? The novel's draw is its plot, but the substance has to be the questions it asks but doesn't answer, the ones we keep asking—even as we dissect, deep-freeze, and microwave marshmallow bunnies. Does desiring and pursuing knowledge endanger our humanity? That question precedes the early nineteenth century by a few thousand years. The Renaissance was obsessed with the potential for knowledge to bring people closer to God and salvation while simultaneously fearing the traps set by demons to lure scholars into the pursuit of knowledge for personal gain and thus endanger their souls. Shelley incorporates this theme and develops a strong case for why scientific knowledge should be grounded in the academy, governed by peer oversight, and responsive to social rather than theological expectations. The novel deliberately distances the pursuit of natural knowledge from its Renaissance twin, the search for divine

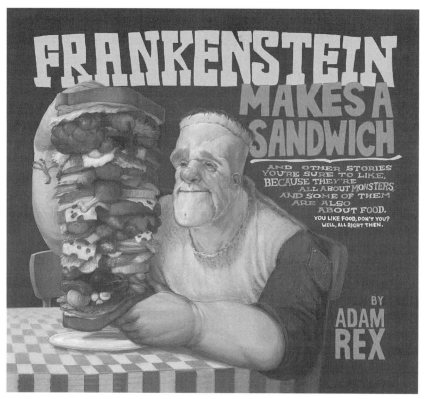

Frankenstein's Creature in a children's book.

understanding; the latter can easily be read as an Enlightenment-driven desire to separate natural and divine knowledge and elevate the pursuit of natural knowledge into an independent and legitimate discipline. It also tends to make scientists look a bit less insane if they are trying to find the cure for cancer rather than the key to eradicating all disease.

In many ways, *Frankenstein* is also a call for a smaller science, where the research questions do not reach beyond the natural world or even beyond the increasingly narrow and defined boundaries of academic disciplines. Thus, Victor should not have attempted to find the secret behind the creation of life, but rather the specific factors separating living from dead cells. Had his search emphasized chemical agents, he would have been a chemist and subject to the rules governing research in his subfield. While that would have necessarily narrowed his investigation and precluded his great discovery, it also would have grounded him in a community of scholars whose work he would have depended on and who would have used his findings in their subsequent research. He might have gone on to a lucrative career in cellular chemistry, married Elizabeth, bored her to tears, been the patriarch of a large and happy family, and died in his bed. Or he might have been denied tenure, which he later blamed on a creature he created in his extracurricular study, a project that had so occupied him that he failed to produce the required number of peer-reviewed articles with correct impact factors and received poor student ratings for being inattentive and slow returning exams. Some fates are impossible to escape.

Shelley's compelling mirror of a novel, filled with questions rather than answers and populated by tropes rather than characters, has far outlasted its original motivating intelligence. A product of Enlightenment-tinged Romantic ideals and a very long, rainy vacation, it has kept pace with the times because it is both a product of its moment and a bellwether for all the scientific-cultural moments that have occurred since. The novel might be less great than the sum of its parts, but one cannot escape its omnipresence. We watch Marshmallow Peeps slip into a vat of liquid nitrogen and wonder at the intelligence that motivates such a hideous act of cruelty committed in the name of human knowledge. Do we really need to know what will happen so badly that an innocent pink chick must suffer?

NOTES

INTRODUCTION

1. Throughout the book, all citations to the novel appear in the text and are from Susan J. Wolfson and Ronald Levao, eds., *The Annotated Frankenstein* (Cambridge, MA: Belknap Press of Harvard University Press, 2012), giving volume and chapter (or letter) and page. For example, (1.1, 99–100) is volume 1, chapter 1, pages 99–100; (L2, 71) is letter 2, page 71.

2. Stephen T. Asma, *On Monsters: An Unnatural History of Our Worst Fears* (New York: Oxford University Press, 2009), 151.

3. Wolfson and Levao, introduction to *The Annotated Frankenstein*, 1.

4. Elaine L. Graham, *Representations of the Post/Human: Monsters, Aliens and Others in Popular Culture* (New Brunswick, NJ: Rutgers University Press, 2002), 62.

5. Joyce Carol Oates, "Frankenstein's Fallen Angel," *Critical Inquiry* 10, no. 3 (March 1984): 546.

6. *New York Times*, October 11, 2015, Arts and Leisure section, 12.

7. Oates, "Frankenstein's Fallen Angel," 548, 546, 548, 550, 550.

8. David Collings, "The Monster and the Maternal Thing: Mary Shelley's Critique of Ideology," in *Mary Shelley's Frankenstein*, ed. Johanna M. Smith (Boston: Bedford/St. Martin's, 2000), 280.

9. Diane Long Hoeveler, "Frankenstein, Feminism, and Literary Theory," in *The Cambridge Companion to Mary Shelley*, ed. Esther Schor (Cambridge: Cambridge University Press, 2003), 45.

10. Anne K. Mellor, *Mary Shelley: Her Life, Her Fiction, Her Monsters* (London and New York: Routledge, 1988), 220; Diane S. Wilson, *Bodily Discursions: Genders, Representations, Technologies* (Albany: State of New York Press, 1997), 108.

11. Ellen Moers, "Female Gothic," in *The Endurance of Frankenstein: Essays on Mary Shelley's Novel*, ed. George Levine and U. C. Knoepflmacher (Berkeley: University of California Press, 1974), 79–80, 83, 81, 87; Mary Shelley's introduction to *Frankenstein*, in Wolfson and Levao, 331.

12. U. C. Knoepflmacher, "Thoughts on the Aggression of Daughters," in Levine and Knoepflmacher, *The Endurance of Frankenstein*, 91; Peter Dale Scott, "Vital Artifice: Mary, Percy and the Psychopolitical Integrity of Frankenstein" in ibid., 201–202.

13. Rebecca Solnit, *The Faraway Nearby* (New York: Penguin Books, 2013), 49.

14. Sandra M. Gilbert and Susan Gubar, *The Madwoman in the Attic: The Woman Writer and the Nineteenth-Century Literary Imagination* (New Haven, CT: Yale University Press, 1979), 221, 224, 222, 224, 222, 224, 245.

15. James Holt McGavran, "'Insurmountable Barriers to Our Union': Homosocial Male Bonding, Homosexual Panic, and Death on the Ice in Frankenstein," *European Romantic Review* 11, no. 1 (2000): 46, 47, 60, 62.

16. Mitch Walker, "The Problem of *Frankenstein*," YouTube, http://www.youtube.com/watch?v=7brHgazFSNI.

17. Chris Baldick, *In Frankenstein's Shadow: Myth, Monstrosity, and Nineteenth-Century Writing* (Oxford: Clarendon Press, 1990), 165–166.

18. David A. Hendrich Hirsch, "Liberty, Equality, Monstrosity: Revolutionizing the Family in Mary Shelley's Frankenstein," in *Monster Theory: Reading Culture*, ed. Jeffrey Jerome Cohen (Minneapolis: University of Minnesota Press, 1996), 129.

19. Judith Weissman, "A Reading of *Frankenstein* as the Complaint of a Political Wife," *Colby Library Quarterly* 12, no. 4 (December 1976): 177, 178.

20. Fred Botting, "Reflections of Excess: Frankenstein, the French Revolution, and Monstrosity," in Smith, *Mary Shelley's Frankenstein*, 435.

21. H. L. Malchow, "Frankenstein's Monster and Images of Race in Nineteenth-Century Britain," *Past and Present*, 139 (May 1993): 91.

22. Susan Tyler Hitchcock, *Frankenstein: A Cultural History* (New York: Norton, 2007), 89; Wolfson and Levao, introduction to *The Annotated Frankenstein*, 24.

23. Anne K. Mellor, "*Frankenstein*, Racial Science and the Yellow Peril," in *Frankenstein: A Norton Critical Edition*, ed. Paul J. Hunter, 2nd ed. (New York: Norton, 2012), 486–487.

24. Edith Gardner, "Revolutionary Readings: Mary Shelley's *Frankenstein* and the Luddite Uprisings," *Iowa Journal of Cultural Studies* 13 (1994): 70–91; Paul O'Flinn, "Production and Reproduction: The Case of Frankenstein," in *Horror: The Film Reader*, ed. Mark Jancovich (London: Routledge, 2002), 72.

25. Fuson Wang, "Romantic Disease Discourse: Disability, Immunity, and Literature," *Nineteenth-Century Contexts* 33, no. 5 (December 2011): 473.

26. Steven Earl Forry, *Hideous Progenies: Dramatizations of Frankenstein from Mary Shelley to the Present* (Philadelphia: University of Pennsylvania Press, 1990), 43.

27. Franco Moretti, *Signs Taken for Wonders: Essays in the Sociology of Literary Forms*, rev. ed. (London and New York: Verso, 1988), 85.

28. Elise B. Michie, "Frankenstein and Marx's Theory of Alienated Labor," in *Approaches to Teaching Shelley's Frankenstein*, ed. Stephen C. Behrendt (New York: MLA, 1990), 93–94.

29. O'Flinn, "Production and Reproduction," 105, 108.

30. Warren Montag, "The 'Workshop of Filthy Creation': A Marxist Reading of *Frankenstein*," in Smith, *Mary Shelley's Frankenstein*, 394–395.

31. Anca Vlasopolos, "Frankenstein's Hidden Skeleton: The Psycho-Politics of Oppression," *Science-Fiction Studies* 10, no. 2 (July 1983): 129, 132.

32. Michael Moore, "We Finally Got Our Frankenstein . . . and He Was in a Spider Hole," blog post, December 14, 2003.

33. Michael C. Dorf, "Spandrel or Frankenstein's Monster? The Vices and Virtues of Retrofitting in American Law," *William & Mary Law Review* 54, no. 2 (2012): 339.

34. Elizabeth Young, *Black Frankenstein: The Making of an American Metaphor* (New York: New York University Press, 2008), 7, 5, 6.

35. Paul Root Wolpe, "Knowing and Seeing: Reconstructing *Frankenstein*," in *Health Humanities Reader*, ed. Therese Jones, Delese Wear, and Lester D. Friedman (New Brunswick, NJ: Rutgers University Press, 2014), 420, 428.

36. Oates, "Frankenstein's Fallen Angel," 545.

CHAPTER 1   IN A COUNTRY OF ETERNAL LIGHT

1. William Eamon, *Science and the Secrets of Nature: Books of Secrets in Medieval and Early Modern Culture* (Princeton, NJ: Princeton University Press 1994); Steven Shapin, *A Social History of Truth: Civility and Science in Seventeenth-Century England* (Chicago: University of Chicago Press, 1994); Allison Kavey, *Books of Secrets: Natural Philosophy in England, 1550–1600* (Urbana: University of Illinois Press, 2007); Tara Nummedal, *Alchemy and Authority in the Holy Roman Empire* (Chicago: University of Chicago Press, 2007).

2. Samuel Vasbinder, *Scientific Attitudes in Mary Shelley's Frankenstein* (Ann Arbor, MI: UMI Research Press), 17.

3. Charter of the Royal Society, 1662, https://royalsociety.org/about-us/governance/charters/.

4. Accademia Nazionale dei Linci, www.lincei.it; l'Académie des sciences, "Histoire," http://www.academie-sciences.fr/archivage_site/academie/histoire.htm.

5. Constance Martin, "William Scoresby, Jr. (1789–1857) and the Open Polar Sea—Myth and Reality," *Arctic* 41, no. 1 (1988): 39–47.

6. For an interesting discussion of the ways maps change to accommodate new places for imaginary places, see Hyunhee Park, "The Imagined among the Real: The Country of Women in Traditional and Early Modern Chinese Geographical Accounts and Maps," in *Imagining Early Modern Histories*, ed. Allison Kavey and Elizabeth Ketner (Burlington, VT: Ashgate, 2015), 101–124.

7. Royal Society Council minutes, 1769–1782, 6:158.

8. Ann Savours, "'A Very Interesting Point in Geography': The 1773 Phipps Expedition to the North Pole," *Arctic* 37, no. 4 (1984): 402–428, 408–409 quoted.

9. Sherard Osborn, Richard Wells, and A. Petermann, "On the Exploration of the North Polar Region," *Proceedings of the Royal Geographical Society of London* 12, no. 2 (1867–1868): 97.

10. Wolfson and Levao say that these texts likely included Richard Hakluyt's *Principal Navigations, Voiages, Traffiques, and Discoveries of the English Nation* (1598–1600) and Samuel Purchas's *Hakluytus Posthumus; or, Purchas his Pilgrimes* (1625). There were other books available in the mid-eighteenth century that would have dealt more clearly with the Arctic, but these two were certainly classics, and their publication in the late sixteenth/early seventeenth century correlates well with the texts that influenced Victor. Susan J. Wolfson and Ronald Levao, eds., *The Annotated Frankenstein* (Cambridge, MA: Belknap Press of Harvard University Press, 2012), 66.

11. Anne K. Mellor, "*Frankenstein*, Racial Science, and the Yellow Peril," *Nineteenth-Century Contexts* 23, no. 1 (2001): 1–28, rpt. in *Frankenstein: A Norton Critical Edition*, ed. Paul J. Hunter, 2nd ed. (New York: Norton, 2012), 481–489; Mellor, *Mary Shelley: Her Life, Her Fiction, Her Monsters* (London and New York: Routledge, 1988); Mellor, "*Frankenstein*: A Feminist Critique of Science," in *One Culture: Essays in Science and Literature*, ed. George Levine (Madison: University of Wisconsin Press, 1987), 287–312.

12. Shapin, *A Social History of Truth*, introduction and ch. 1.

13. Kim Hammond, "Monsters of Modernity: Frankenstein and Modern Environmentalism," *Cultural Geographies* 11, no. 2 (2004): 183.

14. Julia V. Douthwaite with Daniel Richter, "The Frankenstein of the French Revolution: Nogaret's Automaton Tale of 1790," *European Romantic Review* 20, no. 3 (July 2009): 381–411.

15. It is unclear whether the book he read was actually by Agrippa, whose works were still in wide circulation at that time but who also was the spuriously attributed author of several books of black magic. It is possible that he read *De occulta philosophia libri tres* (1531/1533), Agrippa's magnum opus, in which he attempts to revive the pursuit of natural philosophy and magic by making it part of the divine plan, though the five-hundred-plus pages of dense and often difficult-to-comprehend prose make that less likely than the pithy, much more easily read and falsely attributed *Fourth Book of Occult Philosophy*, which began circulating under Agrippa's name in the seventeenth century. He clearly did not read *De incertitudine et vanitate scientiarum et artium*, the skeptical attack on natural philosophy and all human pursuit of knowledge Agrippa penned in 1526 and published in 1530.

16. Wolfson and Levao, *The Annotated Frankenstein*, 93n28.

17. Steven Shapin and Simon Schaffer, *Leviathan and the Air-Pump: Hobbes, Boyle, and the Experimental Life* (Princeton, NJ: Princeton University Press, 2011).

18. Allison Kavey, *Books of Secrets: Natural Philosophy in England, 1550–1600* (Urbana-Champaign: University of Illinois Press, 2007).

19. Dane T. Daniel, "Invisible Wombs: Rethinking Paracelsus's Concept of Body and Matter," *Ambix* 53, no. 2 (2006): 129–142.

20. Allison Kavey, *Agrippa's Magical Cosmology*, forthcoming.

21. Agrippa, *De occulta philosophia libri tres* (London, 1655), 3.1.

22. Daniel, "Invisible Wombs"; Agrippa, *De occulta philosophia libri tres* 1.1.

23. Thomas Aquinas, *Summa theologica*, "Five Proofs of the Existence of God," 1a.2.3, articulates this very clearly and can be understood as the "rule" governing legitimate magical theological practice during the Renaissance.

24. See, for example, Tang Soo Ping, "*Frankenstein*, "Paradise Lost," and the Majesty of Goodness," *College Literature* 16, no. 3 (Fall 1989): 255–260; Joyce Carol Oates, "Frankenstein's Fallen Angel," *Critical Inquiry* 10, no. 3 (March 1984): 543–554; and Burton R. Pollin, "Philosophical and Literary Sources of Frankenstein," *Comparative Literature* 17, no. 2 (Spring 1965): 97–108.

CHAPTER 2   THE INSTRUMENTS OF LIFE

1. *Oxford English Dictionary*, s.v. "daemon."

2. Agrippa, *De occulta philosophia libri tres* (London, 1655), 3.18.

3. Ibid.

4. Jerome J. Bylebyl, "The School of Padua: Humanistic Medicine in the Sixteenth Century," in *Health, Medicine and Mortality in the Sixteenth Century*, ed. Charles Webster (Cambridge: Cambridge University Press, 1979), 335–370.

5. Michel Foucault, *Discipline and Punish: The Birth of the Prison*, trans. Alan Sheridan, 2nd ed. (New York: Vintage Books, 1995).

6. Tim Marshall, *Murdering to Dissect: Grave-robbing, Frankenstein and the Anatomy Literature* (Manchester: University of Manchester Press, 1995).

7. Ruth Richardson, *Death, Dissection and the Destitute*, 2nd ed. (Chicago: University of Chicago Press, 2001), 7.

8. Ibid., 8.

9. David D. Hall, *Worlds of Wonder, Days of Judgment: Popular Belief in Early New England* (Cambridge, MA: Harvard University Press, 1990), 239–274.

10. Richardson, *Death, Dissection and the Destitute*, 14.

11. Ibid., 15.

12. This image is held at the Wellcome Library and was part of the exhibition "Dirt: The Filthy Reality of Everyday Life," which was up March 24–August 31, 2011. The images and text from the exhibition are still available at http://artecony.blogspot.com/2011/05/dirt.html.

13. See, for example, Hillary Marland, ed., *The Art of Midwifery: Early Modern Midwives in Europe*, Wellcome Institute Series in the History of Medicine (London: Routledge, 1994); Merry Wiesner-Hanks, *Women and Gender in Early Modern Europe*, New Approaches to European History, 3rd ed. (Cambridge: Cambridge University Press, 2008).

14. Richardson, *Death, Dissection and the Destitute*, 12, citing T. Brown, *The Fate of the Soul* (Ipswich, 1979) and Bertram S. Puckle, *Funeral Customs: Their Origin and Development* (London: T. W. Laurie, 1926). Note that early modern compendia of preternatural beings also included evil spirits that lived in water, so it could cut both ways.

15. "Burning at the Stake," www.capitalpunishmentuk.org/burning.html.

16. D. P. Walker, *The Decline of Hell* (Chicago: University of Chicago Press, 1964).

17. Richardson, *Death, Dissection and the Destitute*, 29, citing "The Resurrection" (London, 1800), held at the Wellcome Institute.

18. G. J. Barker-Benfield, *The Culture of Sensibility: Sex and Society in Eighteenth-Century Britain* (Chicago: University of Chicago Press, 1996), 1–36.

19. Leonard Barkan, "Cosmas and Damian: Of Medicine, Miracles, and the Economies of the Body," in *Organ Transplantation: Meanings and Realities*, ed. Stuart J. Youngner, Renée C. Fox, and Laurence J. O'Connell (Madison: University of Wisconsin Press, 1996), 221–251, 222 quoted.

20. Jon Turney, *Frankenstein's Footsteps: Science, Genetics and Popular Culture* (New Haven, CT: Yale University Press, 1998), 3; Elaine L. Graham, *Representations of the Post/Human: Monsters, Aliens, and Others in Popular Culture* (New Brunswick, NJ: Rutgers University Press, 2002), 26.

21. Peter Cushing in his autobiography *Past Forgetting*, quoted in, among others, *Frankensteinia: The Frankenstein Blog*, August 27, 2007, http://frankensteinia.blogspot.com/2007/08/dr-frankenstein-peter-cushing.html.

22. Christiaan Barnard and Curtiss Bill Pepper, *One Life* (Toronto: Macmillan, 1970), 397.

23. Cecil Helman, *The Body of Frankenstein's Monster: Essays in Myth and Medicine* (New York: Norton, 1992), 2–3.

24. Emily Swanson, "Americans Have Little Faith in Scientists, Science Journalists," *Huffington Post*, December 21, 2013.

25. Susan Sontag, "The Imagination of Disaster," in *Against Interpretation* (New York: Farrar, Straus & Giroux, 1996), 223.

26. Paul Root Wolpe, "Knowing and Seeing: Reconstructing *Frankenstein*," in *Health Humanities Reader*, ed. Therese Jones, Delese Wear, and Lester D. Friedman (New Brunswick, NJ: Rutgers University Press, 2014), 419.

27. Lennard J. Davis, *Enforcing Normalcy: Disability, Deafness and the Body* (London: Verso, 1995), 146.

28. Martha Stoddard Holmes, "Disability in Two Doctor Stories," in Jones, Wear, and Friedman, *Health Humanities Reader*, 64.

29. Ibid., 67.

30. David T. Mitchell and Sharon L. Snyder, *Narrative Prosthesis: Disability and the Dependencies of Discourse* (Ann Arbor: University of Michigan Press, 2000), 47.

31. Mark Mossman, "Acts of Becoming: Autobiography, *Frankenstein*, and the Postmodern

Body," *Postmodern Culture* 11, no. 3 (May 2001), http://pmc.iath.virginia.edu/issue.501/11.3mossman.html.

32. Chris Gayomali, "The Amazing Bionic Hand That Can Tie a Shoe," *The Week*, March 13, 2013.

33. Arthur Mokin Productions, " 'Frankenstein' and the Heart Machine (The Pacemaker)," documentary, 1988.

34. Wolpe, "Knowing and Seeing," 425.

35. Rebecca Solnit, *The Faraway Nearby* (New York: Penguin Books, 2013), 106.

CHAPTER 3   A MORE HORRID CONTRAST

1. Joyce Carol Oates, "Frankenstein's Fallen Angel," *Critical Inquiry* 10, no. 3 (March 1984), 548.

2. Delmore Schwartz, "In Dreams Begin Responsibilities," in *"In Dreams Begin Responsibilities" and Other Stories*, 3rd ed. (New York: New Directions, 1978).

3. Oates, "Frankenstein's Fallen Angel," 545.

4. William Godwin, *Enquiry concerning Political Justice* (Oxford: Clarendon Press, 1971), 56, 79–80.

5. Percy Bysshe Shelley, *Selected Poetry* (Oxford: Oxford University Press, 1968), 29–30.

6. This line comes from the 1931 film, not from Shelley's text; see Susan J. Wolfson and Ronald Levao, eds., *The Annotated Frankenstein* (Cambridge, MA: Belknap Press of Harvard University Press, 2012), 111n15.

7. Letter to Leigh Hunt, September 9, 1823.

8. Steven Earl Forry, *Hideous Progenies: Dramatizations of Frankenstein from Mary Shelley to the Present* (Philadelphia: University of Pennsylvania Press, 1990). This anthology is the source for quotations from the plays below: Richard Brinsley Peake, *Presumption; or, The Fate of Frankenstein*, 135–160; [D. O'Meara], *Frank-in-Steam; or, The Modern Promise to Pay, 177–186;* Henry M. Milner, *Frankenstein; or, The Man and the Monster!*, 187–204; John L. Balderston, *Frankenstein*, 251–286.

9. Letter to Leigh Hunt, September 9, 1823.

10. See the chronology in Forry, *Hideous Progenies*, 121–123.

11. Ibid., 31.

12. Ibid., 5.

13. Forry, however, does not mention that the 1910 Edison silent film (discussed in a later chapter) might have influenced Webling's play in this regard, which David Skal suggests could well have been the case. David J. Skal, *The Monster Show* (New York: Faber and Faber, 2001), 97.

14. Ibid., 101.

15. Ibid., 96.

16. Ibid.

17. Forry, *Hideous Progenies*, 93.

18. Frederick C. Wiebel Jr., *Edison's Frankenstein* (Albany, GA: BearManor Media, 2010), 215.

19. Jeanne Tiehen, "*Frankenstein* Performed: The Monster Who Will Not Die," *Popular Culture Studies Journal* 2, nos. 1–2 (2014): 66–67.

CHAPTER 4   IT'S STILL ALIVE

1. Frederick C. Wiebel, *Edison's Frankenstein* (Albany, GA: BearManor Media, 2010). 4.

2. Ibid., 147, 224, 230.

3. Christopher Frayling, *Mad, Bad, and Dangerous? The Scientist and the Cinema* (London: Reaktion Books, 2005), 11.

4. Ibid., 127–128.

5. Anthony Tudor, *Monsters and Mad Scientists: A Cultural History of the Horror Movie* (Cambridge: Blackwell, 1989).

6. Stephen Prince, "The Horror Film," in *An Introduction to Film Genres*, ed. Lester Friedman et al. (New York: Norton, 2014), 389.

7. Joss Whedon interview, *Entertainment Weekly*, December 26, 2014, 47.

8. Stephen King, *Danse Macabre* (New York: Everest House, 1981), 65.

9. Paul Jensen, *Men Who Made the Monsters* (Collingdale, PA: Diane Publishing, 1996) 57.

10. Stephen Prince, "The Horror Film," 382.

11. Christine Gerblinger, "James Whale's *Frankensteins* Re-animating the Great War," *Cineaction* 82/83 (2010): 2–9.

12. James B. Twitchell, *Dreadful Pleasures: An Anatomy of Modern Horror* (New York: Oxford University Press, 1995), 59.

13. Julie Grossman, *Literature, Film, and Their Hideous Progeny: Adaptation and ElasTEXTity* (New York: Palgrave Macmillian, 2015).

14. Lester D. Friedman, "The Blasted Tree: *Frankenstein* from Mary Shelley to James Whale," in *The Classic English Novel in Film*, ed. Michael Klein and Gillian Parker (New York: Ungar, 1981), 60.

15. Gary J. Svehla and Susan Svehla, eds., *We Belong Dead: Frankenstein on Film* (Baltimore, MD: Midnight Marquee Press, 1997) 31.

16. David Lugowski, "James Whale," *Senses of Cinema*, October 2005, http://sensesofcinema.com/2005/great-directors/whale/.

17. Rick Worland, *The Horror Film: An Introduction* (Malden, MA: Blackwell Publishing, 2007) 157.

18. Robert Horton, *Frankenstein* (London: Wallflower Press, 2014), 46.

19. Frayling, *Mad, Bad and Dangerous*, 114–115.

20. Horton, *Frankenstein*, 67.

21. Worland, *The Horror Film*, 66; Bram, Madison, and Dante in "She's Alive! Creating the Bride of Frankenstein," bonus material, *Frankenstein: The Legacy Collection*, DVD, Universal, April 27, 2004.

22. Susan Sontag, "Notes on 'Camp,'" in *"Against Interpretation" and Other Essays* (New York: Farrar, Straus & Giroux, 1996), 286–287.

23. *Will & Grace*, "Fagmalion Part Three: Bye Bye Beardy," February 20, 2003.

24. Harry M. Benshoff, *Monsters in the Closet: Homosexuality and the Horror Film* (Manchester: Manchester University Press, 1997), 37, 48.

25. Caroline Joan S. Picart, Frank Smoot, and Jayne Blodgett, *The Frankenstein Film Sourcebook* (Westport, CT: Greenwood Press, 2001), ix; Reynold Humphries, *The American Horror Film: An Introduction* (Edinburgh: Edinburgh University Press, 2002), 16.

26. Robin Wood, "The American Nightmare: Horror in the 70s," in *Hollywood From Vietnam to Reagan* (New York: Columbia University Press, 1986), 79.

27. Jonathan Bailey, "How Universal Re-copyrighted Frankenstein's Monster," *Plagiarism Today*, October 24, 2011, https://www.plagiarismtoday.com/2011/10/24/how-universal-re-copyrighted-frankensteins-monster/.

28. Bruce G. Hallenbeck, *British Cult Cinema: The Hammer Frankenstein* (Baltimore: Midnight Marquee Press, 2013), 55–57.

29. Ibid., 55.

30. Wheeler Winston Dixon, *The Charm of Evil: The Life and Films of Terence Fisher* (Lanham, MD: Scarecrow Press, 1991), 224.

31. Ibid., 236.

32. Hallenbeck, *British Cult Cinema*, 110.

33. Caroline Joan S. Picart, *The Cinematic Rebirths of Frankenstein: Universal, Hammer, and Beyond* (Westport, CT: Praeger, 2001), 135.

34. Hallenbeck, *British Cult Cinema*, 155.

35. Dixon, *The Charm of Evil*, 282.

36. Picart, *The Cinematic Rebirths*, 102.

37. Campbell Dixon, review of *The Curse of Frankenstein*, *Daily Telegraph*, May 4, 1957.

38. Twitchell, *Dreadful Pleasures*, 191.

39. Brian Wilson, "Notes on a Radical Tradition: Subversive Ideological Applications in the Hammer Horror Films," *CineAction* 72 (2007): 53–54.

CHAPTER 5   MARY SHELLEY'S STEPCHILDREN

1. Caroline Joan S. Picart, *Remaking the Frankenstein Myth on Film: Between Laughter and Horror* (Albany: State University of New York Press, 2003), 2.

2. Caroline Joan S. Picart, *The Cinematic Rebirths of Frankenstein: Universal, Hammer, and Beyond* (Westport, CT: Praeger, 2001), 197.

3. Rick Worland, *The Horror Film: An Introduction* (Malden, MA: Blackwell Publishing, 2007), 13.

4. Paul Wells, *The Horror Genre: From Beelzebub to Blair Witch* (London: Wallflower, 2000), 53.

5. Picart, *Remaking the Frankenstein Myth on Film*, 1.

6. "*Young Frankenstein* (1974)," *AMC Networks*, http://movies.amctv.com/movie/1974/Young+Frankenstein.

7. Linda Hutcheon interview, *The Parody Blog*, June 1, 2010, http://theparodyblog.blogspot.com/2010/06/interview-linda-hutcheon.html.

8. Morris Dickstein, "The Aesthetics of Fright," in *Planks of Reason: Essays on the Horror Film*, rev. ed., ed. Barry Keith Grant and Christopher Sharrett (Lanham, MD: Scarecrow Press, 2004), 54.

9. Nicki Gostin, "The Pride of Frankenstein," *Newsweek*, November 3, 2007; "Babbling Brooks," *Newsweek*, December 23, 1974.

10. Jacoba Atlas, "New Hollywood—Mel Brooks," *Film Comment* 11 (March–April 1975): 57.

11. *Playboy* interview, February 1975, reprinted at *The Daily Beast*, February 16, 2014, http://www.thedailybeast.com/articles/2014/02/16/mel-brooks-is-always-funny-and-often-wise-in-this-1975-playboy-interview.html.

12. Christopher P. Toumey, "The Moral Character of Mad Scientists: A Cultural Critique of Science," *Science, Technology, and Human Values* 17, no. 4 (Autumn 1992): 433.

13. Judith Halberstam, *Skin Shows: Gothic Horror and the Technology of Monsters* (Durham, NC: Duke University Press, 1995), 162.

14. Michael Mulkay, "Frankenstein and the Debate over Embryo Research," *Science, Technology, and Human Values* 21, no. 2 (1996): 157, 159.

15. Kimberly Jackson, *Technology, Monstrosity, and Reproduction in Twenty-first Century Horror* (New York: Palgrave Macmillan, 2013), 128.

16. Elaine L. Graham, *Representations of the Post/Human: Monsters, Aliens and Others in Popular Culture* (New Brunswick, NJ: Rutgers University Press, 2002), 12.

17. Worland, *The Horror Film*, 244–245.

18. Shane Denson, *Postnaturalism: Frankenstein, Film, and the Anthropotechnical Interface* (Bielefeld, Germany: Transcript-Verlag, 2014), 26.

19. Donna Haraway, "A Cyborg Manifesto: Science, Technology and Socialist-Feminism in the Late Twentieth Century," in *Simians, Cyborgs and Women: The Reinvention of Nature* (New York: Routledge, 1991), 180.

20. Robert W. Anderson, "Body Parts That Matter: *Frankenstein*, or the Modern Cyborg?" October 5, 1999, http://www.womenwriters.net/editorials/anderson1.htm.

21. Haraway, "A Cyborg Manifesto," 149–150, 154, 177.

22. Slavoj Žižek, *Looking Awry: An Introduction to Jacques Lacan through Popular Culture* (Boston: MIT Press, 1992), 22.

23. *Flesh + Steel: The Making of "RoboCop,"* dir. Jeffrey Schwarz, 37 min., Automat Pictures/ MGM Home Entertainment DVD, 2001.

24. Ibid.

25. Despina Kakoudaki, *Anatomy of a Robot: Literature, Cinema, and the Cultural Work of Artificial People* (New Brunswick, NJ: Rutgers University Press, 2014) 4.

26. Martin Ford, *Rise of the Robots: Technology and the Threat of a Jobless Future* (New York: Basic Books, 2015); *USA Today*, May 3, 2015.

27. Reddit AMA with Bill Gates, January 28, 2015, quoted in *The Week*, February 13, 2015, 16.

28. Stephen Hawking interview, BBC, December 2, 2014, http://www.bbc.com/news/technology-30290540.

29. Kakoudaki, *Anatomy of a Robot*, 72.

30. "Innovation of the Week: An Emotional Robot," *The Week*, June 27, 2015, 18.

31. "In Love with a Bot," *The Week*, December 5, 2012, 40.

32. Timothy Shanahan, *Philosophy and Blade Runner* (New York: Palgrave Macmillan, 2014), xi.

33. Scott Tobias, interview with Ed Neumeier, *The Dissolve*, February 13, 2014, https://thedissolve.com/features/movie-of-the-week/415-robocop-writer-ed-neumeier-discusses-the-films-ori/.

34. Mark Williams, "Real-Time Fairy Tales: Cinema Prefiguring Digital Anxiety," in *New Media: Theories and Practices of Digitextuality*, ed. Anna Everett and John T. Caldwell (New York: Routledge, 2003), 160, 168.

35. Robin Marantz Henig, "Death by Robot," *New York Times Sunday Magazine*, January 11, 2015.

36. Shanahan, *Philosophy and Blade Runner*, 11–21.

37. "In Love with a Bot."

CHAPTER 6   FIFTY WAYS TO LEAVE YOUR MONSTER

1. "Peep and Marshmallow in a Vacuum Pump," uploaded March 29, 2011, https://youtu.be/YD_uixZoVuc?list=PLVm4Tx5ckSqEtfup14ocluQIUndURJs5K; "Fun with Peeps: Liquid Nitrogen," uploaded October 3, 2011, https://youtu.be/BUhXhQQtM_c.

SELECTED BIBLIOGRAPHY

Adams, Carol, Douglas Buchanan, and Kelly Gesch. *The Bedside, Bathtub, and Armchair Companion to Frankenstein*. New York: Continuum, 2007.

Aldiss, Brian. *Billion Year Spree: The True History of Science Fiction*. Garden City, NY: Doubleday, 1973.

———. *The Detached Retina: Aspects of SF and Fantasy*. Syracuse, NY: Syracuse University Press, 1995.

———. *Frankenstein Unbound*. Looe, Cornwall, UK: House of Stratus, 2001.

Anderson, Robert W. "Body Parts That Matter: *Frankenstein*, or the Modern Cyborg?" October 5, 1999. http://www.womenwriters.net/editorials/anderson1.htm.

Asma, Stephen T. "Monsters and the Moral Imagination." *Chronicle of Higher Education*, October 25, 2009. http://chronicle.com/article/Monstersthe-Moral/48886.

———. *On Monsters: An Unnatural History of Our Worst Fears*. New York: Oxford University Press, 2009.

Baldick, Chris. *In Frankenstein's Shadow: Myth, Monstrosity, and Nineteenth-Century Writing*. Oxford: Clarendon Press, 1990.

Bantinaki, Katerina. "The Paradox of Horror: Fear as a Positive Emotion." *Journal of Aesthetics and Art Criticism* 70, no. 4 (Fall 2012): 383–392.

Barkan, Leonard, "Cosmas and Damian: Of Medicine, Miracles, and the Economies of the Body. In *Organ Transplantation: Meanings and Realities*, edited by Stuart J. Youngner, Renée C. Fox, and Laurence J. O'Connell, 221–251. Madison: University of Wisconsin Press, 1996.

Barnard, Christiaan, and, Curtis Bill Pepper. *One Life*. Toronto: Macmillan, 1969.

Benshoff, Harry M. *Monsters in the Closet: Homosexuality and the Horror Film*. Manchester: Manchester University Press, 1997.

Bloom, Harold. "The Internalization of Quest-Romance." In *Romanticism and Consciousness*, edited by Harold Bloom, 3–24. New York: Norton, 1970.

———, ed. *Bloom's Modern Critical Interpretations: Mary Shelley's Frankenstein*. Updated ed. New York: Chelsea House, 2007.

Botting, Fred. *Making Monstrous: Frankenstein Criticism, Theory*. Manchester: Manchester University Press, 1991.

———. "Reflections of Excess: *Frankenstein*, the French Revolution, and Monstrosity." In Smith, *Mary Shelley's Frankenstein*, 435–449.

Briggs, Katharine. *The Fairies in Tradition and Literature*. 2nd ed. London: Routledge, 2002.

Bylebyl, Jerome J. "The School of Padua: Humanistic Medicine in the Sixteenth Century." In *Health, Medicine and Mortality in the Sixteenth Century*, edited by Charles Webster, 335–370. Cambridge: Cambridge University Press, 1979.

Cantor, Joanne. "The Psychological Effects of Media Violence on Children and Adolescents." Paper presented at the Colloquium on Television and Violence in Society, Centre d'Études sur le Media, HEC Montreal (Canada), April 19, 2002.

Cantor, Joanne, and Mary Beth Oliver. "Developmental Differences in Responses to Horror." In Prince, *The Horror Film*, 224–259.

Carroll, Noël. *The Philosophy of Horror; or, Paradoxes of the Heart*. New York: Routledge, 1990.

———. "Why Horror?" In Jancovich, *Horror*, 32–45.

Clover, Carol J. "Her Body, Himself: Gender in the Slasher Film." In Jancovich, *Horror*, 77–89.

Cohen, Jeffrey Jerome, ed. *Monster Theory: Reading Culture*. Minneapolis: University of Minnesota Press, 1996.

Collings, David. "The Monster and the Maternal Thing: Mary Shelley's Critique of Ideology." In Smith, *Mary Shelley's Frankenstein*, 280–295.

Conrich, Ian. "Traditions of the British Horror Film." In *The British Cinema Book*, edited by Robert Murphy, 226–234. London: British Film Institute, 1997.

Cooney, Eleanor. "Gore Wins! The Politics of Horror." *Mother Jones*, May/June 2006. http://www.motherjones.com/media/2006/05/gore-wins.

Creed, Barbara. *The Monstrous-Feminine: Film, Feminism, Psychoanalysis*. London: Routledge, 1993.

Daniel, Dane T. "Invisible Wombs: Rethinking Paracelsus's Concept of Body and Matter." *Ambix* 53, no. 2 (2006): 129–142.

Davis, Lennard J. *Enforcing Normalcy: Disability, Deafness and the Body*. London: Verso, 1995.

Denson, Shane. *Postnaturalism: Frankenstein, Film, and the Anthropotechnical Interface*. Bielefeld, Germany: Transcript-Verlag, 2014.

Dickstein, Morris. "The Aesthetics of Fright." In Grant and Sharrett, *Planks of Reason*, 50–62.

Dillard, R. H. W. "The Pageantry of Death." In Huss and Ross, *Focus on the Horror Film*, 36–41.

Dixon, Wheeler Winston. *The Charm of Evil: The Life and Films of Terence Fisher*. Lanham, MD: Scarecrow Press, 1991.

Dorf, Michael C. "Spandrel or Frankenstein's Monster? The Vices and Virtues of Retrofitting in American Law." *William & Mary Law Review* 54, no. 2 (2012): 339–369.

Douthwaite, Julia V., and Daniel Richter. "The Frankenstein of the French Revolution: Nogaret's Automaton Tale of 1790." *European Romantic Review* 20, no. 3 (July 2009): 381–411.

Eamon, William. *Science and the Secrets of Nature: Books of Secrets in Medieval and Early Modern Culture*. Princeton, NJ: Princeton University Press, 1994.

Evans, Walter. "Monster Movies: A Sexual Theory." In Grant, *Planks of Reason*, 53–64.

Evans-Wentz, W. Y. *The Fairy Faith in Celtic Countries*. 1911; New York: Citadel Press, 2003.

Fischoff, Stuart, Alexandra Dimopoulos, and François Nguyen. "Favorite Movie Monsters and Their Psychological Appeal." *Imagination, Cognition, and Personality* 22, no. 4 (June 2003): 401–426.

Ford, Martin. *Rise of the Robots: Technology and the Threat of a Jobless Future*. New York: Basic Books, 2015.

Forry, Steven Earl. *Hideous Progenies: Dramatizations of Frankenstein from Mary Shelley to the Present*. Philadelphia: University of Pennsylvania Press, 1990.

Foucault, Michel. *Discipline and Punish: The Birth of the Prison*. Translated by Alan Sheridan. 2nd ed. New York: Vintage Books, 1995.

Frayling, Christopher. *Mad, Bad, and Dangerous? The Scientist and the Cinema*. London: Reaktion Books, 2005.

Friedman, Lester D. "The Blasted Tree: *Frankenstein* from Mary Shelley to James Whale." In *The English Novel and the Movies*, ed. Michael Klein and Gillian Parker, 52–66. New York: Ungar, 1981.

Freud, Sigmund. "The Uncanny." In *The Standard Edition of the Complete Psychological Works of Sigmund Freud*, edited and translated by James Strachey, 17:219–252. London: Hogarth, 1955.

Gardner, Edith. "Revolutionary Readings: Mary Shelley's *Frankenstein* and the Luddite Uprisings." *Iowa Journal of Cultural Studies* 13 (1994): 70–91.

Gehring, Wes D., ed. *Handbook of American Film Genres*. New York: Greenwood Press, 1988.

Gerblinger, Christiane. "James Whale's *Frankenstein*s Re-animating the Great War." *Cine-Action* 82/83 (2010): 2–9.

Giles, Dennis. "Conditions of Pleasure in Horror Cinema." In Grant and Sharrett, *Planks of Reason*, 36–49.

Gilbert, Sandra M., and Susan Gubar. *The Madwoman in the Attic: The Woman Writer and the Nineteenth-Century Literary Imagination*. New Haven, CT: Yale University Press, 1979.

Gilmore, David. *Monsters: Evil Beings, Mythical Beasts, and All Manner of Imaginary Terrors*. Philadelphia: University of Pennsylvania Press, 2003.

Glut, Donald F. *The Frankenstein Archive: Essays on the Monster, the Myth, the Movies, and More*. Jefferson, NC: McFarland, 2002.

Godwin, William. *Enquiry Concerning Political Justice*. Edited by K. Codel Carter. Oxford: Clarendon Press, 1971.

Gottschall, Jonathan. *The Storytelling Animal: How Stories Make Us Human*. Boston: Houghton Mifflin, 2012.

Graham, Elaine L. *Representations of the Post/Human: Monsters, Aliens and Others in Popular Culture*. New Brunswick, NJ: Rutgers University Press, 2002.

Grant, Barry Keith, ed. *Planks of Reason: Essays on the Horror Film*. Metuchen, NJ: Scarecrow Press, 1984.

Grant, Barry Keith, and Christopher Sharrett, eds. *Planks of Reason: Essays on the Horror Film*. Rev. ed. Lanham, MD: Scarecrow Press, 2004.

Green, Melanie C., Timothy C. Brock, and Geoff F. Kaufman. "Understanding Media Enjoyment: The Role of Transportation into Narrative Worlds." *Communication Theory* 14, no. 4 (November 2004): 311–327.

Halberstam, Judith. *Skin Shows: Gothic Horror and the Technology of Monsters*. Durham, NC: Duke University Press, 1995.

Hall, David D. *Worlds of Wonder, Days of Judgment: Popular Belief in Early New England*. Cambridge, MA: Harvard University Press, 1990.

Hallenbeck, Bruce G. *British Cult Cinema: The Hammer Frankenstein*. Baltimore: Midnight Marquee Press, 2013.

Hammond, Kim. "Monsters of Modernity: Frankenstein and Modern Environmentalism." *Cultural Geographies* 11, no. 2 (2004): 181–198.

Haraway, Donna. "A Cyborg Manifesto: Science, Technology and Socialist-Feminism in the Late Twentieth Century." In *Simians, Cyborgs and Women: The Reinvention of Nature*, 149–181. New York: Routledge, 1991.

Haynes, Roslynn D. *From Faust to Strangelove: Representations of the Scientist in Western Literature*. Baltimore, MD: Johns Hopkins University Press, 1994.

Helman, Cecil. *The Body of Frankenstein's Monster: Essays in Myth and Medicine*. New York: Norton, 1992.

Higgins, David. *Frankenstein: Character Studies*. New York: Continuum, 2008.

Hirsch, David A. Hendrich. "Liberty, Equality, Monstrosity: Revolutionizing the Family in Mary Shelley's *Frankenstein*." In Cohen, *Monster Theory*, 115–140.

Hitchcock, Susan Tyler. *Frankenstein: A Cultural History*. New York: Norton, 2007.

Hoeveler, Diane Long. "*Frankenstein*, Feminism, and Literary Theory." In *The Cambridge Companion to Mary Shelley*, edited by Esther Schor, 45–62. Cambridge: Cambridge University Press, 2003.

Hollyfield, Jerod Ra'Del. "Torture Porn and Bodies Politic: Post–Cold War American Perspectives in Eli Roth's *Hostel* and *Hostel: Part II*." *CineAction* 78 (Winter 2009): 23–31.

Holmes, Martha Stoddard. "Disability in Two Doctor Stories." In Jones, Wear, and Friedman, *Health Humanities Reader*, 63–76.

Horton, Robert. *Frankenstein*. London: Wallflower Press, 2014.

Humphries, Reynold. *The American Horror Film: An Introduction*. Edinburgh: Edinburgh University Press, 2002.

Hunter, Paul, J., ed. *Frankenstein: A Norton Critical Edition*. 2nd ed. New York: Norton, 2012.

Huss, Roy, and T. J. Ross, eds. *Focus on the Horror Film*. Englewood Cliffs, NJ: Prentice-Hall, 1972.

Hutcheon, Linda. *The Politics of Postmodernism*. London: Routledge, 1989.

Jackson, Kimberly. *Technology, Monstrosity, and Reproduction in Twenty-first Century Horror*. New York: Palgrave Macmillan, 2013.

Jameson, Fredric. *Postmodernism; or, The Cultural Logic of Late Capitalism*. Durham, NC: Duke University Press, 1992.

Jancovich, Mark, ed. *Horror: The Film Reader*. London: Routledge, 2002.

Jennings, Wade. "Fantasy." In Gehring, *Handbook of American Film Genres*, 249–265.

Jensen, Paul. *Men Who Made the Monsters*. Collingdale, PA: Diane Publishing, 1996.

Jones, Stephen. *The Frankenstein Scrapbook: The Complete Movie Guide to the World's Most Famous Monster*. New York: Citadel Press, 1994.

Jones, Therese, Delese Wear, and Lester D. Friedman, eds. *Health Humanities Reader*. New Brunswick, NJ: Rutgers University Press, 2014.

Joshua, Essaka. *Mary Shelley: Frankenstein*. London: Troubador, 2008.

Kakoudaki, Despina. *Anatomy of a Robot: Literature, Cinema, and the Cultural Work of Artificial People*. New Brunswick, NJ: Rutgers University Press, 2014.

Kavey, Allison. *Books of Secrets: Natural Philosophy in England, 1550–1600*. Urbana: University of Illinois Press, 2007.

King, Stephen. *Danse Macabre*. New York: Everest House, 1981.

———. "Why We Crave Horror Movies." In *Models for Writers: Short Essays for Composition*, edited by Alfred Rosa and Paul Eschholz, 460–463. 8th ed. Boston: Bedford/St. Martin's, 2004.

Kipnis, Aaron. "Men, Movies, and Monsters." *Psychological Perspectives* 29 (1994): 38–51.

Knight, Amarantha. *The Darker Passions: Frankenstein*. Cambridge, MA: Circlet Press, 2003.

Knoepflmacher, U. C. "Thoughts on the Aggression of Daughters." In Levine and Knoepflmacher, *The Endurance of Frankenstein*, 88–119.

Langford, Barry. *Film Genre: Hollywood and Beyond*. Edinburgh: Edinburgh University Press, 2005.

Lauristen, John. *The Man Who Wrote Frankenstein*. Dorchester, MA: Pagan Press, 2007.

Levine, George, and Knoepflmacher, U. C., eds. *The Endurance of Frankenstein: Essays on Mary Shelley's Novel*. Berkeley: University of California Press, 1982.

Lowenstein, Adam. *Shocking Representation: Historical Trauma National Cinema, and The Modern Horror Film*. New York: Columbia University Press, 2005.

Lugowski, David. "James Whale." *Senses of Cinema*, October 2005. http://sensesofcinema .com/2005/great-directors/whale/.

Magistrale, Tony. *The Moral Voyages of Stephen King*. Rockville, MD: Borgo Press, 2008.

Malchow, H. L. "Frankenstein's Monster and Images of Race in Nineteenth-Century Britain." *Past and Present* 139 (May 1993): 90–130.

Mank, Gregory William. *It's Alive! The Classic Cinema Saga of Frankenstein*. London: Tantivy Press, 1981.

Marland, Hilary, ed. *The Art of Midwifery: Early Modern Midwives in Europe*. Wellcome Institute Series in the History of Medicine. London: Routledge, 1994.

Marshall, Tim. *Murdering to Dissect: Grave-robbing, Frankenstein and the Anatomy Literature*. Manchester: Manchester University Press, 1995.

Martin, Constance. "William Scoresby, Jr. (1789–1857) and the Open Polar Sea—Myth and Reality." *Arctic* 41, no. 1 (March 1988): 39–47.

McGavran, James Holt. "'Insurmountable Barriers to Our Union': Homosocial Male Bonding, Homosexual Panic, and Death on the Ice in *Frankenstein*." *European Romantic Review* 11, no. 1 (Winter 2000): 46–67.

Mellor, Anne K. "*Frankenstein*: A Feminist Critique of Science." In *One Culture: Essays in Science and Literature*, edited by George Levine, 287–312. Madison: University of Wisconsin Press, 1987.

———. "*Frankenstein*, Racial Science, and the Yellow Peril." In Hunter, *Frankenstein: A Norton Critical Edition*, 481–489.

———. *Mary Shelley: Her Life, Her Fiction, Her Monsters*. London and New York: Routledge, 1988.

Michaud, Nicolas, ed. *Frankenstein and Philosophy: The Shocking Truth*. Chicago: Open Court, 2013.

Michie, Elsie, B. "*Frankenstein* and Marx's Theory of Alienated Labor." In *Approaches to Teaching Shelley's Frankenstein*, edited by Stephen C. Behrendt, 93–98. New York: MLA, 1990.

Milton, John. *Complete Poems and Major Prose*. Edited by Merritt Y. Hughes. New York: Odyssey Press, 1957.

Mitchell, David T., and Sharon L. Snyder. *Narrative Prosthesis: Disability and the Dependencies of Discourse*. Ann Arbor: University of Michigan Press, 2000).

Moers, Ellen. "Female Gothic." In Levine and Knoepflmacher, *The Endurance of Frankenstein*. 77–87.

———. *Literary Women: The Great Writers*. New York: Oxford University Press, 1977.

Montag, Warren. "The 'Workshop of Filthy Creation': A Marxist Reading of *Frankenstein*." In Smith, *Mary Shelley's Frankenstein*, 384–395.

Moretti, Franco. *Signs Taken for Wonders: Essays in the Sociology of Literary Forms*. Rev ed. London and New York: Verso, 1988.

Mossman, Mark. "Acts of Becoming: Autobiography, *Frankenstein*, and the Postmodern Body." *Postmodern Culture* 11, no. 3 (May 2001). http://pmc.iath.virginia.edu/issue.501/ 11.3mossman.html.

Mulkay, Michael. "Frankenstein and the Debate over Embryo Research." *Science, Technology, and Human Values* 21, no. 2 (1996): 157–176.

Mulvey, Laura. "Visual Pleasure and Narrative Cinema." *Screen* 16, no. 3 (Autumn 1975): 6–18.

Nelson, John S. "Horror Films Face Political Evils in Everyday Life." *Political Communication* 22, no. 3 (2005): 381–386.

Nummedal, Tara. *Alchemy and Authority in the Holy Roman Empire.* Chicago: University of Chicago Press, 2007.

Oates, Joyce Carol. "Frankenstein's Fallen Angel." *Critical Inquiry* 10, no. 3 (March 1984): 543–554.

O'Flinn, Paul. "Production and Reproduction: The Case of *Frankenstein.*" In Jancovich, *Horror.* 105–113.

Osborn, Sherard, Richard Wells, and A. Petermann. "On the Exploration of the North Polar Region." *Proceedings of the Royal Geographical Society of London* 12, no. 2 (1867–1868): 92–113.

Park, Hyunhee. "The Imagined among the Real: The Country of Women in Traditional and Early Modern Chinese Geographical Accounts and Maps." In *Imagining Early Modern Histories,* edited by Allison Kavey and Elizabeth Ketner, 101–124. Burlington, VT: Ashgate, 2015.

Picart, Caroline Joan S. *The Cinematic Rebirths of Frankenstein: Universal, Hammer, and Beyond.* Westport, CT: Praeger, 2001.

———. *Remaking the Frankenstein Myth on Film: Between Laughter and Horror.* Albany: State University of New York Press, 2003.

Picart, Caroline Joan S., Frank Smoot, and Jayne Blodgett. *The Frankenstein Film Sourcebook.* Westport, CT: Greenwood Press, 2001.

Ping, Tang Soo. "*Frankenstein, Paradise Lost,* and 'The Majesty of Goodness.'" *College Literature* 16, no. 3 (Fall 1989): 255–260.

Pollin, Burton R. "Philosophical and Literary Sources of *Frankenstein.*" *Comparative Literature* 17, no. 2 (Spring 1965): 97–108.

Pynchon, Thomas. "Is it O.K. to Be a Luddite?" *New York Times,* October 28, 1984.

Prince, Stephen. "The Horror Film." In *An Introduction to Film Genres,* ed. Lester Friedman et al., 369–405. New York: Norton, 2014.

———, ed. *The Horror Film.* New Brunswick, NJ: Rutgers University Press, 2004.

Richardson, Ruth. *Death, Dissection and the Destitute.* 2nd ed. Chicago: University of Chicago Press, 2001.

Robinson, Sarah Libby. "Blood Will Tell: Anti-Semitism and Vampires in British Popular Culture, 1875–1914." *Golem: Journal of Religion and Monsters* 3, no. 1 (2009): 16–27.

Rodriguez, Mario. "Horror-Ritual: Horror Movie Villains as Collective Representations, Uncanny Metaphors, and Ritual Transgressors." *Colloquy: text theory critique* 18 (2009): 208–225.

Roszak, Theodore. *The Memoirs of Elizabeth Frankenstein.* New York: Bantam Books, 1995.

Ryan, Michael, and Douglas Kellner. *Camera Politica: The Politics and Ideology of Contemporary Hollywood.* Bloomington: Indiana University Press, 1988.

Schneider, Steve. "Monsters as (Uncanny) Metaphors: Freud, Lakoff, and the Representation of Monstrosity in Cinematic Horror." *Other Voices* 1, no. 3 (electronic journal, January 1999). http://www.othervoices.org/1.3/sschneider/monsters.php.

Schwartz, Delmore. "In Dreams Begin Responsibilities." In *"In Dreams Begin Responsibilities" and Other Stories.* 3rd ed. New York: New Directions,1978.

Scott, Peter Dale. "Vital Artifice: Mary, Percy, and the Psychopolitical Integrity of *Frankenstein.*" In Levine and Knoepflmacher, *The Endurance of Frankenstein,* 172–202.

Segal, Robert A. *Myth: A Very Short Introduction.* New York: Oxford University Press, 2004.

Seltzer, Mark. "Wound Culture: Trauma in the Pathological Sphere." *October* 80 (Spring 1997): 3–26.

Shanahan, Timothy. *Philosophy and Blade Runner.* New York: Palgrave Macmillan, 2014.

Shapin, Steven. *A Social History of Truth: Civility and Science in Seventeenth-Century England.* Chicago: University of Chicago Press, 1994.

Shaw, Debra Benita. *Women, Science and Fiction: The Frankenstein Inheritance.* Houndmills, Basingstoke, Hampshire, UK: Palgrave, 2000.

Shelley, Percy Bysshe. *Selected Poetry.* Edited by Neville Rogers. Oxford: Oxford University Press, 1968.

Sobchack, Vivian. "Science Fiction." In Gehring, *Handbook of American Film Genres*, 228–247.

———. *Screening Space: The American Science Fiction Film.* New York: Ungar, 1987.

Solnit, Rebecca. *The Faraway Nearby.* New York: Penguin Books, 2013.

Sontag, Susan. "The Imagination of Disaster" and "Notes on 'Camp.'" In *"Against Interpretation" and Other Essays*, 209–225, 275–293. New York: Farrar, Straus & Giroux, 1996.

Sterrenburg, Lee. "Mary Shelley's Monster: Politics and Psyche in *Frankenstein*." In Levine and Knoepflmacher, *The Endurance of Frankenstein*, 143–171.

Sunstein, Emily W. *Mary Shelley: Romance and Reality.* Baltimore: Johns Hopkins University Press, 1989.

Svehla, Gary J., and Susan Svehla, eds. *We Belong Dead: Frankenstein on Film.* Baltimore, MD: Midnight Marquee Press, 1997.

Tarratt, Margaret. "Monsters from the Id." In *Film Genre Reader*, edited by Barry Keith Grant, 258–277. Austin: University of Texas Press, 1986.

Telotte, J. P. "Faith and Idolatry in the Horror Film." In Grant and Sharrett, *Planks of Reason*, 20–35.

———. *Science Fiction Film.* New York: Cambridge University Press, 2001.

Tiehen, Jeanne. "*Frankenstein* Performed: The Monster Who Will Not Die." *Popular Culture Studies Journal* 2, nos. 1–2 (2014): 65–86.

Todorov, Tzvetan. *The Fantastic: A Structural Approach to a Literary Genre.* Ithaca, NY: Cornell University Press, 1975.

Toumey, Christopher P. "The Moral Character of Mad Scientists: A Cultural Critique of Science." *Science, Technology, and Human Values* 17, no. 4 (Autumn 1992): 411–437.

Turney, Jon. *Frankenstein's Footsteps: Science, Genetics and Popular Culture.* New Haven, CT: Yale University Press, 1998.

Twitchell, James B. *Dreadful Pleasures: An Anatomy of Modern Horror.* New York: Oxford University Press, 1985.

Vasbinder, Samuel. *Scientific Attitudes in Mary Shelley's Frankenstein.* Ann Arbor, MI: UMI Research Press.

Vermeir, Koen. "Vampires as Creatures of the Imagination: Theories of Body, Soul, and Imagination in Early Modern Vampire Tracts (1659–1755)." In *Diseases of the Imagination and Imaginary Disease in the Early Modern Period*, edited by Y. Haskell. Turnhout, Belgium: Brepols, 2012.

Vlasopolos, Anca. "Frankenstein's Hidden Skeleton: The Psycho-Politics of Oppression." *Science-Fiction Studies* 10, no. 2 (July 1983): 125–135.

Von Nettesheim, Agrippa. *De occulta philosphia libri tres.* London, 1655.

Walker, D. P. *The Decline of Hell.* Chicago: University of Chicago Press, 1964.

Walters, Glenn D. "Understanding the Popular Appeal of Horror Cinema: An Integrated-Interactive Model." *Online Journal of Media Psychology* 9, no. 2 (Spring 2004).

Wang, Fuson. "Romantic Disease Discourse: Disability, Immunity, and Literature." *Nineteenth-Century Contexts* 33, no. 5 (December 2011): 467–482.

Weissman, Judith. "A Reading of *Frankenstein* as the Complaint of a Political Wife." *Colby Library Quarterly* 12, no. 4 (December 1976): 171–180.

Wells, Paul. *The Horror Genre: From Beelzebub to Blair Witch.* London: Wallflower, 2000.

Wiebel, Frederick C., Jr. *Edison's Frankenstein.* Albany, GA: BearManor Media, 2010.

Wiesner-Hanks, Merry. *Women and Gender in Early Modern Europe.* New Approaches to European History. 3rd ed. Cambridge: Cambridge University Press, 2008.

Williams, Linda. "When the Woman Looks." In Jancovich, *Horror*, 61–76.

Williams, Mark. "Real-Time Fairy Tales: Cinema Prefiguring Digital Anxiety." In *New Media: Theories and Practices of Digitextuality*, edited by Anna Everett and John T. Caldwell, 159–178. New York: Routledge, 2003.

Wilson, Brian. "Notes on a Radical Tradition: Subversive Ideological Applications in the Hammer Horror Films." *CineAction* 72 (2007): 53–57.

Wilson, Diane S., and Christine Moneera Laennec, eds. *Bodily Discursions: Genders, Representations, Technologies.* Albany: State University of New York Press, 1997.

Wolfson, Susan J., and Ronald Levao, eds. *The Annotated Frankenstein.* Cambridge, MA: Belknap Press of Harvard University Press, 2012.

Wolpe, Paul Root. "Knowing and Seeing: Reconstructing *Frankenstein*." In Jones, Wear, and Friedman, *Health Humanities Reader*, 419–429.

Wood, Robin. "The American Nightmare: Horror in the 70s." In *Hollywood from Vietnam to Reagan*, 70–94. New York: Columbia University Press, 1986.

Worland, Rick. *The Horror Film: An Introduction.* Malden, MA: Blackwell Publishing, 2007.

Young, Elizabeth. *Black Frankenstein: The Making of an American Metaphor.* New York: New York University Press, 2008.

Zillmann, D., J. B. Weaver, N. Mundorf, and C. F. Aust. "Effects of an Opposite-Gender Companion's Affect to Horror on Distress, Delight, and Attraction." *Journal of Personality and Social Psychology* 51 (1986): 586–594.

Žižek, Slavoj. *Looking Awry: an Introduction to Jacques Lacan through Popular Culture.* Boston: MIT Press, 1992.

INDEX

Note that page numbers in *italics* refer to illustrations.

Lee, Rowland V., 123, 124
Legally Dead (film), 93
Le Monstre et le magicien (melodrama), 81, 84
Leno, Jay, 165
Leondis, Anthony, 165
Levao, Ronald L., 2, 29
life: artificial vs. natural, 94, 144, 148, 172, 185–190, 194–195, 206; beginning of, 61; creation of, 92–93, 99, 172, 178, 185, 191; spark of, 191
Life without Soul (film), 93, 128
Liveright, Horace, 87
Lochhead, Liz, *Dreaming Frankenstein*, 7
Loew, Rabbi Judah, 3
Lovecraft, H. P., *Herbert West—Reanimator*, 176
Love Doctor, The (film), 94
Lucifer, 35, 38, 40
Lugosi, Bela, 87, 88, 105, 123, 124, 126, 129, 133
Lugowski, David, 107

Madame Curie (film), 98
magic, 29, 32–33, 38, 43, 45, 54, 64, 94, 119
Magician, The (film), 94–95
Mank, Gregory William, *It's Alive! The Classic Cinema Saga of Frankenstein*, 102, 106
Marlowe, Christopher, *The Tragical History of Dr. Faustus*, 3, 42
Marshall, Tim, 10, 51
Martin, Steve, 145
Mary Shelley's Frankenstein (film), 148, 152, 153, 154–155
Maugham, W. Somerset, 94
McAvoy, James, 101, 151
McGavran, James Holt, 152
medicine: assisted reproductive technologies, 172; bioethics, 62, 142, 173; biotechnical operations, 65–66, 67, 94; breakthroughs in, 68, 74, 99; dissection in study of, 48, 51–53, 61; do no harm in, 69; experiments (films), 98, 142–145; heart transplant, 63; life extension technologies, 66, 67–68; organ transplant, 62, 68, 94, 134, 139, 141, 143–145
Mellor, Anne K., 5–6, 10, 26; *Mary Shelley: Her Life, Her Fiction, Her Monsters*, 7
Mengele, Josef, 69, 132
Merle, Jean-Toussaint, 81
Mescall, John, 122
Metropolis (film), 93, 98, 102, 103, 111, 190
Michie, Elsie B., 11

Milestone, Lewis, 106
Miller, Jonny Lee, 151, *151*
Milner, Henry M.: *Frankenstein; or, The Demon of Switzerland*, 81; *Frankenstein; or, The Man and the Monster!*, 84–85
Milton, John, *Paradise Lost*, 34, 38, 40, 77–78, 98, 183
Minaj, Nicki, *120*
mind/body connection, 47, 61, 89
Mindhyam Theatrical Company, 128
Mitchell, David, 67
Moers, Ellen, *Literary Women*, 6–7
Monkey Man, The (film), 94
Monster, The (film), 94
monsters: becoming, 10–11; disobedient angels, 36–37; inside each of us, 185; nature of monstrosity, 3; and people with disabilities, 9, 66–67, 91, 124; physical appearance of, 40; souls of, 40–41, 42, 45; tragedy of, 3–4; and the unconscious, 4. *See also* Creature
Montag, Warren, 11
Moore, Michael, 11
Moretti, Franco, 11
Morrissey, Paul, 150
Motion Picture Association of America, 149
Motion Picture Production Code, 149–150
Mulkay, Michael, 172
Mummy, The (film), 104
Munsters, The (TV), 180, 203, *204*
Murder Act (1752), 50–51, 55
Murnau, F. W., 103

Natali, Vincent, 172
National Library of Medicine, 201–202, *202*
National Theatre, *Frankenstein* (stage), 151–152, *151*
natural philosophy, 15–16, 18, 19–20, 28, 30–34, 37, 38
natural science, 18–26
nature, control of, 15, 16, 34, 42
Neill, Sam, 168, *170*
Nephilim, 34–36, 38
Neumann, Kurt, 174
Neumeier, Ed, 193
Newton, Henry Chance, 82
New York World's Fair (1939), 164
Nietzsche, Friedrich, *Beyond Good and Evil*, 92
Night of the Living Dead (film), 99, 140–141
Nogaret, François-Félix, 28
Normal Heart, The (film), 98
Nosferatu (film), 102, 103

ABOUT THE AUTHORS

LESTER D. FRIEDMAN is a professor and former chair of the Media and Society Program at Hobart and William Smith Colleges. Previously, he taught film classes at Syracuse, Northwestern, and American Universities, as well as the Art Institute of Chicago. He is the author, coauthor, or editor of twenty books on a range of subjects, including American cinema in the 1970s, health humanities, American Jewish cinema, film genres, and British films. His next project is a Clint Eastwood reader, *Tough Ain't Enough.*

ALLISON KAVEY is an associate professor of early modern history at CUNY John Jay College of Criminal Justice and the CUNY Graduate Center. Her published work includes *Books of Secrets: Natural Philosophy in England, 1550–1600* and several edited collections: *World-Building and the Early Modern Imagination; Second Star to the Right: Peter Pan in the Popular Imagination* (with Lester Friedman, 2009); and *Imagining Early Modern Histories* (with Elizabeth Ketner). Her research currently revolves around Agrippa von Nettesheim's magical theology as put forth in *De occulta philosophia libri tres* (1531/1533).